Understanding Loss and Grief

Understanding Loss and Grief

A Guide Through Life Changing Events

Nanette Burton Mongelluzzo

ROWMAN & LITTLEFIELD
Lanham • Boulder • New York • Toronto • Plymouth, UK

Published by Rowman & Littlefield
4501 Forbes Boulevard, Suite 200, Lanham, Maryland 20706
www.rowman.com

10 Thornbury Road, Plymouth PL6 7PP, United Kingdom

British Library Cataloguing in Publication Information Available

Library of Congress Cataloging-in-Publication Data

Mongelluzzo, Nanette Burton.
Understanding loss and grief : a guide through life changing events / Nanette Burton Mongelluzzo.
p. cm.
Includes bibliographical references and index.
ISBN 978-1-4422-2273-1 (cloth : alk. paper) -- ISBN 978-1-4422-2274-8 (electronic)
1. Loss (Psychology) 2. Grief. I. Title.
BF575.D35M66 2013
155.9'3--dc23
2013023012

™ The paper used in this publication meets the minimum requirements of American National Standard for Information Sciences Permanence of Paper for Printed Library Materials, ANSI/NISO Z39.48-1992.

Printed in the United States of America

For Bryan

Contents

Acknowledgments

There are always people who help us along the way. Some help with information and others with support. Still others supportively wait for us to return to normal life. I thank my friends for enduring my absence, my son for his patience, and my clients for their inspiring stories. I learn from everyone around me, and while I was writing this book many people expressed their stories of loss and grief. I thank all of you. I have used some of your stories and have taken care to shield your identity even though many of you said it didn't matter. I thank Grand Canyon University for allowing me a leave of absence for this project. I offer a special thank-you to Grace Freedson for your enduring belief and optimism. I appreciate and thank the wonderful editors at Rowman & Littlefield who worked with me on this book. They were professional, skilled, kind, and available. A special thank you to Bryan R. Burton for his permission to use the photo, Mineral de Pozos, for cover of this book.

Introduction

Understanding Loss and Grief: A Guide Through Life Changing Events is a comprehensive book about loss and grief. More importantly, as the subtitle suggests, it is about owning your loss and grief. In order to own your loss experience it may be helpful to have a look at the way loss crisscrosses your life.

The human condition includes a lifetime of experience with the phenomenon we refer to as loss. Loss is abundantly present almost everywhere. What we do with that loss is referred to as grief. When a loss involves the grieving of a human being who is close to us we refer to that process as bereavement. Mourning is a word to describe the means by which we represent our bereavement or grief. Examples are wearing black to a funeral, going into seclusion, and putting a black wreath on your door.

I have attempted to make this book accessible, something that can be read by anyone across cultures and hold true to the book's primary distillation, whereby loss is seen as an everyday part of life. This book covers the entirety of the concept of loss and grief, including bereavement and mourning. Everyone is touched by loss from early in our life. It will continue through the moment of death. I explore loss in terms of the personal ramifications, theoretical summaries, case vignettes, and fascinating facts on loss and grief within the American cultural landscape as well as within other cultures in the world. I not only explain the comprehensive array of losses that can occur in a lifetime, but I also offer chapters that help the reader with specific types of loss whether it be the loss of a breast through cancer, loss through stillbirth, or the loss of a child, spouse, or entire community.

My book celebrates what it means to be human and alive. I celebrate all that it takes to make the journey of life and endure what will be each of our stories. I offer this book to readers with support, optimism, and encouragement of the continued courage to own your experiences, even those that involve loss and grief.

All vignettes and case study material utilize real-life examples. However, the names, locations, and all information that could be used to identify those people have been altered. In some cases I have changed the gender of the person, and in some situations I have added fictionalized dramatic writing to make the people involved unidentifiable.

Chapter One

Defining Loss, Grief, and Bereavement

The suppression of grief and despair numbs our psyche and soul and drains the energy we need for resilience. —Joanna Macy

Loss, grief, and bereavement carry a heavy responsibility. These words will stare you down throughout a lifetime. These words know they have the upper hand. No one goes through a lifetime without some, or a great deal of, experience with loss and grief. It serves all of us to understand what we mean by loss, grief, and bereavement. By understanding the concepts we are empowered with knowledge, and knowledge can lead to more compassion and understanding toward the self and the other.

EVERYONE IS TOUCHED BY LOSS

Loss begins at the moment of conception. When the male sperm fertilizes the female egg both egg and sperm lose their ability to be independent functioning cellular structures. They give up independent life and embrace death of the individual cell structure in favor of becoming something greater by their combined efforts. They don't die; they become something new. A new life is formed and the human embryo eventually becomes a fetus and grows wildly and happily in the moist, warm, liquid-filled confines of a uterus. All is well until one day the fetus has grown sufficiently. The female body will signal expulsion maneuvers. Labor will begin. Labor is a series of contractions of various intensity, initially with considerable time between the contractions. In time the contractions will become interesting. Interesting is another word for something we don't understand until we find ourselves there. The fetus is now known as a newborn and proceeds to be squeezed through the birth canal (vagina).

You have to wonder how it is for the newborn. Everything was just fine one day. Sitting around in a warm, dark, fully functional uterus doesn't sound all that bad. You can listen to the sounds from outside the muffle of mother's body and you can listen to the heartbeat of your mother. This all must end in order to be born. The newborn arrives; usually head first at the portal that enters the outside world. The infant is taken from the vaginal canal, cleaned, wrapped, and typically placed in mother's waiting arms. She speaks to her newborn. The newborn pays attention. A loss has taken place and something new is offered. We will continue to participate in loss scenarios throughout our lifetime.

Language is designed to help us transition. You can look at the various terms used to describe a human being on his or her way through the changes, losses, and gains of life. Consider: embryo, fetus, newborn, infant, baby, toddler, child, teenager, adult, senior, and elderly. As we transition further we have the following words: dead, dearly departed, those that have passed, souls, ghosts, and spirits. Isn't it simply amazing that we make so many transitions through loss and change during a lifetime?

So, if birth is the first loss and gain, what losses will follow? Let's take a look at what we typically think of when we bring up concepts such as loss and grief.

WHAT DO YOU KNOW ABOUT LOSS?

When you think about loss it is likely that your mind goes to death and those you have lost through death. It is possible that you may also think about the end of a romantic relationship. Perhaps one of your significant losses was loss of a job. For many, losses will surface when thinking about a medical illness such as cancer. We experience loss through disease, illness, and medical interventions. There is no shortage of opportunities to experience loss in a lifetime. Everything that signals change involves loss.

As you read this book it may be helpful to keep a journal. One use of journal pages is putting a date and event in the journal followed by the page number you were reading in this book when a loss was remembered or thought about. If thoughts came up and you reflected on a loss in your life, write down the thoughts in simple words such as: "mom's death," "we moved from New Jersey," "Carla was in New York during 9/11 and she is still having problems." These words and phrases will become useful later on in the book when we begin exploring how to address loss and grief.

You are already an expert on the topic of loss and grief. You were born, you learned to walk and gave up being carried, you learned to eat and gave up breast-feeding or the bottle, you learned to use the toilet and gave up diapers, and you learned to leave home with courage, humility, and grace when you started preschool or kindergarten. These are all huge things, but we don't think of them as that significant because they are a part of life. This is so true. And it is also true that loss is a part of life and the living have a responsibility to learn how to work with the increasingly difficult losses that life offers. We want to wander away from the notion that loss and grief only have to do with death and dying. You may have heard the common saying "There are many things worse than death." It takes considerable courage to stay in life and deal with the multitude of losses that are a part of the tapestry of your life. Loss is an everyday experience. When your son admits to having a drug problem, this is loss. When you found out you had breast cancer, this too is loss. When we age, lose muscle tone, and wrinkles set in like strong sentinels intent on marking time, we are experiencing loss. The point is to understand just how familiar you already are with loss. We have strengths already evidenced and resiliency beyond belief when it concerns loss.

THE DIFFERENCE BETWEEN LOSS AND GRIEF

Loss is something that has changed and grief is the process we attach to dealing with that change.

Loss is a noun. This means it is a main subject all on its own. The verb is *to lose*; we lose something and we call that which we lost, loss. Lose is a transition verb. Lost is an adjective. I think you can see how we want to wrap our minds around the words we are using. Think of all the times in a day you refer to loss, losing something, or something being lost. Related to the word loss is the word misplaced and the word missing. These words evoke a sense of possibility. It may be possible to regain what is now lost once it is no longer misplaced, or missing. Loss usually applies to something fairly significant to us like life or limb, but it also is used when it comes to mental stability or a sense of equilibrium emotionally. Loss of emotional balance can further be connected to a loss of a job, home, financial security, or children leaving home for college or to marry.

Grief is a process. Everyone grieves differently depending on the type of thing, person, or place you have lost. Grief involves settling in with that which is lost. Things that are less significant or more normalized in the everyday are not necessarily pondered through a formal grief process. Take for example going to kindergarten; the child may protest or may be looking forward to it. The child seldom openly and consciously grieves for a return to a younger state. Consider Unger, a young five-year-old. He told his mother he never wanted to grow up or leave home and he was planning to marry his mother once he was older. We think of these as the sweet things young children say. Embedded in all that sweetness are clues around the topic of loss.

The book and movie *Peter Pan* echoes themes around change and loss. Favorite fairy tales such as *Cinderella* and *Snow White and the Seven Dwarfs* both address loss. Another famous tale is the *Pied Piper*. This is the ultimate story of loss and grief. The backstory to the *Pied Piper* is of significance. According to poet and author W. H. Auden the story is based on a real event of an entire town of children dying by disease. The resulting fairy tale was a way to help the surviving parents deal with the loss of an entire village of children. Fairy tales always contain a core of truth around which is wrapped imagination and fantasy. Fairy tales are ways to help touch the subconscious mind and assist people with the issues at hand, especially difficult issues such as loss and grief.

Grief as a process is highly individualized. We bring ourselves to the grief process and with this self comes a history, our social connections, our culture, our issues from the past, our strengths and resilience, and our family. Your wellness in all the realms that apply, including physical, emotional, psychological, intellectual, occupational, spiritual, and environmental, will influence how you navigate through loss.

Robert Burton, in his book *The Anatomy of Melancholy*, stated, "Every perturbation is a misery, but grief is a cruel torment, a domineering passion: as in Old Rome, when the Dictator was created, all inferior magistracies ceased, when grief appears, all other passions vanish."[1]

WHAT IS BEREAVEMENT?

Bereavement is a noun that defines a condition of some type of loss. Bereavement is usually used to talk about being deprived of something or someone. The condition present during bereavement is grief. The bereaved are grieving a loss. The word is most often seen as having a German origin originally meaning "to rob" or "to seize by violence." As you can see, we move from loss to grief and into a condition of grieving known as bereavement. Bereavement can be the condition and state with death, dying, or silent losses such as a miscarriage or stillbirth. Bereavement can take place following surgeries such as mastectomies, bladder removal, or other major disfiguring or life-changing procedures.

There are numerous definitions of bereavement and these definitions usually focus on a particular type of loss. For example, the Joanna Briggs Institute literature review of bereavement defines this term as "the entire experience of family members and friends in the anticipation, death, and subsequent adjustment to living following the death of a loved one."[2]

Lindemann (1944) conducted a follow-up on bereavement after the famous Coconut Grove nightclub fire. He tracked the family members for years after the incident and described the ongoing effect of loss and grief in the process we term bereavement. His study is the first known empirical study of berevement. Lindemann concluded that individuals who do not address grief suffer from greater problems over time. He also found that individuals who found the loss and grief unbearable develop more serious adjustment issues and mental health problems. He was one of the first researchers to point out anticipatory grief—the grief that comes from anticipating the loss or death of a loved one.

The dying process itself may be a state of bereavement. In *The Death of Ivan Ilych*, Leo Tolstoy writes, "From the very beginning of his illness, ever since he had first been to see the doctor, Ivan Ilych's life had been divided between two contrary and alternating moods: now it was despair and the expectation of this uncomprehended and terrible death, and now hope and an intently interested observation of the functioning of his organs."[3]

Mourning is a word often used to describe the rituals associated with bereavement such as funerals, the wearing of black garments, hanging a black wreath on a door, or periods of isolation from public involvement and interaction.

Bereavement is a condition, a process, and a personalized state whereby people come to terms with a loss and their grief about that loss.

WHAT IS THE GRIEVING PROCESS?

When we speak about a process we are referring to many things that take place over a period of time. It is like the process of baking bread or fixing a car. There is process involved in most things in life. There is the process of growing up, the process of going through school, the process involved in getting married, and the process involved in dying. Birth too is a process. Process is different from an event. An event is simply an occurrence such as death, the car broke down, the girlfriend moved out, or the child fell off the swing. All events involve a process, and every process contains events.

Grief involves a process as well. Within the confines of the word grief are many events. There are many theories on how people and even animals process grief. We will review those in the next section. When we speak about the grieving process we are talking about many things that will take place over a period of time. We are talking about events strung together much like Christmas lights on a tree.

The grief process is highly individualized. People grieve in different ways. Most authorities view grief as a universal human experience. In this section grief is spoken about as pertaining to death or a major life-threatening loss. We will be discussing grief as it applies to other significant areas such as relationship endings and geographical moves. How this process of grieving looks will depend on many factors such as the following.

- Who Are the Primary People?

    Who died or experienced something significant and life altering?
    The age of the person who died or experienced a life-changing experience.
    The ages of the people who are grieving, who have lost someone, or who are involved in that person's loss.
    The personalities of the person grieving and the person who is dying or undergoing the change.
    The nature of your relationship with the person affected.
    The quality of your relationship with this person.

- What Was the Context?

    The amount of suffering that was involved in the death or loss.
    How much time you had to prepare for the loss.

- How Did the Person Die or Experience a Major Loss?

    What was the nature of the death or loss?
    What do you know about the person's death and dying process?

- When Did This Take Place?

    What else was going on for you in your life at the time of the death or loss?
    Were you young or an adult?
    Were you home or were you away in the military or otherwise out of the country?

- Where Did This Take Place?

Where things happen is important. Did your loved one die on the highway or in a hospital? Did they die alone or with others? There is a difference between drowning alone, being murdered, and dying from an expected illness in a hospital bed.

The grieving process is complex, individualized, and always significant. We want to look at the who, what, how, when, and where of our grief.

THEORIES ON THE GRIEF PROCESS

There are many theories that have evolved over time that address the universality of the grief process. Some of these theories have also been applied to the study of nonhuman animals such as chimpanzees and birds. The reason there are so many theories is because there is no one proven way people do what they do. When something remains unprovable in its current state, we refer to that as a theory. Let's take a look at the major theories on the grief process.

The Phase or Stage Model of Grief

One of the most well-known theories on grief and death and dying as a process is that of the psychoanalyst Elisabeth Kubler-Ross. Her model is known as the Five-Stage Model of Grief. Many of you are likely familiar with her work. She offered up stages that include: denial, bargaining, depression, anger, and acceptance. Denial is basically saying this isn't happening or this cannot be real. Bargaining is most associated with making promises to God or yourself that if this will pass you promise to do something significant. Statements reflecting apathy, giving up, withdrawal, and perhaps wishing for death to come to end the suffering, characterize depression. Anger is about finding someone to blame and it often asks, why me? Acceptance is a statement of understanding the facts of your situation and being able to move forward with what is next. Sometimes this is about finding the courage to participate in chemotherapy or the courage to accept death as a part of the life process.

At the time her model was introduced, Kubler-Ross was criticized for having a linear approach to grief. She later explained that she did not see individuals moving through the stages one at a time, rather people moved back and forth through the stages, sometimes many times. Her model came from her significant work with death and dying patients. Her model is still embraced today, but some therapists have replaced denial with shock and disbelief. Some notable authors believe the stages are inconsistent with the philosophical belief that grief is individualized. If grief is an individual process, they ask, how can there be steps and stages?

Bowlby (1961) also suggested theories that were stage or phase driven. In his original findings he noted three stages of grief, which he termed protest, despair, and detachment. Later he would add an initial stage termed numbness and disbelief. In the end his four stages would be numbness and disbelief, yearning and searching, disorganization and despair, and reorganization.

Both Bowlby and Kubler-Ross talk about the process of time and healing over time as the most important consideration in the grief process.

Sanders (1989) later introduced the concept of grief clusters. She viewed individuals' grieving responses as occurring in clusters of responses during particular phases. Her clusters included: shock, awareness of the loss, conservation (withdrawal), healing, and renewal.

Many literary authors have touched the topic of grief in their writings. Sometimes it is from these fiction accounts that we learn the most about individual sorrow, grief responses, and ways of grieving not always addressed in the research literature. C. S. Lewis wrote, "For in grief nothing stays put. One keeps on emerging from a phase, but it always recurs. Round and round. Everything repeats. Am I going in circles, or dare I hope I am on a spiral?"[4]

Literature that reflects on grief includes the work of Milton and the grief he records in *Lycidas*. Dostoyevsky examines grief in *Crime and Punishment* and Keats speaks about ecstasy and grief as one and the same with death ending pleasure with a type of climax of extinction. Eugene O'Neill explores grief in *Long Day's Journey into Night*, which portrays the communal grief of a family doomed to loving and destroying one another. The repetition of grief and the inability to resolve it is addressed through the way violence may become interspersed with the grief process. Albee's *Who's Afraid of Virginia Woolf*, Pinter's *The Caretaker*, Pirandello's *It Is So, If You Think It Is So* show the macabre way grief works its way around the relationships between the living. On the other hand, grief is shown as calm and patient in *Waiting for Godot* and *The Blacks*. Literature can assist you in finding where your feelings are in the grief process. Sometimes it helps us feel less crazy during a time of craziness.

C. S. Lewis writes in *A Grief Observed*, "How often—will it be for always?—How often will the vast emptiness astonish me like a complete novelty and make me say, 'I never realized my loss till this moment'? The same leg is cut off time after time. The first plunge of the knife into the flesh is felt again and again."[5]

Evolutionary Theories of Grief—Natural Selection Considerations

J. Bowlby was one of the first researchers to point that grief was a product of natural selection intended to re-create new unions following loss. Bowlby suggests that due to the psychologically devastating reaction to the loss and separation from a loved one, the pain acts as a motivator to secure reunion with another or with others in their family or community. The sheer pain acts to propel the person in grief to be around others and to seek out union. Bowlby believed grief was a maladaptive by-product of a separation reaction, which is seen as an adaptive response to loss. According to Bowlby, the point of grief is that of seeking reunion and moving on in order to preserve the species.

In 1972 C. M. Parkes suggested a notion that we often hear in our everyday exchanges around grief and loss. He was the first to suggest that grief is easier if the relationship with the one for whom you grieve is an uncomplicated relationship. He believed grief was a consequence of having personal relationships. As John Archer explains in his review of Parkes's work,

> The emotional and motivating responses which are essential for maintaining the relationship when the other is alive (felt as love) also operate when the loved one is no longer there (felt as grief): that is, when, in functional terms, they are futile. Grief, then, is the cost we pay for being able to love in the way we do. This view implies that grief will vary according to strength of the lost relationship.[6]

Parkes is saying that grief is a natural consequence of having loved. The more you love and are loved, the deeper the grief. The more complicated the relationship with the one you love, the more complicated the grieving.

Charles Darwin is best known for his research on evolution, species adaptation, and natural selection. Darwin had some things to say about grief as well. His primary research was done with nonhuman animals. However, Charles Darwin and his wife, Emma Darwin, would lose their daughter Annie when she was only ten. Emma Darwin is said to have kept keepsakes, such as locks of hair, to remember her daughter being taken from her at Easter from a fever. Emma would never recover and enter acceptance of her daughter's death.[7] Later, this phenomenon would become known as complicated grief or pathological grieving. We will discuss this in a later chapter.

Ethel Tobach is an evolutionary psychologist. Her work addresses the blend of humanistic and biologic concepts. In her article "The Comparative Psychology of Grief" she writes about the connection between evolution and animal behavior.[8] She states that being human places us within the rest of the animal kingdom. Being animals our responses to social losses are governed by behavioral and physiological responses. She notes the human animal has a more highly developed nervous system that is specialized and "highly plastic." She makes the following conclusion, "To grieve is to be human, and in the absence of human beings there is no grief."[9] Dr. Tobach notes that grief relies on a social-emotional process, which is based on social bonds. Social bonds are not individualistic; rather, they require more than one individual. She defines grief as "An emotional process generated by the irreversible dissolution of a psychosocial bond of the most evolutionarily advanced type."[10] Death disrupts the social organization and death represents the irreversibility of social bond destruction. In the end, she views grief as a way of remaking social bonds. The expression of grief draws others near and by doing so it creates the possibility of new bonds.

The Medical Model of Grief

In the medical model, grief is viewed as similar to an illness or sickness. Here the premise is that grief is something to be "treated" or "managed" rather than allowed its own progression. From this model of grief we have seen many industries spring into view including grief counseling, grief support groups, social work presence in hospitals, and to some extent the concept of hospice. We will discuss hospice in a later chapter.

The medical model of viewing grief will often rely on medical intervention to assist the sufferer with their grief. It is not unusual for stage theories of grief to be incorporated into a medical model. If a person is not seen as moving functionally through the stages of grief then medication or even hospitalization might be recommended.

Major hospitals throughout the United States have units devoted to grief. As increasing numbers of people are diagnosed with cancer and undergo life-changing surgeries such as bladder removal, mastectomy, and lung or kidney removal, the issues around loss have confronted physicians, nurses, and staff. The more complicated the grief in medical situations the more complicated the physical healing process may be.

The Grief Work Model

In this model the main point is that enormous effort is necessary to "make real" the fact of loss in itself. If you don't do your grief work there will be a later price to pay. One hears this sentiment echoed in conversations with others. Friends ask me if they are grieving enough or they say, "I wonder if I am going to have a problem because I didn't cry when my mom died." Many expectations are placed on your process in the grief work model.

Today there is some controversy around this model. Authors such as Ruth Konigsberg, a journalist, discuss the grief work model in her book *The Truth about Grief*. She feels the model approach does not assist people in moving through their loss. Her book is offered as an antidote to the culture of grief she views as the American way. Other authors, such as psychologist George Bonanno, discuss the research on bereavement, pointing out that some people show resiliency and do not grieve or do grief work. They get back to the business of life. He is clear to point out that this doesn't mean people don't have feelings of sadness or that they don't feel a void with the loss of a loved one, however, they go on because it helps them to be fully engaged in their life.

There is a saying that I cannot credit to a source: "A loved one's last gift they give to you is their death." I remember thinking about this when my mother died. I remember asking what gift it was that my mother wished me to now embrace with her passing? I have acknowledged many gifts from my mother and the ultimate gift was in her last words, "Are you going to be alright?"

The Stress and Crises Model of Grief

As the category suggests, this model of grief focuses on grief as a stress and a crises. When a spouse dies this creates stress, as there are so many feelings to address and things to do. For many, life changes in a major way following the death of a partner. Joan Didion's book *The Year of Magical Thinking* shows the way the loss of a life partner is intricately woven into the every-day, producing a myriad of new stresses. Likewise, death and illness, dying and loss all represent crisis. A crisis is anything that represents a turning point. We typically think of a crisis in negative terms; there are situations when a landfall of money through an inheritance presents a crisis. There is also the term "crises of opportunity" which refers to the way it feels to have wonderful opportunities presented and be unclear about the next move you should take.

The Attachment Theory Model of Grief

Attachment theory is credited to the psychoanalyst John Bowlby. His re-search was done with children and their parents. He recorded reactions of children being separated from their parents and vice versa. When applied to bereavement and death, attachment theory says that we grieve when we have lost an attachment and that attachment developed in order to survive. There-fore, when an attachment is lost, so too are we. Some of what we see in terms of a grief response may have evolved as part of the human condition. With-out our attachments our very survival is threatened.

The Freudian and Psychoanalytic Model of Grief

In this model of grief, pain is seen as being repressed. Repressed pain leads to the advent of symptoms that may surface in how one thinks, behaves, feels, or interrelates. In the Freudian and psychoanalytic model of grief the goal may be to give a voice to this repressed material, raise it to conscious-ness, and give the bearer of grief an opportunity to see what was repressed and why. It is at this juncture of understanding that the person is said to now have a choice in the matter. As long as things rumble about in the uncon-scious true choice is not really possible, as the person is acting from a repressed state and unconsciously inspired impulses.

The Psychosocial Transition Theory of Grief

In the psychosocial transition theory of grief, the roles, skills, identities, and relationships that were a part of you, your loved one, or both are called to action toward change. Bereavement behavior requires the changing of the way we socially interface with others due to the psychological changes we have undergone with the experience of loss or bereavement. Grief is not an individual ordeal, but rather one that involves the way we socially construct our self in our world. Our worldview is often called into contemplation and change.

SYMPTOMS OF GRIEF

Many websites and books describe symptoms of grief. To the seasoned mental health therapist these lists look oddly familiar. Most of what is published on the Internet is a combination of different diagnostic categories, such as those that apply to depression, anxiety, or even obsessive-compulsive type of disorders. It is true that while grief has components of mental health disorders, grief is not in itself a mental illness or disorder. So, some clarification is in order here.

Grief, bereavement, mourning, and loss are a part of life. People experience and interpret losses in their own unique way. We never want to judge a person for the style or manner in which they deal with their losses. There are two chapters in this book that address two types of grief responses that are problematic from a mental health point of view. One of these is clinically referred to as complicated grief and the other is traumatic grief. These are mental health concerns.

Symptoms of grief can be thought of as being divided into categories of what is felt, what is thought, what is done, and what is experienced both physiologically and psychologically.

What Is Felt?

We all know about feelings. Typically feelings are the same thing as emotions. We can feel sad and emotionally be sad. We can feel happy and emotionally experience happiness. There are five primary emotions: Anger, Joy, Sadness, Love, and Fear. Secondary emotions include: Hate, Happiness, Shame, Loneliness, and Compassion. When involved with loss and grief symptoms such as sadness, depression, guilt, anxiety, worry, rage, irritation, despair, hopelessness, powerlessness, sorrow, and misery may be common. Most of these emotions are secondary emotions to the primary emotion we call sadness.

What Is Thought?

Thoughts are those things in our mind that come in a singular, plural, or chaos-like fashion. Thinking about dinner tonight? Thinking about the argument you had with a friend or your child? Thinking about having been fired from your job? Thinking about the interview for the new job? Thinking about the mammogram you need to schedule and the appointment with your doctor to follow up on your cholesterol? Perhaps you are thinking about all of it and then your mother is diagnosed with cancer. Thoughts can pile up and be unbearable.

It behooves us through a lifetime to learn how to control our thoughts or, put another way, how to corral them and let them know who is in charge.

When dealing with grief following a loss or even a series of losses there is a tendency for thoughts to take on a life of their own. It is not uncommon with grief for there to be racing thoughts, irrational thoughts, bizarre thoughts, evil thoughts, and thoughts that are a cause for your concern. Some people who verbalize thoughts during a grief process may be shocked to find out that others think their thought process is a bit off. It may be off. However, there is a rhythm to your grief and it may involve some pretty strange thoughts, at least over the short term. How can you tell if you are in trouble?

If you are having thoughts of suicide and the thoughts are more than fleeting you likely need to consult a professional. If you are having thoughts of harming another and find these thoughts to be recurring, you need to speak to a professional. If you are hearing voices and they appear to be coming from outside of yourself / outside your head, you need to consult with a mental health professional. If you cannot stop the thoughts and it is interfering with you ability to sleep, to go places, to leave the house, to function in your life, please call a professional as these are signs your brain and your thoughts are wanting to get stuck. There are medication remedies, talk remedies, support remedies, relaxation techniques, and a host of other options that can help.

What Is Done?

What is done is about what we do and this is about your behavior. Sometimes behavior gets a bad rap. Sometimes it deserves one. Grief can show up in your behavior. This is the way you act, the way you act toward yourself, and the way you act toward others.

It is certainly fine to be withdrawn while grieving and want to isolate from others. It is also fine to not want to be alone and need to be in the presence of others. We all function differently when it comes to grief and loss. Following my mother's death I only wanted to be with my son and with my mom, then with her ashes. I didn't want to have to bother about taking care of others' feelings about my mom's death. I tended toward seclusion. I didn't tell many people my mother had died; those who needed to know knew. I spoke to my mom after her death, and on the way back from the funeral home I put her ashes in the passenger seat of my SUV. I had strapped her in the seat using the seat belt. A vehicle pulled in front of me and I had to hit the brakes to avoid a collision. The first thing I did was to reach with my right arm to secure the passenger from being hurled forward toward the windshield. It made me laugh and it made me cry, again. My behavior toward my mother was always protective, even in death. I was trying to keep her from getting hurt and she was in a box, now ash, in the passenger seat.

How do we know we are in trouble with our behaviors when in a period of grief? Certainly things to note are if your behavior involves hurting yourself or others. If your behavior is way outside of normal this is a concern. Outside of normal might be climbing in the casket and needing to sleep with your dead loved one when she died two months previously. Outside normal is pretending to pet your cat some time after he has died. The rule of thumb is if the behavior is of danger to self or others then the behavior is not appropriate. If the behavior is not dangerous but, rather, bizarre then we want to look at two things: the length of time since the loss and the nature of the loss. Things can be mighty strange in the first few months following a significant loss. It is different to be acting out through behavior with the death of a child versus the loss of a job or the losses entailed in a geographic move. We will be looking more closely at these variables in subsequent chapters.

What Is Experienced Physiologically and Psychologically?

The body is intimately tied to our brain and to our emotions and feelings. We are whole beings where everything relates to everything else. Sometimes we don't know just how interconnected we really are.

The body in grief is much like the body in pain. Psychologist Elaine Scarry wrote a sad but poignant and important book, *The Body in Pain*. She writes about torture and the resilience of human beings to endure the unendurable. The body in grief experiences hardship in terms of things such as heart rate, respiratory distress, blood pressure, temperature fluctuations (hot and cold), sensations such a tingling or numbing, aches in the muscles and/or joints, and at times problems with gait and balance.

The emotions and the way we feel about what has happened in terms of our loss will infiltrate our biological system. Changes can even occur on a cellular level; the immune system can lose its resiliency, and our natural killer (NK) cells may not be able to respond to opportunistic enemies such as cancer cells laying in wait. All stress is experienced emotionally as well as physically. The more extreme the stress, the more insults to the body.

I once met a man who had lost his wife, his dog, his mother, and his financial security all within a period of three months. He said, "I am an emotional wreck." He went on to describe sleep problems, eating problems, anger, anger, anger, and sadness. He also went on to describe playing tennis four days a week, volunteering for the animal shelter, and staying in touch with friends. Sometimes life hits people like an out-of-control locomotive and it will feel like a mess. Strengths are still evident in people if they are still standing. The gentleman I described was in considerable distress and pain. He also had many things working for him that would go far in terms of his eventual return to a state of stability.

Our psychology is comprised of many things such as our intelligence, our unique ways of processing information, our strengths and weaknesses when it comes to cognitive functions, and our general state of mental health. Everything that is true about us becomes a factor in the grief experience. If you had a history of depression or if you were abused as a child, these things will want to be heard through your grief in one way or another. Sometimes grieving individuals tell me things like, "Here it goes again, one more awful thing to deal with." When we look at that sentence the listener wants to understand the meaning of the word *again*.

As a general rule, symptoms of grief that manifest in the body or your psychology might include: problems sleeping, breathing difficulties, increased heart rate or blood pressure, confusion, disorientation, flashbacks to other losses especially if you have a history of posttraumatic stress, and difficulties interrelating with others.

Let's move on and take a look at *Loss As a Lifelong Process*.

NOTES

1. Burton, *The Anatomy of Melancholy*, 259.
2. Christ et al., 554. In Joanna Briggs Institute, www4.rgu.ac.uk/files/BereavementFinal
3. Stone and Stone, *The Abnormal Personality*, 312.
4. Lewis, *A Grief Observed*, 46.
5. Ibid., 56–57.
6. Archer, *The Nature of Grief*, 5.
7. Desmond and Moore, *Darwin*, 386.
8. Schoenberg et al., *Loss and Grief*.
9. Ibid., 348.
10. Ibid., 349.

Chapter Two

Loss as a Lifelong Process, Life Events, and the Loss Continuum

> Who knows that life be that which men call death, and death what men call life. —Euripides

We know about loss. Everyone who lives has experience with loss. We can look at loss on a continuum. This line, or continuum, runs from the moment of conception to our death or death of conscious awareness. Loss does require consciousness. Loss is a feeling that relies on awareness of change.

Cells are alive and reproduce in our bodies throughout a lifetime. The cells that will come together by way of sperm and egg give up their unique identity in favor of a combination that will produce a growing embryo and eventually a life if all goes well. This is the first loss. We don't perceive this as a loss, as the outcome is so unique and most often one celebrated with joy and hopefulness. Consciousness is also not afforded an embryo or cells. Most losses go unnoticed throughout our lives, as they are the type of changes that bring us something that is perceived as better than a former state or condition.

The newborn will cry until hearing mother's voice and calm is restored. A loss took place in terms of emerging from mother's inner place of safety. The new world outside mother's uterus is loud, bright, different, and frightening. Change has taken place and change is loss. What assists a newborn in making the transition from inside mother to outside mother is mother. We all hope to have a mother who welcomes us during this transitional period. It isn't always the case and other problems ensue, which we will address later in this book.

As we grow and develop we are introduced to new life events. There may be preschool, elementary school, junior high school, and then high school.

While these social and cultural transitions are taking place we are also developing physically, intellectually, and emotionally. Our parents, friends, neighbors, and family are also changing. They change in terms of their life events, which are tied to our own loosely or closely. They change physically, intellectually, and emotionally as a result of life events including those that have to do with the aging process.

In therapy sessions with couples I hear a statement with some regularity. Often it is the man who will say this. It is said with confidence, assurance, and belief. He thinks he is making a pronouncement that will explain the difficulty he and his wife or partner is experiencing.

He says, "I am the same person I was when we married. It is her that changed. I'm not the problem; she changed and I didn't."

When I hear this commentary my first feeling is that of empathy. I do care that this gentleman sees change as the problem. Secondly I am aware of how painful it is for his partner, as she knows it is a true statement and wonders what it was she did wrong by changing with the course of events that life offered her. Lastly I see it as an opportunity to explain to them the concept of change and loss and how we need to step up to the plate and be ready to let go of the way things were in favor of new things, however ill-defined in the beginning. This is one of our life goals; to be able to change over a lifetime. If we can do so with grace we have achieved the pinnacle of meaning as a human being. We will look more at this later.

Life exists on a continuum from birth to death. All changes, life events, experiences, happy times, traumatic events, physical or emotional events will be recorded and we will need to adapt in order to survive. Some people will adapt better than others. Some have more support and more choices.

You can take a sheet of paper and mark the day of your birth. Draw a line from the date of your birth to the first event that comes to mind for you. Perhaps this is when you were told you first spoke or took your first step. Continue on drawing lines between all the life events and changes that come to mind. Depending on your age this may take more than one sitting to accomplish. It will be pages long. Now, reflect on the paper or papers in front of you. All of what you have experienced in terms of changes you have also experienced in terms of loss. Change is about giving something up to obtain something else. Change involves loss. Loss may be simple and almost invisible as an experience or it may be traumatic.

WHY LOSS HURTS

Loss is a complicated composite that includes physical experiences, emotions, intellectual activity, and spiritual reflection. At times the loss is so normalized that we are unaware that we are actually dealing with a loss. Take for example the first day of school. Many children cry upon separation from mother or father. We urge our children on and tell them this is a great new experience. We console them and persuade them that it is a good thing and they will enjoy it. In the end it is difficult for the young person to leave known environs and embark into a collective experience with what can be viewed as other tribes. A child has a tribe or family. School represents the coming together of many tribes with rituals, beliefs, interaction styles, and manners that are not identical. One child may fare well and another not so well in the mixing of groups or tribes. Most children find it a challenging adjustment, however most parents do not mark this transition as one of loss that involves grief and giving up the old in favor of something else. Kenneth P. Nunn of the John Hunter Hospital in Australia notes, "The capacity to change is critical to the ability to adapt to a changing environment. Our brains help us to manage change by constructing possible futures and enabling us to behave in a way that prepares us for those futures."[1]

Loss hurts emotionally and physically. This is because loss is an emotion and an emotional state. Emotions have both emotional and physical components. It was once a notion that the feelings and physical sensations shared about loss of a loved one were metaphorical rather than actual. Our language and the languages of the world express how loss hurts. Take for example: hurt feelings, broken heart, ache in your heart, not feeling like yourself, or something is missing or absent. There is a commercial on television for an antidepressant. It is an emotional commercial. The narrator says, "Where does depression hurt?" The photos that follow in the commercial make it clear to the viewer that depression is a feeling and a state of body discomfort and pain.

The person experiencing loss may complain about body aches and pains, organ pain, head pain, and generalized neuralgia. Naomi Eisenberger, Matthew Lieberman, and Kipling Williams studied rejection and hurt by way of fMRI studies. What they found was, "the same neural machinery recruited in the experience of physical pain may also be involved in the experience of pain associated with social separation or rejection. Because of the adaptive value of mammalian social bonds, the social attachment system, which keeps young near caregivers, may have piggybacked onto the physical pain system to promote survival."[2]

Ethan Kross et al. studied social rejection and physical pain.[3] Their study also concluded that social rejection (such as the breakup of a romantic relationship or death of a loved one) and physical pain share the same affective components in the brain.

Loss hurts physically and emotionally. Depending on the type of loss, whether the death of a loved one or a move to a new and unknown country, there will be things experienced in the physical body and through our emotions. We know that the brain records things of significance to us.

The limbic system, where centers such as the hippocampus and amygdala of the brain reside, is part of a twenty-four-hour surveillance system in what has been referred to as the "reptilian brain" or our more instinctive animal brain. This part of our brain has a job to send and receive information about how things felt by way of sensations such as smell, taste, texture, and sound. The limbic system does not interpret what it processes. It simply receives and sends. The sending part has to do with coupling things of like kind. If a smell permeated the air when you were hit by a car at age five and that same smell or one similar to it is received by your olfactory sense, the limbic system will send that information to you. How it sends the information will not make sense. It will act to have you experience odd sensations or feelings. You might have a sudden change of mood or your heart might begin racing for no apparent reason. There is a reason, but the limbic system's job does not include making things make sense. It is the job of another part of your brain to do that. The prefrontal cortex is located behind your forehead. This part of the brain handles reasoning, right and wrong, decision making, and interpretation of signals being sent from the limbic structures. One has to work with the prefrontal cortex in order to master how to mediate with the limbic structures.

Let's look at Carl. Carl was in the Iraq War. He was not injured physically, but he did witness three of his friends be blown apart by IEDs (improvised explosive device). He remembers a vague human sound, the sight of blood, and a shoe. He smelled smoke and other smells of burning fabric. He remembers a bitter taste, which he could not tie to anything in particular. He recalls the temperature and heat in the Iraq desert and a constant state of thirst, which he felt he could never quench. It was during the summer months. Carl finished his tour of duty and returned to the United States. Waiting for him was his wife of five years and their two-year-old son. Carl went to counseling and worked on loss, grief, anxiety, and aspects of PTSD (posttraumatic stress disorder). Two years after returning home and completing counseling, he and his wife and son were in a shopping mall. It was around the first of July. They had a fun day of shopping and had eaten in the food court at the shopping center. He had fried rice, a curry chicken plate, and a small salad. His son had pizza and his wife had a mixed salad. All was well. They left the shopping center and headed toward the parking lot to retrieve their car and return home. Five sudden bursts of firecrackers snapped loudly. Carl hit the ground and put his hands over his head. He started screaming, "We need help, we need help here." His wife and son watched as Carl relived a time held in his emotional and physical memory.

It all happened in less than five seconds. This is the work of our very well developed limbic structures. Its job is to send and receive and it did just that. Loud explosions or a near-enough sound of fireworks would cause Carl's limbic system to receive the sound, find an association of like kind, and send information to Carl's sympathetic nervous system. The limbic system's job is to protect Carl by informing him quickly of any information useful to his well-being. The limbic system will do this with big traumatic events such as Carl's experience being in the military. It will also send us more subtle information if what is stored is not necessarily associated with something traumatic. For example, the smell of grandmother cooking homemade pasta sauce is stored in the limbic system too. When you smell a similar homemade version a sense of calm or joy may come over you.

THE SIGNIFICANCE OF GRIEF FOR ADDRESSING LOSS

Loss is an emotion and grief is the process by which we deal with that emotion. Grief is individual in nature. Some people will have an involved grieving process and others will feel better using moving on as a way to grieve. Although we described some of the theories of the grief process in the preceding chapter, not everyone will grieve according to a theory.

If grief is the process by which we address a loss there will be many factors influencing how we do this. Culture plays a role in showing us how a large number of people we identify with will go about grieving. Further afield from culture is the world. In the world as we know it all cultures say something about how grief is handled. On the nightly news, in newspapers and magazines, in the online news features and blogs, and in motion pictures produced in Hollywood or throughout the world, the subject of grief is shown to us. We see mention of grief in literature, poetry, art, architecture, and science.

Harry Harlow was a researcher who studied baby monkeys in the 1950s.[4] In his experiments around attachment he separated infant monkeys shortly after birth from their mothers. They were given the choice between a surrogate wire mother monkey with food but no padding or a surrogate wire monkey with padding (soft terry cloth) and food (milk in both cases). The infants chose padding over food when given the chance, even though both wire mother surrogates were capable of providing mild nourishment. Although these studies were about attachment, emotional bonding, and even adoption we can see that grief played a role in the choice of attachment. The infant monkeys preferred, when given the choice, to be next to a wire surrogate that felt like a body. But attachment and a subsequent loss of attachment will become a loss that will need to be grieved in some manner. We see the infant monkeys grieve by way of holding on to the soft terry cloth and rubbing against it for comfort.

Grief will allow a person or animal to move through a loss in whatever manner will be most helpful to them at the time. In addition to a worldview, animal view, and cultural view of grief, we also can look at learning about grief as a familial factor. Families have ways of expressing grief. We learn about grief by watching our parents, siblings, and other relatives as they grieve. Sometimes we will emulate what we have seen and other times we will discard what we have learned and choose something different.

I lived in a small colonial town in central Mexico for a year in 1989/90. There was a small expatriate American community in the town as well as Canadian, European, and South American communities. All of these people lived interspersed with the native Mexicans of the area. When someone in a Mexican family died the family would put a black wreath, black flowers made from ribbons, or another black object on the front door of the house. This signified a death had taken place. It was understood that vendors or beggars were to stay away. It was understood that anyone who did not have a close association to the family was to let them grieve in peace. I had the occasion to know an American family who had a family member die while I was living in this town. Although they were from the United States they adopted the ritual and grief emblem of the black wreath. The wreath would stay on the door until the family concluded their grieving. For some, this would last for several months and for others the black flowers would stay for a year or longer. Sometimes we borrow customs of grief from other families.

We learn about grief from our friends, our schools, and from the animal life we observe. It has been observed that dogs know when their owner is close to death, and don't leave their owner's side, either to eat or to go outside to urinate. It seems that we learn about grieving from the animals with which we share our lives.

Grief is an individual experience that may be informed by family, culture, world culture, friends, and our own attitudes. In psychotherapy I hear about grief on a regular basis. I have observed that conflicted relationships at times lead to more grief. The more the issues have been settled between you and the one you have lost, the better. Better yet if they are settled within your own heart.

THE IMPORTANCE OF RITUALS FOR DEALING WITH LOSS

Rituals are actions performed for symbolic significance. Our lives are filled with rituals, especially at holidays. Think of Christmas, Hanukah, New Year's Eve, Easter, the Fourth of July, Memorial Day, Labor Day, Halloween, and Thanksgiving. We have rituals associated with major events such as the Super Bowl, the Tour de France, the World Series, the US Open, the Wimbledon Championships, and so on. There are rituals involved in joining the military, attending college, entering a fraternity or sorority, and in graduating from high school and college. Certain age markers involve rituals such as the *quinceañera*, the celebration of turning fifteen in the Mexican and Hispanic American cultures. Death involves rituals as well. Following a death in the United States it is common to decide on an obituary that will be in the local newspaper. This is a ritual. Deciding on cremation, burial, or interment are rituals as well. A memorial service or Catholic requiem mass are rituals. Different religions support different rituals for addressing death. Although there is no one time frame for mourning following a death, many people hold the belief that one full year must pass in order for the loss to have completed a calendrical cycle of all holidays, birthdays, and special events that would have been celebrated with that person had they lived. Throughout the world there are many rituals that have come to be associated with death. Everything from how one is buried, such as burial at sea or by being placed on towers, to hanging coffins found in China on the cliffs,[5] and to whether a headstone or marker will be set in place or whether a secret burial or family plot on private property will be used.

We use rituals as a way to help us grieve. There is something about stepping through the many parts involved in a process that organize things and delay the onset of the reality of life without that person. The rituals also act to infuse respect, by way of ceremony, into the life of the one who has died, while also giving the survivors a memory of that respect offered. Rituals help us to note a passing from what was to something new. In death or in other transitions rituals help us to mark, celebrate, mourn, respect, note, acknowledge, and let go of what was.

Rituals are also used with illness and disease. When I was growing up, my paternal grandmother believed in whiskey, honey, and lemon juice for a sore throat. She believed in putting a knife or spoon in the freezer and then applying it to a bump on the head to take down the swelling. She believed in chicken soup for the flu and letting a fever burn itself out by piling on blankets until your body broke the fever by way of an intense sweat. These were all rituals that were used on a regular basis. The doctor would only be called if the rituals did not result in the desired outcome.

I have known many people diagnosed with a terminal disease such as cancer. There are rituals associated with the dying process. Often friends and family come to see and speak to the person who is ill. Food is brought for the family and people take turns helping care for the loved one. Sometimes projects are started such as videotaping messages to children or others who will survive. Other times belongings are individually distributed to family and friends as part of a special token. All of these things are rituals or ways by which we help handle our grief and assist others in their grieving.

When I was working on my doctoral dissertation in central Mexico, I interviewed dozens of elderly women beggars. I focused in on three women who would form a case study of the elderly women beggars of San Miguel de Allende. All of the women were over the age of sixty-five and had been begging on the streets for several years. They took to begging following a traumatic event or loss.[6] Some of their rituals involved praying in church. If they felt they had been afflicted with *susto*[7] or soul loss they might seek out the help of a local healer or *curandera* to help the emotional trauma or loss leave the body so the soul would return.

One of these rituals involves the woman lying on the floor in her dwelling or the home of the healer. Aluminum-foil strips were placed around her body. She was doused with *aqua para susto* or *susto* water. The healer then prayed over her body asking for relief for the afflicted one. It is believed that any significant trauma or loss causes the soul to temporarily leave the body, because the soul cannot stand this type of pain. If the soul stays away too long, a life threatening condition known as *espanto* can occur. *Espanto* is when the soul has gone far away, cannot be found, and the person will become weak and eventually die.[8] We will discuss the interesting cross-cultural perspectives on loss and grief in other chapters.

Rituals help us deal with loss. They help in the grief process and they provide a sense of the familiar when difficult life events take place.

HOW WE LEARN TO GRIEVE AND EXPERIENCE LOSS

The first place we will learn about loss is likely in our family of origin. We see the look on mother's face when she learned her mother was hospitalized. We saw how father looked and responded when he took the phone call that said his brother had died in an automobile accident. We remember how our parents told us that our family pet was going to be "put down." We may recall when your kitty never came home or when the puppy ran out in the street and was struck by a car.

We first learn about loss and grief from the people who took care of us when we were small. This may be parents, grandparents, a foster home, an orphanage, or multiple family settings. Most often, we learn that loss is a sad phenomenon. There are times when children in therapy have explained that they were shocked that dad didn't seem to care when he put the dog down by shooting it in the head or when the cat disappeared and mother said, "Good riddance."

We may learn about loss and the variance in grieving styles from our first caregivers. We also learn by way of friends and acquaintances. Later we learn through the media such as television and the Internet.

Learning about loss and learning to grieve requires attachment and attachment is connected to what we know to be love. Can a human being experience loss and enter into a grief process without there being an attachment or an attachment of love? Love is a complex topic beyond the scope of this book, however it is worth mentioning that love is not a singular experience of lovers, partners, spouses, siblings, friends, or parents and children. Love can be felt toward strangers or those where our involvement may have been temporary or fleeting.

ANTICIPATORY GRIEF

Anticipatory grief is as the phrase implies. When we await a loved one's death we are anticipating their death and the loss and grief that will come. While we wait for death we are already grieving. In some ways the words are confusing as we are already in a grief process as we anticipate death.

Consider the case of Carl and Margie. Carl was diagnosed with colon cancer. He was given about one year of life as a projection by the oncologists if he went through prescribed oncology treatments. If he chose not to do the chemotherapy he would live about four months. Carl chose not to do the chemotherapy and he lived eighteen months. His wife, Margie, was grieving his loss long before he died. She fretted about finances, bills, changing titles, and giving special belongings away to his adult children. She worried and she planned his funeral. She was involved in the grief process before Carl died. She and Carl spoke about his impending death. His wishes were heard and so were hers. In the end he died relatively peacefully. For Margie it marked the beginning of another type of grief. Here she entered emotional areas she did not experience in her anticipatory grief. She was angry at cancer and angry that he would die so young from cancer (age seventy). She began doubting herself and whether she had shown up for Carl in all the ways possible as he was dying.

Anticipatory grief also refers to grieving a loss that has already taken place.[9] In our example above, a loss took place long before Carl's actual death. He lost the ability to connect socially. He no longer attended church. He was not having lunch with friends or going for hikes. The family dog was relegated to Margie for her morning and afternoon walks. Carl was already gone before he died. It is important to note that anticipatory grief is used in our culture both ways. We wait for death and also accept or address losses as they come in the process of dying. We see this in nursing-home patients with dementia. The loss of who they once were already took place and the grieving began long before the body died.

NOTES

1. Nunn, "Neurofuturity," 183–190.
2. Eisenberger, Lieberman, and Williams, "Does Rejection Hurt?" 290–292.
3. Kross et al., "Social Rejection," 6270–6275.
4. Harlow, "Love in Infant Monkeys," 68, 70, 72–74.
5. China Ministry of Culture, *Hanging Coffins in Gongxian.*

6. Mongelluzzo, "Street Stories," 55–58.
7. Avila and Parker, *Woman Who Glows*.
8. Rubel, O'Nell, and Collado-Ardón, *Susto: A Folk Illness*, 106–111.
9. Walter, *On Bereavement*, 50.

Chapter Three

An Overview of Some Personal Losses

The bitterest tears shed over graves are for words left unsaid and deeds left undone. —Harriet Beecher Stowe

PERSONAL LIFE EVENTS

Personal life events include all things we encounter on the journey through life. We want to highlight your personal life events in order to show how many things you have experienced and where loss has taken place throughout your life span.

Being born is a personal life event we do not remember, but our parents and other relatives do. We will be informed of that special day through stories, some of which we will incorporate into our understanding of who we are.

All of our childhood experiences are personal life events. My son loves to talk about parts of his childhood. He remembers experimenting in the garage with a collection of pieces of broken things. There were blow-dryers that were broken, parts of a long-abandoned radio, a watch that grandmother didn't want because it no longer worked, and lots of screws, nails, tools, and wood. There were old tricycles and an old tire or two. Leftovers from a garage sale offered odds and ends and plenty of curiosities. He had a desk and workstation and would, in the summer months, take things apart and put them back together again. He was a six-year-old inventor. He engaged in the world of creating by way of things that had become lost. In time he would lose interest in these things, which then found a home in another garage sale, the trash, or landfill.

What personal life events do you recall?

I remember playing as a child at Columbus Park in the inner city of Chicago. There was a large sand play area and my brothers and I would build castles and I imagined we were living at the time of Sir Lancelot and Guinevere. There was a part of the park called the Council of Rings. I remember standing in the center of the Council of Rings and pretending it was at the time of King Arthur and the Knights of the Round Table. I would become lost in imagination and play. Books I had read merged into my conscious creative play. Then there was a day when we no longer went to the park. Our family moved to Colorado. I remember Colorado and the clean, clear, crisp air. I would become a runner in high school and the air was part of what I remember. I loved the way my lungs burned as air was inhaled. In time I would give up running in favor of hiking and skiing.

Try to remember the small parts of the everyday. What was interesting or remarkable as a child, a teenager, a young adult, and an adult? What was remarkable about your siblings or parents and your grandparents? What do we have to lose in order to grow, change, and develop?

Through a lifetime we are busy experiencing life, recording moments, letting go, and moving on to new experiences. Consider the case of Max. Max was born into a wonderful family where he felt loved. His mother became ill when he was six, and off and on she deteriorated and improved. He loved his mother. He remembers feeling anxious. He noted he could not fully relax when reading a book or playing with friends. He had this nagging thought taking his peace away. His mother was diagnosed with cancer, but it was the type of cancer that did not pose an immediate threat. Max grew up and his mother lived until he was twenty. Max recalls his mother's illness coating most of his childhood experiences. He remembers not doing things for fear of being gone too long from his mother. He gave things up to be with her. He experienced loss of engaging more spontaneously in his childhood. There wasn't anything he could have done differently. It was the way it was. How this has influenced his adult life is that he savors every moment as though it was the last moment. He figures the best gift his mother gave him was the influence of focus on the here and now. His here and now experience was mother's illness. Around that fact all else revolved. He does not feel cheated out of a thing from childhood and he has grown to recognize anxiety as a whisper reminding him of his love of his mother.

THE HUMAN DEVELOPMENTAL PROCESS

Children and adults will experience loss differently. They will also grieve in their own unique way. Human development influences certain parts of the loss and grief process. An infant, for example, cannot understand either loss or grief. An infant does not know death. However, an infant does experience loss without knowing what the experience means. The infant knows if something is not given to them and it once was. If an infant is fed every three hours and suddenly is being fed every twelve hours, she will make herself heard. If a diaper is left to cause a rash, burning, and irritation, the infant will announce his discomfort. If mother no longer comes and someone else has taken her place, the infant knows of this but does not have the type of brain development necessary to process loss.

Infants do not have sufficient cognitive abilities to understand death. They function very much in the here and now. They will react to changes in their care, caretaking, and routines. Let's take a look at some of the developmental stages and the corresponding ability to understand death, loss, and grief.

The psychosocial stages of development refer to the psychological and social development of human beings through the life span.[1] There are many developmental theorists and theories on development. This is one model that focuses in on physical, social, and relationship development. This model is based on the work of Margaret Mahler, a physician who would later work in psychiatry on the development of the self.[2]

Normal Autism is the stage of development that begins at birth and lasts to about three months of age. We think of autism as a developmental disorder affecting communication and personal interaction. Normal autism refers to the time in all of our lives where our interrelating skills were in their infancy and communication skills were primitive. The goal of this stage is that of developing a symbiotic relationship with the primary caretaker, who is generally the mother. Mother and infant are one from the perspective of the newborn. The infant was once one with mother when she rested in mother's uterus attached by a feeding tube (umbilical cord) to mother. Following birth the conception of being a part of the mother continues for a few months. Normal autism involves many self-stimulating behaviors such as the infant examining his own hand as he lifts it in front of his face. Normal autism involves staring into space and seeming to be engaged in some inner world of preoccupation. If all goes well an infant will achieve the beginning structure of bonding. Bonding leads to the development of trust, and trust will become essential in terms of relating to the larger world.

Infants in this stage of development do not know death. They can experience loss through change in routines. They have already developed a basic preference for the caregiver and recognize mother's voice from when she was inside the uterus. Just like we know how a baby smells, the infant knows how mother smells and is already differentiating smells that are not the same as mother's. An infant in this stage can perceive of loss and may grieve as reaction to a change. The grief is limited in its expression and most often is handled by crying, problems eating, and stomach upsets.

The **Hatching Phase** is the stage of development that begins at three months and will continue to about six months of age. During this phase of development the infant is becoming aware of others as distinct from self. Strangers are now known as others. Bonding will continue to be strengthened during this phase of development and the infant has established clear caretaking preferences. One should see the infant be more engaging and less involved in solitary self-stimulation.

Death is still not something cognitively possible to understand at this age. The infant in the Hatching Phase of development is aware of strangers and has established bonds with a caretaker. If the caretaker is suddenly gone, the infant will not be able to know the person died. The infant can detect someone else is caring for him and this someone is not the other caregiver. They can discern differences in smell, taste, touch, and the manner in which they are held. They can discern voice differences as well as loudness and tonal differences. An infant in this developmental stage will experience loss and can react to that loss by crying, upsets, and resisting being held by another. An infant in this stage may also resist eating or may overeat due to anxiety caused by change. Remember all change is loss.

Practicing is a phase of development that begins at six months and lasts until about twelve months of age. The young infant/toddler is practicing being in the world. This stage is best known for exploration of things in the environment, as mobility is taking place with crawling and walking during this time frame. The child will also begin developing language during the practicing phase, as language typically follows walking. The young child practices physically creating space between him and mother. This is part of learning trust and object constancy (that things stay even if you leave), and games such as peek-a-boo are popular at this age and exhilarating to a young child because inadvertently object constancy is being practiced. The child shrills loudly with delight when you hide your face behind the couch only to reappear in a moment. It is like magic to the child and it is essential to learn that things will still be there even if you cannot see them. The child will pile toys on mother or father's lap, practicing the skill of collecting things, giving gifts, exercising the power of obtaining things, and looking for approval or disapproval in order to learn about things and things in relation to others. The child is also learning to be in a relationship.

The child in this age range still has no concept of death. Remember, a child of this age is just developing object constancy—that things stay put. How would they be able to handle that mother went behind the couch and never came back? It is developmentally out of sequence and outside of a young toddler's cognitive ability. However, attachment and bonding have taken place by now. Serious distress would take place upon a child losing a caretaker. There would be little significance or understanding in the loss of a family pet, but a caretaker such as father or mother would be distressing. The toddler can feel loss because she can acknowledge change. Distress would be shown in temperament, eating, sleeping patterns, and overall mood.

The **Separation Individuation Phase** of development is one of the most important developmental stages. It begins around twelve to eighteen months of age and ends around age three. It is a vital stage for many reasons, but mainly because it is at this juncture in development that we first see a true sense of self, will, spirit, and intention. In ways, the flower is opening.

In my clinical practice I find parents have the most difficult time with this age range. It is frustrating to parents due to the will of the child. Many parents are of the belief that they have to instill discipline now or forever deal with a small tyrant. We want to allow emotional and interpersonal growth to take place while setting limits and boundaries. We don't want to squash the toddler. At the same time we want the child to feel secure in a safe and fair structure.

The separation individuation stage is characterized by walking, rapid speech development, and an overall mastery evidenced by the child over her environment. We often refer to this time in a child's life as the "terrible two's." It can be terrible, but it isn't always. During this stage the child goes back and forth between having temper tantrums and willful displays of omnipotence and good-natured behavior with lots of love.

In American culture this is the age range when children are often engaged in some fairly serious negotiations around body, space, and emotions. The child is typically in the toilet-training years during this phase and a test of wills may be seen around elimination issues. Sometimes young children protest, "But it's my poop and I will put it where I want." To the toddler it is a magical creation to first witness that a bowel moment comes from inside that tiny body and is disposed of in the diaper and then the toilet. Most parents don't think much about what their child thinks about the little act of creation their child produced. Toddlers of this age are also being weaned from the breast or bottle and speech begins with the learned power of the word "no." Additionally this age is characterized by the introduction of increased socialization through day care and other opportunities for interaction with children. All of this can be daunting for the little guy or gal. When you think of it from the child's perspective there is considerable loss going on. The child can walk and is not carried as often. The expectations have increased concerning child behavior. The child is no longer given a bottle or the breast and is instructed on where to eliminate and when. This all involves considerable loss and loss is about change.

Parents may also change during this phase of development. It appears they become more worried when the newly emerging self of their child makes himself known. They worry that the child will "get worse" if they don't eliminate bad behavior or willfulness. Willfulness and some disruptive behavior are necessary for a formation of the self and self-concept.

This developmental stage is about the child asking if you will still love her and be there for her even as she changes moment by moment from the good-natured little girl into the wailing, defiant toddler. If the child does not experience extremes then all will be well.

When a major loss such as a death of a family member occurs during this phase of development, the child will not understand the death as death. They are aware of the absence of someone significant. They will grieve. Their grief is informed by an inability to understand the permanence of death. All they know is that death means the loved one has left them. They will feel abandoned by the deceased loved one more than having an ability to feel sadness about something having happened to the loved one. A loss is personalized and children in this age range may think the loss has something to do with their own behavior. The separation individuation phase is about being all-powerful and exerting that power. A little one doesn't know if his or her power could also extend to making someone leave, as through death.

The **Oedipal Stage** of development is typically first evident around age three and will conclude somewhere around age seven or eight. Sigmund Freud first identified this stage of psychosexual development, as part of his developmental theory of psychoanalytic sexual drive theory.[3] However, for our purposes, we are using this stage to denote the time in the young child's life when the little boy "falls in love" with his mother and is engaged in rivalry with the father. Conversely, the little girl "falls in love" with her father and creates rivalry with the mother. In this stage we see the child learn about rivalry and it is further applied to relationships with siblings and later between friends. In essence the child is learning about how to love by "being in love." The normal resolution of this stage is that of the child not being able to obtain the goal of securing mother or father as a mate, but being rejected and accepting the loss. It is in this stage that we learn about love, loving, competition, rivalry, and the consequences of all of the above.

Loss that takes place at this age will be felt, especially loss through death. The three-to-eight-year-old understands death in a simple manner. The child in this age range will most likely associate death as impermanent. They will expect the person to come back and death is most like going to sleep or going away and returning from a long trip. There is a sense that death is reversible for a child in this stage of development.

The **Latency Stage** of development picks up around age eight and lasts until about twelve years of age. These years are years of wisdom, balance, and great abilities for both compassion and thoughtfulness. The child in latency is often quieter and more withdrawn, preferring to think and observe. Children in this age range are intelligent and can tell parents many things about life, the world, and their observations of parental choices and unfairness. A latency age child may withdraw from one or both parents, preferring their own solitude. At times parents confuse these choices with independence and maturity. The child is still a child emotionally and intellectually. It is a time for parents to engage and stay engaged with the child. It is important to stay firm with boundaries and structure and not overburden the child with adult-like responsibilities such as extended caretaking of younger siblings.

The latency age child understands death as not reversible, and children of this age range will experience a full blow where loss and grief is concerned. They worry, cry, and try to make deals with whatever power they believe owns death. The one thing that sets this age apart from the other childhood age ranges is that the view of death often revolves around doing something wrong or "getting caught by death" by doing something wrong. The latency age child understands the permanence involved in death, but still does not understand its inevitability. This may be a remnant of the earlier omnipotence that hangs on a bit longer until the child reaches adolescence where it is gradually replaced with an understanding of the universality of mortality. As a result, the grieving process with a child this age often involves blaming others or even blaming the one who has died.

On a cold December day some years ago I saw a ten-year-old child who was dealing with his mother's illness from a malignant and fierce form of cancer. I had an initial session with the boy and explained who I was. I had asked him if he knew why he had come to see me. He said, "No." I explained in simple terms that I often tried to help people with their problems, with things that might feel sad or bad to them. He said, "I really need help. Are you always able to help the people that come here?" I explained that many people felt better after coming here. He explained, "The problem I need help with is my mother is dying from cancer. I don't understand cancer. I want you to stop her from dying. That is my problem." I explained that I could help him with his feelings about his mother being sick. He didn't want help with his feelings. He wanted me to stop her from dying. When eventually I explained I could not keep her from dying he shouted at me, "Then what good are you?" This is part of the dilemma with this age range. Someone owns death in their minds and if they can figure out who it is that controls it then perhaps there could be a reprieve.

Adolescence is the most spoken-about developmental stage. Adolescence begins at age thirteen and will end when the teen years conclude at the close of a young person's nineteenth year. Adolescence and the Separation Individuation Phase of Development have much in common. Both are about separating and individuating. Both are about a struggle with dependence and independence. Both involve a combination of good-willed relating and tantrums or uproar. Development is individual and not all children have "terrible two's," just like not all teenagers will have a difficult adolescence. The main skill to be accomplished besides that of reconciliation of the independence/dependence struggle is that of building adult skills. Adult skills are necessary for when the youth departs home. This includes interpersonal skills, morality, decision making, ethics, functional skills such as managing money and paying bills, and working at jobs. In its best sense adolescence is a dry run at adulthood where parents and adult friends can hone in on the strengths and weaknesses evidenced during these years in order to offer assistance and guidance.

Many physiological changes take place during adolescence, including hormonal changes and the development of the prefrontal cortex, which will be useful in mediating some of the influences of the limbic structures of the brain where trauma and high-charged emotional experiences are stored.

Parents sometimes think that adolescence marks a completion of childhood. It does not. Adolescents need supervision and they need someone to talk to. This is the age range where I have the most referrals and it is the most useful time of therapy.

Loss is deeply felt during this age and an adolescent processes loss and grieves very much like an adult. They understand the permanence of death, the inevitability of death, and the consequences of death for the living. The huge emotional life of a teenager interprets death in an acute, vivid, and loud manner. It is usually the teenagers who organically set about designing altars for a friend or adult who has died. They grieve in their own ways, but it is always a bit bigger than it may appear on the outside. We want to be sure to be available for support with teens when they have lost a friend, loved one, or close acquaintance, as they won't always show what they are feeling. There is a lonely aspect to much of their internal processing about significant things.

During **Adulthood** and what we term as **Late Adulthood** there are many skills being honed and shared with others. The adult is busy building a career, a family, and embarking on a deeper understanding as to what their purpose is in life. Community takes on a new and important significance, as does family.

Late adulthood typically begins when the work years start to wind down. This is for many around the age of sixty-five. However, in recent years many adults are postponing or eliminating retirement from their repertoire of choices for the advanced years. The person in late adulthood is often challenged with illness either with self or others they care about or for. Loss and grief become constant companions. As more and more relatives and friends die, it becomes difficult for the late adult to stay steady.

Nancy was an eighty-four-year-old when she began therapy. She had lost four husbands and had survived cancer twice. She had lost two of her four children and she was using counseling to dialogue about her own mortality and what she would like to accomplish before dying. She was in good health but she said, "How many more years could I really have?" Her most significant issue was learning to let go of some old shame and anger. She also wished to show herself that she could accomplish something she had wanted to do her entire life. She wanted to be a musician. Once all of her caretaking of others had ended, due to their deaths, she began taking piano lessons. In two years she was playing remarkably well and was writing her own music. She had a performance at one of the local churches and received a standing ovation. Nancy wasn't waiting for death; Nancy was trying to outrun it.

LEAVING, BEING LEFT, AND LETTING GO

Personal losses also involve choices we make by leaving. If we make a decision to move to a different geographic area we will experience a loss of the familiar and those we are leaving will experience loss as well. Some people stay in the same geographic area for their entire life. In areas such as towns throughout the Midwest, South, and the East, we see generations of families still in the same city.

In Yonkers, New York, there are many families whose grandparents and great grandparents first settled there. Families grow up around one another and the thought of leaving to go elsewhere creates havoc.

I live in Arizona and most of the people I know are from somewhere else. People in the West have migrated from the East or Midwest over the years. Loss is involved every time a person or a family moves. Loss is involved for those we leave behind.

It may take years to let go of some personal losses. Take Jeanine, for example. She moved from Ohio to Arizona about fifteen years ago. She still lovingly speaks of Cleveland, her family, and her friends. She doesn't want to go back, but she has never fully embraced living in Arizona. For Jeanine this is about several things. She does not want to go back and fit neatly into the expected niche that she feels the past holds for her. However, she misses the daily connections with family, friends, and neighbors. Although she has made friends here, it is not the same. Jeanine also feels it would be a sign of failure to return to her hometown. It has been difficult for Jeanine to let go.

When my mother was ill in the last few years of her life, she and I spoke a good deal about death and dying. My mother, Inez, was not afraid of dying. She did, however, wish for the dying process to be acceptable. By acceptable she meant an end without undue suffering, pain, or hardship to her adult children, her survivors. Often she would ask me, "Are you going to be alright?" What she meant was, would I be OK following her death. I always reassured her that I would be. Up until the day before she died, she still asked me if I would be OK. I was humbled by her last thoughts being about my well-being. Sometimes letting go is intimately tied to the ones we leave behind.

DREAMS, EXPECTATIONS, AND FANTASIES

It may be helpful to think of loss in a holistic manner. This is what we have been discussing up to this point in this book.

Consider Katie, who dreamed of being a ballerina from the age of five. She went to dance classes without fail three days a week, every week, through elementary, middle school, and into high school. She was talented and accomplished. She was a butterfly and flower in one as she moved across the dance floor effortlessly with grace and artistry. During her junior year in high school she was on her way to work at a local bakery. She was due to arrive at 7 a.m. on a Saturday morning. She had been out the night before with friends and was working on about four hours of sleep. She fell asleep at the wheel of the car. The car rolled four times and then came to a silent stop upside down. Katie was unconscious and paramedics and EMTs arrived at the scene with the daunting task of extracting her from her tiny compact car. The Jaws of Life were called in and the car was disassembled on the side of the highway. Katie lived. Her right hip, both legs, both ankles, and both arms were broken. Her neck was broken. It would take about a year for her to heal and be able to walk again. She would never dance again. Katie had to deal with the loss of a dream. Katie was also able, a few years later, to deal with the creation of a new dream. She became a successful interior designer. As George Bonanno explains, "Resilience in the face of loss is real, prevalent, and enduring."[4]

Expectations are intimately tied to loss as well. Have you ever anticipated something such as someone returning your love or friendship only to have your hopes dashed? Have you ever been expecting a promotion at your job and found it being given to someone else who was less qualified than yourself? Or, have you expected to pass an exam and found you failed it? Loss is a part of life and if we are living we are addressing loss. This does not mean we curl up in a ball and cease to exist or interact. It means we have considerable experience with loss in most things we do in life and in every day during a lifetime. We may take for granted our significant experience with loss and the grief process that will be uniquely our own.

Fantasies abound in a lifetime. We can fantasize about great wealth, fame, winning the lottery, or marrying that beautiful or handsome someone. We engage in fantasizing as a way of projecting desires and wishes, but also as a calming device when under stress or facing disappointment. Sometimes fantasies have a way of reducing anxiety. Fantasy time is about projecting into the future with dreams about what you might like to see happen. Some fantasies become intentions and some intentions certainly do manifest in our lives. Other fantasies remain fantasies, and for some this is a loss and grief may be a part of the process.

One spring about fifteen years ago I met a woman who lived for the future. Her childhood had been unspeakable where abuse was concerned and her adulthood exemplified the lack of discernment that became her consequence following traumatization. She went through five marriages. She had a fantasy she would meet a man who was perfect and she would be cared for and loved unconditionally by him. She had considerable therapeutic work to do including working on the child abuse and incest issues. She was a beautiful and beguiling woman who could attract men easily. Once she was with them, however, her panic around intimacy, abandonment, and being out of control surfaced. Neither she nor the men could sustain the tension and each relationship ended. Until she thoroughly works on the early issues, it is unlikely she will have her fantasy become a reality.

GROWTH AND CHANGE

Life is about growth, change, loss, grief, and more growth and change. All of our life experiences prepare us to take on the challenge of letting go and moving on. Some losses are quite different than others. The loss of a geographical residence is different than the loss of a child. The loss of the family pet is different than the loss of youth through aging. In the chapters to follow we will explore some of the more difficult losses and ways people grieve. The first three chapters helped to set the stage for thinking about loss and all the ways you have worked through losses in you life so far. You have also learned your own way for handling grief and expressing it. There is no right way to grieve and there are no wrong ways.

NOTES

1. Mongelluzzo, *The Everything Guide to Self Esteem*, 28–31. Mongelluzzo first printed material on the psychosocial stages of development in this edition. The wording was changed for inclusion in the current book.

2. Mahler, Pine, and Bergman, *The Psychological Birth*.

3. Freud and Strachey, *Three Essays*.

4. Bonanno, *The Other Side of Sadness*, 195.

Chapter Four

As Loss Relates to the Action of Another

We pass through this world but once. Few tragedies can be more extensive than the stunting of life, few injustices deeper than the denial of an opportunity to strive or even to hope, by a limit imposed from without, but falsely identified as lying within. —Stephen Jay Gould, *The Mismeasure of Man*

There are losses that involve the actions of another. These include things such as child abuse, widowhood, elder abuse, domestic violence, and substance abuse and dependence. These types of losses are difficult because they involve people, often those we love most dearly and intimately. The grief process will be more complicated for some with these types of losses.

CHILD ABUSE

Child abuse and neglect are worldwide problems. Child abuse includes the physical, sexual, or emotional abuse of a child. This is far ranging and can include beatings, hitting, slapping, throwing, shoving, burning, breaking bones, intercourse, fondling, pornography, and emotional cruelty that leads to a breakdown of emotional coping skills and ends up producing a mental disorder or emotional problems as a consequence.

Losses are involved with being abused. A child may lose the trust they had in a loved parent; she may lose trust in people in general. Think about what happens to a child who lives in fear of the next time. Anxiety, or a fear about something that has not yet happened, becomes a staple of childhood. Confusion runs rampant, as the child isn't sure what it was that caused the abuse. Children are not capable of understanding that being abused has nothing to do with them, but rather everything to do with the abuser.

A child who is being abused has lost safety, consistency, predictability, and the carefree aspects of childhood. A child being abused within the family has no safe place and must create constructs in his mind to stay alive and keep from fragmenting emotionally. Dissociation, a common defense, can lay the groundwork for future problems, with an inability to discern safe from unsafe in the larger world.

Typically a child who is being abused will not grieve until the abuse has ended and more typically not for many years afterward. The American Academy of Pediatrics article on behavioral and emotional consequences of child abuse states, "Early maltreatment can significantly alter a child's normal developmental arc and leave the victim with significant long-term impairments."[1] Additionally, these authors believe there is significant evidence to support an association between early child abuse and major illnesses such as stroke, cancer, heart disease, depression, suicide, hypertension, substance abuse, and diabetes.[2] Child abuse has long-term consequences that linger well into adulthood. Posttraumatic stress disorder as a result of child abuse presents difficulties in childhood with sleep, anxiety, oppositional behaviors, violent behaviors, school difficulties, and relational problems with both adults and peers. An abused child will typically develop attachment issues. Without the ability to attach, the child is sentenced to a life of inability to connect in meaningful ways.

Often the first sign of grieving a childhood of abuse happens in psychotherapy. If the child is no longer in danger of abuse and attends counseling there is a good chance they can be assisted in grieving the losses and healing some wounds. Due to the developmental experience of abuse, children will often need to go to counseling throughout their childhoods at key times and then again during adolescence and adulthood. Each developmental stage only allows for so much processing. We can only process what each developmental stage will allow and understand.

Child abuse creates loss on an emotional, social, intellectual, spiritual, physical, and relational level. Grieving these losses often results in a lifetime of processing, acceptance, and rebuilding.

WIDOWHOOD

When a person loses their spouse or partner we refer to this as widowhood. A woman who loses her husband is a widow and a husband who loses his wife is a widower. Depending on the strength of the bond and the length of the relationship this can be a devastating loss. There are many stories of couples that lived together for forty-plus years and when one dies the other often follows within a year or less. People develop close relationships over a lifetime. The parent-child relationship and the couple relationship are often the strongest relationships we will have.

Widowhood also carries with it a host of other problems that confuse and complicate the grief process especially for women throughout the world.[3] According to the Pan American Health Organization (PAHO), the American Association of Retired People (AARP), and the World Health Organization (WHO), Latin America and the Caribbean are not subject to contradictory plural legal systems.[4] The "machismo" or male chauvinistic climate keeps women in subordinate roles.[5] With widowhood the low status of women only worsens. Poverty increases and loneliness, low self-esteem, and isolation become paramount as issues affecting survival.[6] In Latin America and the Caribbean, widowhood disturbs cultural identity as traditional ways of life become fragmented and family systems disintegrate.[7]

Ken Tout cites a number of studies in his book on aging in developing countries. He notes, "But in mass it is elderly women who are most likely to suffer problems accruing not only from a current state of abandonment but also from earlier disadvantage."[8]

In a United Nations report of 2005 the following finding was reported:

> In South Asia, widowhood is viewed not as a period of the life cycle of a woman, but as a personal social aberration, to be devoutly wished away. This attitude to a great extent governs the social, cultural, and even economic implications of widowhood. Widows are invisible; or rather society keeps them so. Above all a widow is doubly traumatized as a woman and as a widow. She is victimized as a woman and because she is a woman she is marginalized as a widow.[9]

In India and Nepal, within Hindu society, a woman who is a widow is considered physically alive but socially dead. In most third world countries society and culture orient around men, husbands, and sons. Widowhood for the woman is a dangerous enterprise. In India, a now forbidden ritual referred to as sati (or suttee) involves the burning of widows.[10] Following the death of her husband a widow was expected to throw herself on her deceased husband's funeral pyre. Sati was considered a form of suicide related to preserving honor and demonstrating loyalty to her deceased spouse and his family.

Millions of widows throughout the world endure extreme poverty, ostracism, violence, homelessness, ill health, and discrimination in both law and custom.[11] Widows in developed countries are more likely to be elderly whereas widows in developing countries may be young or old. One of the consequences of wars, the world over, is that of increased numbers of widows. Women who have been widowed by war and ethnic cleansing in countries such as Angola, Bosnia and Herzegovina, the Congo, Indonesia, Kosovo, Mozambique, Rwanda, and Sierra Leone have never been counted.[12]

The concepts of loss and grief become exponentially complicated when addressing the issues of widowhood throughout the world. Loss of a spouse can and does mean loss of financial security and even loss of safety from assault and rape. Even in developed countries widows often feel they must find new groups of friends who are also widowed. A woman's socialization changes upon becoming a widow. She may feel shunned by others who have husbands. Death of a husband makes the surviving wife feel as though she has done something wrong when she outlives her husband. She may feel guilty or others may imply she could have done more for her husband and he would have lived longer.

Shunning is the act of deliberately avoiding association.[13] Its origin is in political punishment, exile, and in some religions. Exactly how shunning became applied to widows is not known.

ELDER ABUSE

Abuse of an elder creates as many issues for the elderly as child abuse does for a child. Any abuse of citizens of our world who are more vulnerable due to age (younger or older) is deplorable.

In 2002 WHO and the International Network for the Prevention of Elder Abuse (INPEA) initiated an international cross-cultural study of elder abuse in an attempt to redefine and further classify elder abuse. The study used older persons as informants and this was the first study of its kind.

Elder abuse is not new nor is it a new form of interpersonal violence. In sixteenth-century Europe, elderly women were often suspected of entanglements with Satan or the Devil during the witch craze. The *Malleus Maleficarum* (*The Witch's Hammer*, 1486) was the official guide to finding witches, heretics, and devil workers.[14] It was women and women without mates who were most often singled out. Women without a man were highly suspect as being under the influence of Satan himself. This book was used during the Spanish Inquisition in the Americas including Mexico. Throughout the world there was justification for abusing or killing an older man or woman in the name of heresy.

Patricide and matricide involve killing of the father or mother. In Greek mythology Oedipus killed his own father and Pelias was killed by his two daughters. Child abuse and wife abuse were the first types of interpersonal abuse to emerge in the research literature during the latter half of the twentieth century.[15]

Child abuse was originally referred to as "baby battering," wife abuse was referred to as "wife battering," and elder abuse was known as "granny battering."[16,17]

As defined by WHO and INPEA, "Elder abuse is a single, or repeated act, or lack of appropriate action, occurring within any relationship where there is an expectation of trust which causes harm or distress to an older person."[18] Elder abuse can include physical restraint, physical or sexual abuse, the infliction of pain or injury, physical coercion, chemical restraint, psychological/emotional abuse, infliction of mental anguish, financial or material abuse or illegal or improper exploitation and/or use of funds or resources, nonconsensual contact of any kind, and failure to fulfill a caretaking obligation.[19]

Culture influences the definition of elder abuse. There are traditions and practices of a historical nature that greatly influence normative practice for groups. There are times when acts of violence become imbedded in culture. We still hear news reports, from present-day Afghanistan, of women being killed, often stoned to death, for bringing shame to their family by way of something as innocent as speaking to a man on the street. The same holds true for violence against the elderly.

> Like any other oppressed or enslaved group, women often sought self-protection in elaborate charades of harmlessness, designed to reassure the oppressor than no offense was meant. When old women were declared enemies of God and "man," old women tended to walk careful, speak quietly, hide their bodies in funereal clothes, keep their eyes downcast. From such habits of protective coloration arose today's stereotype of the sweet little old lady, or the granny next door, the acceptable old woman who makes no judgments and speaks only to bubble cheery platitudes. The shrewdly critical, thinking, challenging sort of old woman might be condescendingly termed "feisty," but some men still show as much suspicion of her as centuries ago, when she could be legally mutilated and burned as a witch.[20]

Loss and grief are embedded in what it means to become older. Depending on who you ask, aging is not something most folks look forward to. Some of the reasons for this have to do with losses. As a person ages he often loses his sense of worth and value. My clients in their eighties report feeling that their opinion is not valued and they feel tolerated rather than embraced. There are the obvious losses of youth, estrogenic cheeks, and firm body. There may be losses of their health and certainly the loss of friends. The older we become, the more deaths we encounter. With age comes a loss of status, dignity, youth, health, employment, often a partner or two, the death of children, financial losses, and the loss of a sense of being a sought-after member of the community. A person who makes it to advanced years has profound knowledge of loss and has adapted a manner of grieving. When we add elder abuse on top of a lifetime of losses, and coping with those losses, it can become unbearable. Elder abuse will compound the losses already associated with aging. Elder abuse creates mental health problems (such as depression, anxiety, and acute stress reactions) in a population that has increased physical, emotional, interpersonal, and financial vulnerabilities. Elder abuse attacks one's pride. Elder abuse feels like shame to the victim. Often older persons feel they did something to deserve the abuse, especially if it comes from an angry adult child. Older parents often have trouble speaking up and saying NO to abuse, because they fear not being believed. They also fear repercussions, just as young children do. If intervention on behalf of a child or an older person is not well honed and decisive, the child or the elder may be abused further and may even be killed. Elder abuse is an emotional betrayal. Abuse creates isolation and isolation is dangerous at any age, but deadly at an advanced age. Elder abuse is morally reprehensible. It is simply wrong to harm anyone, but to harm those who are most vulnerable is unthinkable.

It is little wonder that the suicide rate, rate of depression, and substance abuse issues (primarily through alcohol use and prescription drugs) are the highest in this age range.

DOMESTIC VIOLENCE

Domestic violence is also referred to as intimate partner abuse. It is a worldwide problem with devastating consequences for women, men, children, families, culture, and the future of everyone. Domestic violence is a form of violence that can include physical, sexual, emotional, and many other ways one person can harm and do damage to another.

Research into the causes of violence against women have found a high correlation between witnessing domestic violence during childhood, experiencing violence as a child, and later life experiences of a violent nature. [21] In the United States there is a widespread problem with domestic violence. Violence tends to be intergenerational, and children who witness or experience violence are more prone to find violence in their personal lives as adults. All socioeconomic levels are affected by the occurrence of domestic violence; it is not a problem only among the poor. Kaja Finkler, a researcher, found a correlation between domestic violence and physical illness in Mexico. [22]

Any form of violence sets into motion problems with coping, emotional constructs engineered toward survival, and physical strategies also geared toward survival. A person does not walk away from violence unaffected.

Being beaten, sexually coerced, economically controlled, verbally insulted, or harmed in any other way are all examples of domestic violence. There is considerable loss that takes place when another treats one poorly or violently. There is a loss of security, safety, resiliency, trust, and often even a place to stay or money for food. Lives are often threatened in domestic violence cases and death can occur. How does one begin to grieve the loss of an intimate abuse? If the very person whom we looked to for safety betrays that trust, the person who is being abused is in an unenviable position of not being able to trust or relate or discern adequately. This leads to more potential for harm. This is not due to a masochistic nature of the victim, but rather limbic system changes that create a fight, flight, or numbing response in most interactions that involve even minor degrees of stress or anxiety. Most often these are not the best responses and would-be predators look for this when hunting for their next victim.

The expected losses in life include the obvious ones of the death of friends, loved ones, and others. There are losses associated with marriage. The beginning of a marriage holds promise of security, where one is loved and perhaps even cherished. Over time the love may lose some of it shine, it may become dull, or it may become angry and hurtful. All of these things are losses because they represent change. It is a loss to be hit or hurt by someone who once adored you. It is a loss to have a husband or wife turn to substance use and abuse rather than turning to you for help. Expected losses involve life, death, marriage, perhaps divorce, changes in jobs, and the economic ups and downs of a lifetime. The expected losses involve illness either in your own life or the lives of others of importance. All of these things keep people busy coping. When we add to that the fear for one's own life and the degradation associated with domestic violence everything requires a Herculean effort. Domestic violence creates shame, low self-esteem, fear, anxiety, panic, depression, posttraumatic stress disorder, and the risk for substance abuse, further victimization, and suicide. Domestic violence creates mental health problems, physical health problems (blood pressure, heart problems, insomnia, hypersomnia, hypervigilance, overeating, anorexia and bulimia, gastrointestinal problems such as acid reflux disease, HIV/AIDS, other sexually transmitted diseases, and chronic pain syndromes), and interpersonal problems. Victims of domestic violence live in fear and relate from a fear base. They may not accurately read the cues of possible danger and place themselves in dangerous situations again and again. They often struggle with parenting their children and helping their children make safe choices. Counseling helps and yet some of these losses will last a lifetime. Long after the children are grown and the abuse has stopped, the victim of domestic violence may physically or mentally suffer the consequences, regardless of any legal intervention on her behalf.

SUBSTANCE ABUSE AND DEPENDENCE

Alcohol, illegal drugs, and prescription drugs are all abused. Individuals can develop a dependence on alcohol, cocaine, heroin, and pain medication. People can become dependent on antianxiety prescription drugs such as many drugs in the benzodiazepine family.

When one is dependent on or abusing substances, loss is a part of their daily experience. Being dependent on a substance means one cannot be doing other things such as relating, listening, learning, remembering, developing life skills, or engaging in real emotional intimacy. Substances alter reality and provide the user with a substitute reality for a period of time. There is most always a reason the individual uses substances. It is not a surface issue such as simply liking to get high. Most often there is a secret beneath the surface about something the user holds dear. It may be guilt or shame. It may be not feeling he can live up to expectations. It may be she experienced child abuse, domestic violence, or witnessed violence growing up. There is always a reason for someone choosing to leave reality and its painful memories. In the words of Edgar Allan Poe, "I have absolutely no pleasure in the stimulants in which I sometimes so madly indulge. It has not been in the pursuit of pleasure that I have periled life and reputation and reason. It has been the desperate attempt to escape from torturing memories, from a sense of insupportable loneliness and a dread of some strange impending doom."[23]

For the substance abuser or substance-dependent individual, loss comes in many forms. He might experience the loss of friends, family, or freedom if his abuse creates legal problems such as jail time, loss of professional status, the loss of a license to practice a profession, and loss of financial resources. Loss might take the form of treatment through a drug rehab program or comprehensive treatment center. This is a loss and a potential gain if the treatment works. He may lose his job, his home, his control over his life. And even if he is successful with treatment, he may come to realize the loss of time—time spent on drugs or alcohol and the loss that comes with realizing that life may have been different if not derailed by these choices. Often there is the developmental loss. When someone starts using and abusing substances, especially at a young age, the emotional and interpersonal development of the person stops. It may be years before they are successful with treatment. Once addiction-free, he realizes he is behaving and feeling like a person much younger than he is. This is a known consequence of early addiction to substances. For family members, the loss can be of the child they thought they were raising—the loss and grief over a promising life that may have taken a bad turn. In some cases, when drug abuse is not addressed, family members may lose the person entirely—to death, to the streets, to strangers and bad places. Facing up to those losses can be daunting. Rehabilitation and counseling can help. But often, the loss remains for a lifetime.

NOTES

1. Stirling et al., "Understanding the Behavioral," 667.
2. Ibid.
3. Mongelluzzo, "Street Stories."

4. PAHO, WHO, and AARP, "Midlife and older women."

5. Rosenbaum, "With Our Heads Bowed," 971.

6. Mongelluzzo, "Street Stories." Sections of this chapter were first discussed in this PhD dissertation.

7. Arrom, *Containing the Poor*.

8. Tout, *Ageing in Developing Countries*.

9. WUNRN, "The Status of Widows."

10. Soika, "Sati: A Project on the Indian Ritual."

11. World Bank, "How Poor Are the Old?"

12. UNDAW, Convention on the Elimination.

13. DeVinne, *American Heritage Dictionary*.

14. Kramer and Sprenger, *Malleus Maleficarum*.

15. WHO/INPEA, "Missing Voices."

16. Baker, "Granny Battering," 20–24.

17. Burston, "Do Your Elderly Patients," 54, 55.

18. WHO/INPEA, "Missing Voices."

19. Ibid., 3.

20. Walker, *The Crone*, 144.

21. Doumas, Margolis, and John, "The Intergenerational Transmission," 157–175.

22. Finkler, "Gender, Domestic Violence," 1147–1160.

23. Letter from Edgar Allan Poe to Sarah Whitman, 1848. In Robertson, *Edgar A. Poe: A Study*, 102.

Chapter Five

The Inevitable Types of Loss

> While I thought that I was learning how to live, I have been learning how to die. —Leonardo da Vinci

Inevitable losses are those we cannot escape. These include death, dying, aging, and medical problems. When things are inevitable we fashion loss and grief a bit differently. Sometimes it is the young child who is dying. The child will never know aging, but the child will know death sooner than his parents. Other times people live to be over a hundred. All of their friends have died and perhaps their spouse, relatives, and children. They may find themselves completely alone. Still other times medical problems become a part of daily living for weeks, months, years, or even a lifetime. Let's take a look at some of the inevitable losses.

MEDICAL LOSS

What comes to mind when you think of a medical loss?

If you have been reasonably healthy medical issues may not represent a loss for you. When we think about having a cold with a sore throat, a running nose, a fever, headache, and chills we usually think of these things as unpleasant. During the time of being ill most people wish for a return to a state of health. It feels good to be healthy and it feels good to not have symptoms that warn us something is wrong with our body. If we encounter illness more severe than the cold or flu it can present a challenge and it does represent a loss. Remember, loss is about change. Even illnesses that will run their course with full recovery projected entail loss.

Mary was healthy and active as a child, teenager, and young adult. In her mid-twenties Mary was diagnosed with thyroid problems. She had symptoms such as feeling hot or cold, emotional ups and downs, and problems with her appetite. Sometimes she wasn't hungry at all whereas other times she couldn't get enough to eat. Her relationships suffered due to her emotional moods and she was growing impatient with herself.

Once she had gotten a diagnosis of thyroid nodules and hyperthyroidism she was able to start a process of stabilization. She needed to take medication and have her thyroid checked once a month. The small tumors (nodules) on her thyroid gland would need to be checked periodically as well.

Mary lamented her physical state. She wished she was a kid again and worry free regarding her health. She was angry at times, moody at times, and noncompliant with her physician on occasion. Mary was dealing with loss. She needed to vent the way this felt to her. She needed to count her blessings while at the same time appreciate what she was having to give up to keep on living. She wanted to live, but she didn't like the concessions she had to make in order to continue living. As she accepted the loss of perfect health she eventually came to appreciate other things that had improved, but were also about change. She had a more realistic attitude of illness. Prior to becoming ill Mary thought that people who got ill had made mistakes and poor choices. She no longer believes that.

Some medical issues are simpler, such as thyroid issues which can be addressed. There are other illnesses that present greater challenges. Probably one of the most spoken about illnesses is cancer. Statistics say that one out of every three people will encounter cancer in their lifetime. So, in a room of twelve there will be four individuals with cancer. About every other person I know has cancer.

David Servan-Schreiber is a physician and author who is a cancer survivor.[1] He mentions that all people have cancer cells in their bodies, but not all people will develop cancer. What this means is that cancer cells exist in everyone, but it takes a trigger to activate the growth mechanism that can send cancer out of control in the body. There are many hundreds of different types of cancer. The word itself is capable of making many people weak at the knees.

Cancer changes lives and by doing so loss is incurred. What was life as you knew it is replaced with life addressing cancer. Even for those who beat cancer and go on to lead cancer-free lives, there is grief for the loss of the healthy person one once was. A fear that cancer may return, even if it never does, may always have to be kept at bay, and if a body was physically or functionally changed due to cancer treatments, there will be loss and grief associated with that. Women who have mastectomies may face, first, the emotions associated with the loss of a breast, and, second, the losses associated with one's self-image, sexuality, and changed appearance. They may grieve their lost body part and any feelings tied up with that. A person who has bladder cancer and requires the removal of the bladder will have to use a urostomy bag to urinate. This loss of function can result in a variety of emotions and feelings of loss and grief. Likewise, anyone experiencing cancer who must also undergo surgery to remove cancerous tissue will experience a range of emotions for their loss of health, even if it is eventually regained.

Cancer always represents some kind of a loss. With cancer one has to be mindful for the rest of their life. A friend of mine with breast cancer had a double mastectomy. She went five years without any reoccurrence and then she was diagnosed with a different type of breast cancer than the one she had before. She had weeks of radiation therapy. Then three years later the cancer reoccurred again. She had more radiation and a chemotherapy drug. She has been cancer free for five years again. My friend doesn't live in fear of the cancer returning. She is grateful for her life and for her ability to have gone through all the stages of acceptance, anger, and disillusionment that were a part of her unique process. She enjoys life today more than ever before. My observation is that she is more open and beautiful than ever. Cancer gave my friend a new perspective and she lives each day with joy.

Not everyone fares as well with a cancer diagnosis as my friend. John was diagnosed with leukemia three years ago. He just had his second bone marrow transplant. He operates with the cup half empty, rather than half full. He said, "I don't know what everyone thinks is so great about life." This is how he feels. Life is something to be endured, rather than something to be enjoyed. He feels he wouldn't mind dying. He keeps up with doctors and treatments because his family and friends expect this of him. He would rather not. He says he looks forward to dying and being done with "this joke called life." John also deals with depression and his loss and grief became stuck in the depression part of loss. John continues to work on these issues.

Medical issues can also be created by harm done by others. We know that victims of rape, torture, and other forms of violence and injury can and do create medical problems. The body has the unenviable task of learning how to deal with pain and how to deal with a body in pain. Elaine Scarry wrote an extraordinary book about the body and its vulnerability. She observes, "Regardless of the setting in which he suffers (home, hospital, or torture room), and regardless of the cause of his suffering (disease, burns, torture, or malfunction of the pain network itself), the person in great pain experiences his own body as the agent of his agony. The ceaseless, self-announcing signal of the body in pain, at once so empty and undifferentiated and so full of blaring adversity, contains not only the feeling 'my body hurts' but the feeling 'my body hurts me.'"[2]

Everything that affects the body will affect how we address loss and what will intimately be contained within that loss statement. The grief process, always individually decided upon, will make use of the composite remains of the tincture made from the distillation of loss. Medical losses can be some of the most difficult to address. When our own body appears to turn on us it is the ultimate feeling of betrayal.

AGING AND LOSS

When my mother had reached her sixties she was known for her commentary on aging. Once she was looking in a full-length mirror and proclaimed, "I don't know whose body this is, it surely isn't mine!" Another time she said, "I can close my eyes and I still feel like I did when I was younger, in my twenties or thirties, but when I open my eyes and look in the mirror I don't recognize myself."

May Sarton writes, "I am not mad, only old. I make this statement to give me courage. To give you an idea what I mean by courage, suffice it to say that it has taken two weeks for me to obtain this notebook and a pen. I am in a concentration camp for the old, a place where people dump their parents or relatives exactly as though it were an ash can."[3]

Aging can be a daunting process filled with ample opportunity to practice the art forms of loss and grief. Some people dread aging for the inevitable physical changes including grey hair, loss of skin elasticity, loss of muscle tone, changes in body and body organs, and loss of hair. The physical changes are profound. If you have looked at photos of yourself when you were five and then sixteen, the changes are astounding. The same is true comparing a photo from age forty to one at age seventy. Quite remarkable changes take place over time if we are fortunate enough to live that long to observe the changes.

Aging is not only about the loss of youth, it is also about inching forward toward death. With each year we live we are that much closer to having to entertain the event and process of death. Many of my senior-age clients wonder a good deal about death in their sessions. When some are in their eighties and spry and healthy they wonder what it will be that comes to end their life. Will it be illness or an accident or some random event such as a break-in at their home?

Aging is also about watching many others die and change. The older one becomes, the more people one has known who have died. As one ages one also watches changes in others such as adult children.

Camilla was eighty-six and still working at a local stationery shop. She has four children, one daughter and three sons. Camilla had three marriages. Two ended due to her husbands' death and one ended from divorce many years ago when her children were still young. There was concern that her first husband may have sexually abused one of her sons. As time went on and the first husband died, the son whom we will call Mike started having emotional difficulties. He was dealing with anxiety and severe bouts of depression. His wife of many years was stoically removed and Mike started to have financial problems. Camilla spoke to Mike and in time Mike revealed he thought his father had done things to him when he was little. He hated to put this issue on his aging mother, but he felt he had nowhere else to turn. He wanted to know if Camilla thought it was possible that it had happened.

This was difficult for Camilla for many reasons. For one, she didn't want to revisit the old pain she had known in the relationship with Mike's father, her first husband. She had discovered during their marriage that he had a "thing for boys." Young men populated their home and just seemed to hang out. The husband would also go away for weeks on end. She had no proof of his being either homosexual or a child molester. She simply felt it was a marriage of convenience for both of them. Camilla also did not want her son to suffer, as she wondered if the husband had done things to Mike. Her suspicion was based on instinct and sometimes feeling an air of discomfort when she entered a room that Mike and his father were in. Mike was only four. Sometimes we experience deep loss and grief due to the passage of time and the things left undone or the things that ask for clarification later on.

Aging can be about relinquishing a home and embarking on a journey into a nursing home or long-term-care facility. This is difficult for most that must make this shift. Most third- and second-world countries do not send the old off to be cared for by strangers. But, even in countries such as Mexico this is becoming more common as families resent caring for aging parents and grandparents. In a study, Maribel Blasco and Ann Varley found some striking cultural contradictions. On the one hand, they noted that in Mexico strong family ties are a part of the "national soul." As such, many authors assume that the elderly will receive care from relatives. They noted, "This myth of the ideal family is a persistent one, but many elderly people cannot, in fact, rely on their families for housing and support. Some of those who are housed by relatives are neglected and abused."[4] In the end, this pervasive, mistaken belief that family will support its members has resulted in a gross lack of institutional provision and governmental assistant for the elderly. It is further complicated with beliefs that hold that an elderly mother not cared for by her family must have done something to deserve this fate. The "reap what you sow" attitude is pervasive as an explanation for why bad things happen.

THE DYING PROCESS

Most people appear to fear the dying process even more than death itself. Death is inevitable whereas the dying process is unique and differs from person to person. Some will die in agony and suffer greatly and others will seemingly go peacefully in their sleep.

What is it about the process of dying that influences our understanding of loss and the grief process? I imagine people fear the unknown and being able to stay in control in a process that can be out of control. In the United States we don't have as intimate a relationship with the dying process as some developing countries do. In many countries throughout the world people die in the home without medical assistance, hospice, or any sanitizing of the process by way of medications for pain. Death is real, death is unpleasant, and death invariably involves suffering.

Although I don't advocate for a return to suffering as the remedy, I do believe we have pushed the process of dying away from view, and due to this are ill prepared when it comes time to die or assist those we love in the process of dying. Today in the United States a close family member need not participate at all in the dying of her spouse.

Consider the case of Frank and Maxine. They had been married for over thirty years when Frank was diagnosed with pancreatic cancer. Pancreatic cancer is purported to be one of the most painful cancers. Frank underwent three bouts of chemotherapy in order to buy perhaps nine extra months of life. During the third round of chemotherapy he decided enough was enough. He did not want his dying process to be one of pain, vomiting, constipation, and trips every other day to the emergency room. After he stopped chemotherapy he began feeling better. He could still walk the dogs and drive his car to the grocery store. He and Maxine went to church and had friends over for dinner. Frank and Maxine did not talk about Frank's dying. Frank decided to give his special art collection to his daughters. He decided to give his special gun collection to his sons. He started saying goodbye to friends. He wrote colleagues and told them of the cancer. He would likely have four months to live, at best, according to his oncologist. He and Maxine still did not discuss his cancer or his dying.

Maxine felt it was wrong to talk to her husband about dying. She worried he would think she was urging him on. When asked if perhaps Frank might want to talk about it, she replied, "Then he will have to bring it up directly, because I cannot."

Hospice was eventually called in and the nurses explained to Maxine that Frank would do OK until he fell down. What they meant was not that he would physically fall, but that there would be deterioration in his ability to get around and then one day he would be unable to get up again. From this point forward, he would die fairly quickly.

Well, hospice may have had the same conversation with Frank. Frank did not fall down or sit down much at all. At best he would sit in his recliner in the living room. He could not comfortably lie down on the bed due to pain, and he began to take pain meds daily. Frank and Maxine still did not talk about the dying.

About two weeks before Frank died, hospice told Maxine that he had perhaps a month left. Although his heart was strong they suspected any day now he would "fall." Frank did not fall and Maxine and Frank never had that discussion about how Frank felt about dying.

Frank sat down one afternoon in front of the television. He never got up. He died in about three hours.

Maxine wished she had spoken to Frank. She was afraid of doing so. She didn't want emotions or tears, from herself. She wonders what he was thinking and feeling. She wonders if he thought she didn't care. But some people are unable or unwilling to face up to an impending loss. For some, just the mention of it can be akin to giving up; for others the very acknowledgment of the impending loss may be too much to bear.

My mother and I were close in her last years of her life. She would tell me that she wished she could "just leave this body." She said, "Do you think it is suicide to want to die and leave your body?" My mother had been ill for some years and not well off and on for much of her adult life. It wasn't that she didn't like life; she often didn't know how to live life happily.

Mother was fond of saying, "I wish you could tell me how to get out of this body."

One day I said, "Mom, you have had a number of strokes, have a stroke, but this time make it work." She looked at me in amazement, as though I had provided her with an exit strategy and a map.

I didn't want my mother to die, not at all. However, my mother did voice feeling finished with life. She had diabetes that was not well controlled, she had had a number of strokes, and she had chronic problems with uncontrollable diarrhea and loss of urinary control. She was unhappy and suffered from depression. She was noncompliant with her medical doctors more often than she was a willing participant in her own health care.

My mother died five days after I uttered those words about the stroke. She had a stroke, her kidneys failed, and she was dead in less than one hour. It was a perfect death for my mother. She had always said she didn't want to be a burden to her children and wished for a quick and painless death. One wonders how much of the dying process is in our control and how much isn't.

My mother dealt with loss openly most of her life. She was candid about what she didn't like about life as she aged. My father had preceded her in death and she didn't have a direction or goals or things she felt she still needed to accomplish. She grieved the losses that came with her aging and most of these had to do with simply terrible health and not feeling able to do almost anything that required physical exertion. This is what she meant when she said, "Whose body is this anyway?"

The dying process is an opportunity to grieve and to share with others. For some it is a very private affair and for others it is very open. Sometimes we don't have to be there for loved ones because so many specialty services exist that help and help us stay back from the process.

DEATH

Death is the final loss. It represents a change as well. It is here that we go from living to no longer being alive. Depending on your beliefs death may be a transition as well. Many believe an afterlife is on the other side of death. Others believe in reincarnation and still others believe there is nothing.

What one believes about death, as a finality or a transition to another place, does influence how one looks at this loss and what type of grief will be a part of the loss process. Sherwin Nuland writes about death in his 1995 book *How We Die*. He asserts, "It is a dignity that proceeds from a life well lived and from the acceptance of one's own death as a necessary process of nature that permits our species to continue in the form of our own children and the children of others. It is also the recognition that the real event taking place at the end of our life is our death, not the attempt to prevent it."[5]

Death is often thought of as the worst thing that can happen. However, many people who suffer with disease, who have survived torture, or those who have witnessed the torture of others would assert death is not the worst thing that can happen. Death is an end of life and due to this end there is no more that can be done. We cannot love the person more or tell them of their importance. We won't have an opportunity for apologies or for the asking of forgiveness. Time stops when death occurs and the relationship we had with the deceased ends with the cessation of their heart.

The grief process with death can be difficult. Saying goodbye always is. It has been said that conflicted relationships make for a more difficult grief process. The less complicated our relationship is with the one who is dying, the easier it is to let go.

We will discuss the special types of relationships in the following chapter and how loss enters into family relationships. Each intimate relationship carries a unique responsibility and experience at death.

NOTES

1. Servan-Schreiber, *Anticancer*.
2. Scarry, *The Body in Pain*, 47.
3. Sarton, *As We Are Now,* 3.
4. Blasco and Varley, "Intact or in Tatters?"47–55.
5. Nuland, *How We Die,* 255, 256.

Chapter Six

The Family Constellation of Loss Scenarios

There is no tragedy in life like the death of a child. Things never get back to the way they were. —Dwight D. Eisenhower

COURTSHIP AND DATING

People aspire to find someone with whom they can form a bond and live out life comfortably with a safety net formed by a special connection. We are drawn to being in relationships from the moment of our birth. It is through others that we often come to see ourselves more clearly and help the other be more clearly seen. It is true that unhealthy relationships can have a negative impact on the self and how we view self and others. Here we are speaking about the ideal reason we seek connection with another.

When we meet that special someone we are, by ritual, drawn into some form of a dating scenario. Even within the American culture this ritual is different in different regions throughout the United States. The dating ritual also differs from a public high school setting to a private boarding school setting. There is not one way that young people will come together and spend time with one another. Dating, if successful, leads to courtship, another ritual. During courtship the intentions are for permanency if it can be a mutual desire. Courtship is the process by which two people come to know one another and ascertain if there is sufficient chemistry, similarities, conflict styles, and overall belief-system similarity in order to sustain a long-term relationship with one another. During courtship the ideal is that things such as money, work, whether children are desired, and other particulars such as religion and family of origin are discussed. In some cultures courtship is quite formal, as in arranged marriages. In some cultures courtship is barely discernible.

Jenny and Jeff were both seventeen. They met in photography class and both attended a private day and boarding school facility. They were day students and lived in the local town. Dating amounted to eating meals in the dining hall together and studying at the same table in study hall. They would go for hikes together during breaks in their schedule. They held hands and they stole kisses on occasion. In time they had a sexual relationship, but they had never gone on an actual date. They hadn't gone to the movies or to a dinner at a restaurant. Jeff didn't bring Jenny flowers and they didn't exchange cards or love notes. They dated through their junior and senior years in high school and then parted ways when both were accepted to different colleges. They kept in touch, but theirs was not a relationship either was intent on keeping. It was still an important relationship with a strong bond. Years later Jenny was diagnosed with breast cancer. She was married to a financial advisor and had one child. Jeff flew to be with her during her surgery and recovery. Jenny's husband was fine with this. Jenny has been cancer free for a couple of years and she and Jeff remain in touch and close.

There are no wasted moments in life if those moments have to do with another individual, with loving, sharing, giving, receiving, laughing, and wondering. Each person who crosses into our lives has value. The value may be short term in nature or it may last a lifetime with either its direct influence or a more indirect affect. We grieve the loss of relationships. We grieve breakups with boyfriends, girlfriends, and special partners, whether the relationship became physically intimate or not. It is important to take time and reflect on the love and loves that have passed through all of our lives. Every gesture of kindness impacts our lives. Every offer of compassion and love impacts another.

MARRIAGE AND LOSS

In today's world marriage is spoken about with a mix of sentiments. Some believe it is unnecessary to place a contract on a relationship whereas others believe the contract needs to be binding. Then there are those somewhere in between.

Many marriages last for years and others end early on. A divorce is a significant loss, but so too is a marriage. Marriage represents a change from single life to married life and this represents a loss. Many losses give way to wonderful opportunities and marriage can often be one of these opportunities.

As a therapist who works with many couples, I have come to view marriage as the ultimate experience of potential for growth and change. In the marital connection the vulnerability expressed from partners can be used to understand things that could never have been understood through another path of experience. All couples have conflict, but those who can stay with the tension of the conflict, and find what it is in that conflict that will set each of them free, revel in what I view as true emotional freedom.

Kathy and Bob were married for thirty years when they presented in couples counseling. About five years earlier they had largely stopped having physical intimacy. Neither was happy about this, but neither had the answer to how to make a change back to intimacy or to understand the true reason for the loss of intimacy. Neither wanted a divorce and a lack of sex was not going to be a deal breaker for either of them. They had a deep love and respect for each other. Bob could accept living out his life without sex. Kathy could do the same. They were committed to keeping their friendship, marriage, financial security, and history. So what do they do? They had been to many therapists off and on in their marriage and evidenced a psychological and emotional sophistication. What would be discovered was that the very acceptance of a lack of intimacy was key to the issue they had not uncovered. Bob would discover that he was punishing his wife by accepting a lack of sexuality. He was punishing her for old things that had happened much earlier in their relationship. Kathy was punishing Bob for other things, also dating back to the very beginning of their time together. It wasn't until the last of their four sons moved out that they took up residence in separate beds and bedrooms. Why now?

Not unlike many couples that aspire to create large and wonderful families, Kathy and Bob learned early on to compromise certain individual needs in favor of couple and family needs. Bob had affairs with other women early on in their relationship. He took responsibility and corrected this problem. He had been faithful for over twenty years. Kathy felt shamed and humiliated, but for the sake of the family and Bob's change of behavior, she was willing to move forward and continue with the family and relationship intact. The problem for both of them was that the underlying issues surrounding the infidelity were never addressed and there were many issues. Sexuality took on a life of its own; it became a macabre mascot for everything unspoken. Both were willing to sacrifice physical intimacy because deep down it kept alive the old hurt and anger.

Loss and grief became embedded in the very fabric of Bob and Kathy's marriage. This is not unusual, and something that marriage counselors encounter every day. For Bob and Kathy there was something about their brutal honesty with one another that loosened both of their positions. Bob realized ways he had historically hurt his wife and Kathy realized she was using intimacy and the lack of it to take a stand against old hurts. This insight made it possible to call a truce, and they did. They are closer now than ever before. Insight-oriented counseling can work very well with many people.

PREGNANCY

The prospect of carrying a life inside of you is just short of a miracle. The idea that two of you created this new life is almost beyond comprehension. It is delicious, overwhelming, frightening, and powerful as an experience. It is also the perfect template for loss, grief, and a lifetime of frothy joy mixed with angst and suffering.

Sometimes a pregnancy will end within a month or two. We refer to this as a miscarriage. Our bodies are smart machines with all sorts of checks and balances in place to oversee functions within the body. The same is true when it comes to pregnancy and the growth of a fetus into a full-term neonate. At times there are genetic issues and our bodies recognize when things do not come together properly after the joining of egg and sperm. A miscarriage is the body's way of aborting a fetus that is not determined to be well. There can also be reasons due to the mother's health. If she is sick, under enormous stress, or has suffered a significant trauma, the miscarriage is a way to keep mother alive. It is as though the body decides who is at risk and why and makes a decision for us. There is always loss involved, even if a pregnancy last a short time. Expectations, wishes, plans, other family members, and the future are all tied up in the prospect of this little life joining yours after birth. When a death takes place you have no choice but to change the dreams and the thoughts about the future, at least with regard to this pregnancy. Miscarriage can be devastating. The loss and grief may not even be apparent to others, who often encourage a grieving mother to move on and try again, without properly working through the feelings bound up in the loss.

Stillbirth is when a fetus grows to full term or near full term but dies at some point during the birth process or just prior. The fetus will be delivered vaginally or through cesarean section. In either event, it is an overwhelming experience to feel a life growing inside and then to know it has died. According to the American Pregnancy Association, stillbirths affect approximately twenty-five thousand families each year.[1] As with many types of loss, stillbirth can involve shock and disbelief. There is often blaming of self or others for what has taken place. The mother has the additional loss and issue of dealing with hormonal changes, breast milk that will not be used, and the aftermath of healing from a full-term pregnancy. The partner or husband may blame himself. They too were expectant fathers and a death is difficult in any situation. There is something particularly shocking when a near newborn dies just before making it to life. For those affected by stillbirth it often feels like a betrayal of something sacred. It is easy to blame self or those close to you, but blaming is not the solution.

Often, following a stillbirth parents are allowed to spend time with their stillborn infant. This is an important part of the grief process. You can hold your child, take photos, have handprints or footprints made, and even name the infant. A child can be baptized and you can receive a baptism certificate. Culture and one's cultural beliefs dictate how comfortable individuals may be with embracing a dead infant. It is important to choose what would be best for you and your family. Some families hold a memorial and have funeral services. Other families choose not to do this. It is important to remember grief is a process. For some, it will assume a form of stage progression such as shock, anger, depression, and acceptance. For others, it will not be linear at all. Still others may experience depression followed by acceptance. Some people will lead with sadness blended with acceptance. There are many ways to grieve. Later we will discuss when grief has become a problem

CHILDREN, PARENTING, AND LOSS

Becoming pregnant is both a loss and a gain. The loss aspect of giving up life as a couple without children is a part of what it means to form a family. Once that decision has been made and a child is born, most parents would agree that their lives are changed forever. Most parents would also agree that parenting is the singularly most important activity they have engaged in during their lifetime. Still others find (affectionately or not) that parenting is a life sentence.

In the big picture of what it means to be a parent most parents would endure any nightmare, all forms of torture, unending anguish, and anything else life wishes to toss in their face in order to keep their child or adult child alive. There is a bond in parenting and it is a uniquely powerful bond of love and protection. So, imagine what is felt when a child is taken from you by way of death. The natural order of life is disturbed. Children follow their parent's death, rather than precede them in death. This is what we are told is supposed to be.

Losing a child is likely the most difficult loss one can endure. The road to acceptance is long and hard in many cases. It is intimately tied to how the child died, whether there was advance warning, if suffering was involved, and the age of the child. Our children, whether age five or fifty are always our children. Death is one form of loss, but there are numerous other losses that have to do with parenting a child. If a child develops a mental illness many parents view this as a loss. Likewise, physical disabilities are seen as losses. Indeed, both emotional and physical limitations are losses. That is, they are a change from what was. As a change it requires the parent to change as well. As with all losses there is great potential in using that loss in some powerfully advantageous way. Imagine all the brilliant people in history who struggled with emotional or physical limitations. They made contributions despite their limitations. And, perhaps their contributions were due in part to the losses they were asked to address.

A common saying recurs when people consider death: "There are many things worse than death." When one ponders this statement there are things that immediately come to mind for each of us. Certainly I have known many clients who have felt death would have been easier than certain things they were asked to address as a parent.

Connie was a single mother with one son. Connie and her estranged husband, Ramon, put up with one another. They divorced when Chad was five. When Chad was sixteen he was going down that feared path of drugs, alcohol, risk taking, and playing around on the dark side of life. By the time he was twenty he had an arrest record. One night, while intoxicated and using drugs, he attempted to rob an elderly couple. He ended up killing the woman by accident and the man had a heart attack and died. Chad was sentenced to two consecutive sentences of twenty years each. It was a blow to his parents who, without question, loved their son. Connie visits her son every other month at the prison where he resides. Ramon visits when he can. It is heartbreaking for all those involved in scenarios such as this. Loss is the operative word and many lives were affected. Loss can have a ripple effect on many others besides the direct participants.

Cindy and Paul had five children. All of their children were bright, engaged in sports and community, and the entire family attended and volunteered in church activities. One of the five children was a girl, Candace. Candace married another bright and promising person. They had three of their own children and were well on their way by their mid-thirties to creating a life where dreams are realized and put into reality. One night following a rare argument with her husband, Michael, she became so angry that she ran to the bedroom and removed a revolver in the nightstand drawer. Michael had followed her to the bedroom. She shot him, killing him instantly. She then turned the gun on herself. The children were in the house and the responsibility for calling 911 fell to the six-year-old. Both parents were dead and the three children took up residence with the grandparents. Both sets of grandparents committed to raising the children. The level of loss and grief is unthinkable in situations such as this. Yet everyday people are killed, someone comes undone, and actions are taken that cannot be taken back.

Our children are in our care, but we are not responsible for what they become. We influence outcome, but do not determine it. In any event a parent will grieve the loss of his child. A parent's life will be forever changed if a child dies or is taken away.

Children are also our teachers. They teach us about our struggles, our failings, our inadequacies, and they encourage introspection. All it takes is a look of fear or horror on a child's face as a result of a parent misstep for most parents to step back and wonder what they just did. It is humbling to learn from a child and yet I believe children enter our lives to teach as much as to be taught. If a parent is open they will grow by leaps and bounds through the experience of parenting. There will be many losses, things to give up, ideas to toss away, and reconsideration after reconsideration. Every "I will never" will become a "perhaps." And every "never" will be asked to be reconsidered.

WHEN CHILDREN BECOME ILL

Dealing with children and illness is always a difficult and heartbreaking experience. Even in situations where a child is sick with a bad cold or a stubborn flu virus, the child is vulnerable and does not understand illness. They feel bad and parents and other loved ones feel bad for them.

When a child has a serious illness such as a terminal condition, cancer, or other potential life-threatening medical issues such as kidney failure, juvenile diabetes, or bipolar disorder first evidenced in childhood, parents are in for a landslide of loss, chaos, confusion, and emotional upheaval.

When I was an infant I had pertussis or whooping cough. I don't remember being ill, but my mother would occasionally bring up this early illness. She always said the same things each time the subject was broached. She said, "It was awful, you couldn't breathe, you almost died." I remember thinking it was certainly terrible that I almost died, but because I couldn't remember almost dying and an infant has no concept of death, my interests turned to my mother's fear that I almost died. It was clear she felt powerless to do anything for me as an infant in that state. I was hospitalized for a time and did regain my health. Every time I got a cold that involved a cough or when I had bronchitis and later when I once had pneumonia the look of terror on my mother's face was clear. It was as though the first insult of her infant almost dying was experienced as a traumatic event. Each time I was ill she reexperienced the trauma along with all of the fears and worries that she had the first time.

Not all parents react the same to a child being ill. I think it is safe to say that most parents feel powerless, upset, perhaps angry, certainly confused, and always terrified. Parents fear losing their child to death. Parents feel responsible, even when they aren't. There is a bond that exists that is just short of crazy making. A parent will go to almost any length to intervene on their child's behalf. That said, on the other hand, I have met and worked with parents who were coolly detached, but this is less common.

Parental reactions to severe or terminal childhood illness can include anxiety, depression, obsessive-compulsive behaviors, panic attacks, and a combination of all of these. Obsessive worry can be maintained even when a child successfully completes treatment for cancer. Rumination, worry about the return of the disease, and troubling thoughts often remain for parents after a disease is even cured.[2] Parental stress levels climb when they care for and worry about a child who is sick. Parental stress levels are associated with later parent-child quality of life following treatment for a child.[3] Conversely, when a parent is ill it poses a host of problems for the parent, the family, and the parent-child relationship. Parents often feel ill-equipped to manage parenting when they are dealing with a personal illness; they worry about the effect their illness will have on the children and later repercussions for the child, and they may neglect their own self-care during illness due to these stress levels.[4]

It is important to keep in mind that children who are ill and being treated for life-threatening illnesses often endure trauma as a result of that treatment. It is an unintentional consequence of saving lives. It is no fun to be poked, prodded, given enemas, injected, incised, or given chemotherapy. The very things that may save a life can and do produce trauma.[5] These are scary things for children and the emotional component of dealing with a sick child adds to the stress levels for parents, the ill child, siblings, and the entire family network.

Lastly, we don't choose if or when our child or children become ill. When illness in a child takes place it takes place in a family with already existing dynamics. There may be alcoholism in the family or drug use and abuse. There may be mental health problems for one or both parents. Either parent may have been physically or sexually abused in childhood, and the ill child may have been abused. It is important to address all of the things that accompany us into a state of illness. A comprehensive inventory will assist caregivers, doctors, your child, and you.

WHEN CHILDREN DIE

Earlier we discussed the death of children. The loss of a child is capable of producing a tsunami of emotions. It may take weeks, months, years, or a lifetime to stabilize after such an event. Research has shown that the adjustment to loss of a child is determined by many factors. There are factors inherent in the parents such as personality, history of significant loss, existing coping skills, mental health history, and specifics to do with how the child died. In addition to how a child dies, parents are greatly influenced by the care they perceive they received if their child died from an illness or accident.

When a child dies over time from an illness, there is time to begin the grief process. This does not mean it is simple or easy in any way. When a doctor tells parents their child may have six months to live the parents attempt to engage in a letting-go and staying-present scenario. Parent and child will often grieve together. There are numerous variables because each situation is unique.

Children who die suddenly in an accident or by way of violence present an unthinkable challenge to those that love them. Unexpected death is more difficult because it is shocking and disbelief is the first round of challenges encountered. I have known parents mull over and over the "if only I had driven her to school," "if only she had taken my car," "if only he hadn't walked to school that day." A sudden death by accident, violence, and abduction creates a context of "what if" and this is emotional torture. Most parents lovingly accept the lifelong responsibility of caretaker for their child and even adult children. Parents feel responsible even when they are not. The instinct to protect is so strong that parents feel they could have somehow divined an intervention that would have saved their child. Indeed, any harm that comes to a child will place a burden on the parents as to any and all of their choices. The most difficult thing to accept is that we can't be the protector all the time and bad things do happen to innocent children.

While the loss of a young child is horrific, the loss of an adult child can be just as devastating. An adult child is still a child and if your adult child dies it is still an emotional insult. As children grow up, their exposure to more dangerous situations (like driving, drinking, or even going off to war) makes them more vulnerable in some ways. It seems rather like a miracle to make it to an older age. Imagine how many proverbial bullets had to be missed in order to have made it to age eighty.

When children die it is important to watch the entire family and the functioning of all involved in loving the child. Mother, father, siblings, and extended family will all be affected, as well as family friends, neighbors, and teachers. It is not uncommon for one family member to grieve more openly and emotionally than others. This does not mean others are not in pain. Everyone grieves differently and sometimes when one is grieving more openly, other family members step back to allow for that expression.

Many times I have had the occasion to work with grieving parents. It may be mother who is inconsolable in her loss regarding the death of her child. Father may hang back and appear to be going on with life. This is usually very far from the truth. While working in the garage the father is building furniture. With each swipe of the sandpaper over the new wood he thinks of his daughter. Each movement he is reminded of her and the times they spent in the garage when she was small, working alongside her daddy. His tears fall to the wood and he sands them into the deepest contours. In time he will apply a stain and then varnish or a light lacquer. His daughter is inside the furniture and his heart. We all grieve differently. It may be difficult for a more openly grieving wife and mother to see her husband's pain, but that does not mean it is not there. The death of a child can ruin marriages, even the strongest ones, so therapy and counseling and the support of friends and family is paramount in the grieving process.

Joanna lost her son twelve years ago from a drug overdose. He was an adult, married, and had three small children. Her son loved birds. He would bring home wounded birds when he was little for his mother to fix. Often she could render first aid and equally as often the birds would die. Joanna and her son, Steven, would dig a grave and bury the little bird. Steven would cry big tears. Joanna would cry because Steven was so upset. After Steven died, Joanna started a bird sanctuary. It grew. Then she opened a pet store catering only to birds. Then she began a rescue organization saving birds such as doves that are often released by unknowing wedding planners at weddings. It is through working with hundreds of birds that Joanna finds peace and communion with her son.

Parents who lose a child are vulnerable to marital tensions and divorce. There is a tendency following the death of a child for parents to blame one another for their respective humanness. It is seldom a parent's fault for the death of their child. Parents may not know where to place all the hurt and anger and they choose to place it on the person nearest to them. This is likely one's spouse or another child in the family. One expects anxiety, stress, anger, irritability, depression, and a deep sense of loss following the death of a child. The concept of acceptance of the event is possible, but for most it takes considerable time.

Keep in mind that the manner in which one's child died influences the grief process. Accidents and illness are often somewhat easier to deal with than murder, war, and terrorism. The reason for this is that illness is a process and it blends well with grief as a process. Accidents are not typically intentional and therefore there is no culprit or enemy. Murder, war, and terrorism differ because they are personal. In these cases someone set out to intentionally harm or kill. The intentionality is what makes the grief process more complex. Healing from any death that involves a child will be difficult. However, when you know your son fell asleep at the wheel of his car on his way to classes at the local college this will be experienced much differently than when you learn your son was raped and murdered walking home from college to the dorm at night. Even the sentence I just wrote evokes anger as the words pass from falling asleep at the wheel to rape and murder. An accident is no one's fault, and violence against another is always someone's fault. Healing will be a complex and individual journey. Some people find that individual counseling and group counseling with other parents of children who have died helps them find a place to begin sorting through all the confusion. Later chapters will offer other suggestions on this.

NOTES

1. American Pregnancy Association, "Stillbirth."
2. Duran, "Developing a Scale," 154–168.
3. Kazak and Barakat, "Brief Report," 749–758.
4. Altschuler and Dale, "On Being an Ill Parent," 23–37.
5. Shemesh et al., "Comparison of Parent," e582–e589.

Chapter Seven

Special Considerations about Loss Suicide

Sometimes even to live is an act of courage. —Lucius Annaeus Seneca

Taking one's life may be the ultimate act of desperation. In order to arrive at such a decision there would have been many losses counted up by the one who contemplates an end to life. Suicide is a process and an event. It is the process aspect of suicide that allows us to intervene. Once the event is completed it is too late.

The World Health Organization (WHO) identifies depression and suicide as worldwide problems. One million people die each year by suicide. This is approximately one suicide every forty seconds. According to WHO, worldwide suicide has increased by 60 percent over the past forty-five years. It is the leading cause of death for people aged fifteen to forty-five. It is the second leading cause of death for those in the ten to twenty-four age range. WHO notes that suicide represents 1.8 percent of the total disease global burden as of 1998. [1]

The major risk factor for suicide in Europe and North American is mental disorders, specifically depression and alcohol-use disorders. In Asian countries impulsiveness was identified as a risk factor. [2]

Suicide is a process and a complex continuum involving social, biological, cultural, and environmental factors. Determining a suicide risk involves an in-depth understanding of risk factors, protective factors, psychosocial stressors, warning signs, variables, symptoms, and signals. [3] It is wise to consult a professional if you are concerned about yourself or someone else.

Symptoms or warning signs can include insomnia, hypersomnia, crying spells, loss of appetite, weight gain or loss, apathy, despondency, moodiness, hostility, anxiety, agitation, indecisiveness or impulsiveness, inability to concentrate, physical or psychological exhaustion, and noticeable personality change.[4]

Signals are behaviors that may include threats or hints about self-destruction, preoccupation with aspects of death or impact on others, truancy or running away, disruptive or rebellious behaviors, abuse of alcohol or other drugs, reckless driving, excessive risk taking, accident proneness, sexual promiscuity, social isolation, neglect of personal appearance, putting affairs in order, giving away personal belongings or prized possessions, and revising wills or insurance policies.

Variables or personal and family factors, traumatic events, and life changes can include many things. Some personal factors would include:

- Family relationship; the quality of those relationships
- Lack of close friends
- Alcohol or other drug abuse
- A previous suicide attempt[5]
- Impulsive or dangerous behaviors
- School dropout; school underachievement
- Perfectionism; difficulty handling failures, disappointments, or rejection
- Extreme mood swings
- Signs of depression; poor appetite, sleep problems, and physical complaints

Family factors may include:

- A family history of suicide or a suicide attempt
- A family history of a severe mental disorder
- Alcohol or other drug abuse in the family
- Poor family communication
- Child abuse, incest, neglect, or other harm to the child
- Conditions that reduce the family's stability, including financial difficulties

Traumatic events and life changes may include:

- Recent loss of a family member through death or divorce
- Recent loss of a romantic involvement
- Pregnancy
- Child abuse, incest, sexual assault
- A family move; new town, new friends, new school, new job; no support system
- Earthquakes, tsunamis, wild fires, a tornado, and other natural disasters

- Any event, situation, or change in which loss is involved; in which change and readjustment are involved; in which the dominant theme is loss accompanied by feelings of helplessness, hopelessness, and powerlessness

These factors all have one thing in common. They all represent loss of one kind or another. The loss may build and result in feelings of helplessness, hopelessness, and powerlessness. These feelings may lead to further depression. As depression sets in more heavily, the person may give up or may become angry at himself rather than at others who may be the source of pain or discomfort. The person is then a risk for suicide. If no intervention takes place, the process toward possible suicide continues.

It goes without saying that losing a loved one, friend, or even a colleague to suicide places the survivor at risk. Suicide is a significant loss and the grieving may last a lifetime. In terms of assessing for a suicide risk, knowing someone who did commit suicide in your close circle places you at more risk for a suicide. Suicide is confusing. Even if it comes to be understood (the process leading to the event of suicide) it will still be confusing to those most affected. All death is difficult, but death by suicide combines the worst of all scenarios for those who will grieve. We know it is awful to lose a child, spouse, close friend, or relative. When someone we love ends their own life, it adds the further dimension of "what if" to the picture. Surviving family and friends will question, often for the rest of their lives, what they might have done to prevent the suicide. They will wonder what they did wrong, why the loved one didn't turn to them for help, and endless torturous questions. Suicide ends with an event, but is usually a long-term process. The key to intervening rests with understanding the warning signs and behavioral indicators, risk factors, and life-event variables that can all coalesce in a cascade of powerlessness and choice of death.

Dealing with suicide as a friend, family member, parent, or even a co-worker is difficult. I find my clients do best to educate themselves about what a suicide is and isn't. Starting with the facts helps reduce and often eliminate the tendency to blame one's self. Group counseling and individual counseling are extremely valuable for teaching coping skills and for letting the pain and grief find words and support from others. It is crucial that teenagers and preteen children be given the opportunity to have counseling if one of their friends dies by suicide. It need not be a close friend; the suicide of any person they knew well will impact your child. We don't know what children and teens are thinking. We don't know if they had some last words with the person who died or if an argument took place a week before the suicide. We don't know if the boy that hung himself was in love with your daughter, but she did not return the affection. The suicide of a friend can impact another child for the rest of her life. It can result in the surviving child or children assuming adult lives of depression, anger, and an inability to embrace life.

COMBAT

War means death, disfigurement, disability, and emotional scars that may well last a lifetime. War hurts the person in combat and those who love him. War hurts everyone.

Tim O'Brien writes, "War is hell, but that's not the half of it, because war is also mystery and terror and adventure and courage and discovery and holiness and pity and despair and longing and love. War is nasty; war is fun. War is thrilling; war is drudgery. War makes you a man; war makes you dead."[6]

And war is a major loss. Loss carries responsibility as well. One responsibility is that of carrying the memory, carrying the pain, carrying the love, despair, disappointment, and the hope that the combat was not more than your loved one could carry or more than you now carry for him.

Our loved ones can die in combat and this is a loss to be addressed with all the similarly ugly emotions that have a way of accompanying loss. If a loved one returned home there are losses to be endured as well. These losses are often silent losses that take the form of a changed person. Your husband may no longer smile. He might be staring at the wall or out the window. Perhaps he no longer initiates lovemaking. He may be quick to express anger or go into a rage. All of these reactions represent loss because they represent a change of what was. Returning veterans are often different, altered from the essence of their basic core. We weren't meant to kill even in the name of country, freedom, and safety. But it is done for all these reasons. The point is that it is against what we are taught, told, and believe. When one must turn on their own basic values it creates a state of disharmony and disruption internally. Whether a soldier kills or witnesses killing, it is the same. We were not meant to be active players in the deaths of others. Most humans have family, loved ones, people who will miss them and grieve terribly upon hearing of their passing. Jonathan Shay writes, "If military practice tells soldiers that their emotions of love and grief—which are inseparable from their humanity—do not matter, then the civilian society that has sent them to fight on their behalf should not be shocked by their 'inhumanity' when they try to return to civilian life."[7]

Dying in combat will require the surviving family to have great strength. They may have to help raise children not their own, or support surviving spouses. They may have to raise their children as single parents, and help those children navigate their own grief. Finding resources for families who lose spouses or children or siblings to combat is essential to the recovery process.

On the other hand, surviving a tour of combat duty has its own set of challenges, and requires strength as well. Depression, anxiety, posttraumatic stress disorder, and substance dependence and abuse are just some of the basics that many military men and women may have to deal with. They need love, support, and lots of expert help. They need to know we will help them through an unthinkable ordeal. Resources are more abundant now than ever before. In prior times, such as during the Vietnam War, returning veterans came home to an angry and uninviting populace protesting the war. Since veterans were a part of the war they were blamed as well. Today the Veteran's Administration in hospitals, clinic settings, and outpatient offices offers a wide variety of individual and group services for veterans. Services outside the VA are also available to veterans from private practice mental health professionals. Family counseling is available, as well as individual and group counseling through most community mental health centers.

The returning combat veteran will have many challenges when they return home. Challenges can be grouped into those experiences that took place while in service as a military professional, any physical traumas that resulted, emotional traumas, ongoing home-related issues the service person heard about while serving in the military, and life at home when they return. Additionally, life at home did not stay exactly the same over the passage of time. Changes took place at home during a tour of duty. Children may have grown or were born. Wives or husbands may have become ill or suffered from accidents or face their own emotional issues. Parents and siblings have had issues in their lives as well. Life did not stand still the day the military serviceman embarked to a war zone. All of these things need to be processed and yet a return home may feel like everyone needs something from the returning veteran. It is important to take time to debrief emotionally, to seek counseling even in the absence of significant issues, and to eventually pull your family into the counseling as well. If there are significant issues, trust that this is the best time ever to seek help for anxiety, depression, posttraumatic stress disorder, and any other mental health concern.

PETS AND ANIMAL FRIENDS

People who are not animal people may have a difficult time understanding the significance of the death of an animal friend. People who have pets whom they consider family members understand this loss very well. The Humane Society states, "Animals provide companionship, acceptance, emotional support, and unconditional love during the time they share with you. If you understand and accept this bond between humans and animals, you've already taken the first step toward coping with pet loss knowing that it is okay to grieve when your pet dies."[8] Those who grieve the loss of a pet, grieve a dear loved one and often go through a grief process similar to the passing of another person.

I would like to share a story about Abigail Goodspeed and Oliver Twist, who are two cockatiels that live with me.[9]

Last fall I had Abigail and Oliver outside for a few moments of cool sunshine. We were at a bird feeder and they were taking in the sun and mild breeze. Abigail was on one shoulder and Oliver was on the other. They have been clipped and do not have the ability to fly upward, but they can fly level and downward.

Oliver was a rescued bird whose name is about his little twisted foot. As a toddler his foot was grabbed by a conure and broken. He was taken to the veterinarian and his foot was put in a cast. He hobbled around in the pet store for a time, falling over and being trampled by other cockatiels. He was stepped on and urinated on and was in need of being placed somewhere so he could recover and learn to be a bird. The storeowner gave us Oliver to get him out of the chaos. He needed to learn to walk, to step up, to climb, to clean himself, and to be a bird.

Abigail is the voice of reason. She is a proud bird who thinks through every move before she makes it. She is beautiful and wise. She took to watching over Oliver. Oliver needed some watching over in the beginning.

We have a resident female Cooper's hawk who lives between our property and the neighbor's in a two-acre tract of land that is heavily treed. We have outdoor water and the hawk has a wonderful place to hunt. She has lived in my backyard for some years.

The hawk watches me and comes fairly close. She is comfortable being less than twenty feet away at the birdbath where she drinks, the woodpile where she sits, or in the sycamore tree where she watches for rodents, baby quail, and other critters that live here as well. We have had conversations of the silent kind. I enjoy her presence.

On this afternoon the hawk flew in from the northeast part of the property, heading south. Oliver caught a glimpse of the hawk as she flew by into the neighbor's property. He panicked. He flew off my shoulder and in the direction of the Cooper's hawk. Abigail screamed and flew in the opposite direction, away from the hawk. I was stuck in the middle. Who do I rescue first?

I went for Abigail as she was closer and I held her close as I took off in a sprint over rocks and a ravine to get to the neighbor's property where I had to jump a high wall. I heard Oliver screaming. I saw the hawk circling and beginning her descent. Just as I was about to hurdle the rock wall, Abigail got loose and flew to the chamomile patch. She was almost invisible and hiding beneath generous dense sprays of daisy-like chamomile.

I thought for a split second. "Leave her there, she is hidden, get to Oliver, Abigail will be fine hiding."

I didn't interrupt my hurdle over the rock wall. Oliver was on the ground and the hawk was within ten feet. I snatched up Oliver and held him to my chest as I ran back to the chamomile patch to retrieve Abigail.

I heard Abigail screaming. This is the scream only heard when very bad things are happening. It is a death scream. Abigail was gone from the chamomile patch and in the talons of the hawk, now over twenty feet above in the air.

Oliver answered each of Abigail's screams with an ear-piercing scream. He wrestled to get loose from my hold as he watched the hawk with Abigail up high. He wanted to fly toward her and the hawk. He screamed like an angry and frightened animal.

The hawk was heading to the top of the Arizona cypress, the tallest tree on the northeast side of the property. I was running as fast as I could. I reached the base of the tree, looked up at the hawk, and screamed one word, "NOOOOOOOOOOOOOOOOOOO."

The hawk looked at me. Abigail stopped screaming. Oliver bit into my left fore finger and couldn't let go as he trembled and made a low guttural noise.

The entire world stopped for a moment.

Blood was dripping from my finger and Oliver's little face was stained red with my blood. The hawk dropped Abigail and flew away.

I found Abigail in the next tree over sitting silently on a branch perfectly still. I called out her name. She looked at me. I held out my finger for her to step up. She stepped up to my finger and I put her on my shoulder and we three went into the house.

Abigail was not physically harmed. Oliver couldn't look at Abigail for several hours.

This story has many stories within the story. I find the same is true with all of us as people. We live in relation to each other and occupy different roles as we interact, caretake, or love one another, including our animal friends.

I don't know why the hawk didn't kill Abigail. I don't know why she dropped her, following my very long and loud "No."

Oliver is now grown up, strong, and proud. Abigail is still the voice of reason. The hawk sometimes comes to the tree outside the window where the birds have their inside play area. She looks at them for a few minutes and then flies away. They run and hide under the bed or take off into another room in the house. They had an encounter with a Cooper's hawk.

Animals entrust us with their very survival. They are in many ways children that will never grow into independence and leave the nest to start lives of their own. Their entire life will be spent with us. It is a daunting responsibility and it entails loss for those who have opened not only their homes but also their hearts to the small creatures of the world. We experience loss, depression, anxiety, and fear when they die. We long to have them back and people may feel they didn't do enough for their beloved animals while they were here. It follows the same grief course as losing a human friend or companion.

WHEN PARENTS AGE AND DIE

We come to see our parents in an evolving way over a lifetime. How we view them when we are five is different from how we view them at age fifteen. It will change again by age twenty-five and be nearly unrecognizable by age fifty. By the time parents have reached an advanced age and sit near death's door there is a transformation that has taken place. Our parents are very real, vulnerable, and, for some, parents do not seem real until advanced age.

Many clients comment on how different their parents are as grandparents than they were as parents. Often what they mean is that as grandparents they are kinder, more compassionate, and patient. Grandparents comment on being able to love their grandchildren in ways they couldn't love their children due to responsibilities and little time to actually enjoy the daily interactions, antics, and growth taking place. Parents express frustrations with all the questions their children ask whereas grandparents revel in the dialogue.

What has happened is that the people in question have changed. Parents change and become grandparents. Children change and become parents. We are all in the business of changing and change means loss. Loss means a level of grief and learning to let go in favor of something else or something ahead, whether we want to or not.

Some people will handle their feelings of guilt, depression, and helplessness by emotionally withdrawing from an ill and dying parent. It sounds cruel; yet it is one way people manage overwhelming feelings. It has often been said that in the face of an overwhelming situation or trauma a person has but three choices: fight, flight, or numb to the experience. Emotional distancing is a form of numbing or flight. Children who are adults now watching their aged parent leave life may be filled with a host of unresolved feelings. They may not have treated their parents well or they may have held them as emotional hostages over the years. Often there is financial exploitation and cruelty. Early Freudian psychology took a general position in its infancy to speak about all the problems parents would cause for their children. It would not be until the late 1990s that research would be created to look at how parents endure the abuses of their children.

Kenneth was in his fifties when his mother died of pancreatitis. She was in the hospital for two weeks before dying a fairly painful death. Kenneth was partying with friends and did not want to bother going to the hospital. Kenneth was an adopted only child. He did not wish to remember his mother as suffering and he feared the memory of her in a hospital bed would stay with him forever as a phantasm of torture during his already numerous sleepless nights. His mother died with her husband by her side.

Kenneth's father declined steadily following his wife's death. He was a smoker and he lived alone. He didn't prepare much for himself in the way of nutritious meals and he had few visitors except the occasional lawyer, trust advisor, or banker. Kenneth seldom went to visit his father even though they lived in the same town. On one occasion Kenneth went to see his dad and found him sitting in the dark alone in the house. He learned his father had not eaten for two days. A cigarette burned in the ashtray near his recliner chair. Kenneth told his dad he would get him some food. He went to a fast-food restaurant for fried chicken, mashed potatoes, and coleslaw. He brought the meal to his dad and left, as he was late for a concert and party to follow. His dad died alone that night in the chair next to the untouched Styrofoam container of chicken and an ashtray filled with cigarettes that had burned themselves into dainty ash cylinders.

Kenneth struggled with guilt and shame following his parents' deaths. He felt he had been selfish and was now punishing himself by way of nightly intoxication. He was left a sizeable amount of money and yet he felt he was undeserving of the inheritance. Kenneth was intent on destroying himself as punishment for his uncaring attitude toward his parents. This too is an example of loss and the grief process.

Before my mother died she told me she would come back in another form to let me know she was OK on the other side. My mother had a sense of humor! I became slightly concerned, because my mother had an intensity about her, and I felt if anyone could come back in another form it would likely be her.

I told her, "Don't, please don't come back in the form of a ghost or phantasm at the end of my bed!"

She said, "Don't worry, I will come back in a way you can recognize it is me."

I said, "How?"

She said, "You love ravens, I'll come back as a raven."

I said, "But, mom, ravens are everywhere." (I live in the Southwest.)

Mom said, "Precisely, honey!"

And every time I see a raven I think of my mother. And, it is good.

Everyone has a story to tell about their parents and their parents' passing. It is one of the most common stories I hear as a therapist. It is more common than stories about how spouse, children, animals, or even friends have died. I suspect there is something about losing a parent that makes all of us orphans. It is rather daunting to go through life with parents and then one day not have them anymore.

Loss of our grandparents is also significant. I remember living near my paternal grandmother, Josephine. She was always available and my grand instructor on all the dark things in life. I could ask grandmother any question and she would honestly answer. It is important for a child to have someone who is unafraid to answer the darker questions. Grandma Jo would explain child molestation, rape, abduction, and suicide before I was ten years old. She was careful about how she explained these things. We lived in the inner city of Chicago and the darker aspects of life and loss were everywhere. I trusted her and she never failed to help me understand the difficult things in life. She added to that a love of cooking, sewing—and singing, which she and I did on afternoons on the back porch.

Whatever your situation with a dying parent or grandparent, remember it is never too late to revisit what worked in those relationships. Seldom is life so simplistic as things being all good or all bad. All relationships are made up of sweet and bitter things. It is important to acknowledge that both exist, but equally important to choose your position. Just because there are problems, do we throw the person away? Every relationship has good components. Even an alcoholic father who raged at his children when he was drunk had times he wasn't drinking when he took his children to the park or helped them change the tire on a bicycle. Father may have entered treatment and entered sobriety as a way of life for the last thirty years of his life. In therapy we work to understand that relationships challenge us to grow past hurt, suffering, judgments, and to grow toward acceptance of what was and is reality. What worked in relationships refers to what was sane, healthy, caring, and honest. We all know what doesn't work such as abuse, rage, hurt, excess anger, and expectations that diminish one's light and self-esteem. If we balance the two it tends to feel better and we tend to choose to lead a life with what works for us and those we love.

NOTES

1. WHO, "Suicide Prevention (SUPRE)."
2. Ibid.
3. Burton, *Entering Adulthood*.
4. Ibid., 73.
5. Ibid., 75.
6. O'Brien, *The Things They Carried*, 86.
7. Shay, *Achilles in Vietnam*, 67.
8. Humane Society, "Coping with the Death."
9. Mongelluzzo, "Abigail Goodspeed and Oliver Twist."

Chapter Eight

Extended Loss

I know this: fire blooms, blooms again, marking us, dismantling what we believed inviolable. At times we can do nothing but record its stunning reck-lessness. Later, we sift through the ashes by hand. —Nancy Reisman, *House Fires*

FRIENDSHIPS THROUGH A LIFETIME

Do you recall the friends you had in elementary school, middle school, or high school? How many of those people are still your friends? Some people will keep friends for a lifetime, especially if they stay in place geographical-ly. Much of the mobility of modern times accounts for a fracturing of rela-tionships, home, towns, and communities. People move for many reasons. But, people do move and relationships are lost in the move.

I kept two elementary school friends until college even though my family moved from Chicago to Denver when I was in the sixth grade. I corre-sponded with these two girlfriends, following their progression into college as well. Then, for some reason, we no longer wrote letters. This was before the Internet, e-mail, cell phones, and our instant-access culture.

I have no college friends to speak of, as I moved yet again. I do have many friends who have been in my life for over twenty or thirty years, but they were not classmates. They were colleagues, people I met in the work-place, and they became close friends.

Everyone's story is a bit different where friends are concerned. What we do know is that we lose friends and learn about loss, but also about memory and how we hold those we once knew in our thoughts and our hearts. A type of eternity exists within. Do people die in spirit or energy? Is that even possible? If we can hold their image and conjure up feelings as real as if they were still with us, have we created a type of immortality and eternity? I doubt we will ever have scientific evidence of any of this, but I take comfort knowing I keep friends alive in an ample space within my heart.

We learn to love, extend our self, receive from others, share time with others, and eventually let go of those same people. As this book repeatedly suggests, we know considerably more about loss than we may have thought, and we have well-honed skills for a personalized grieving process. There will always be those things that can impact us and we may temporarily forget what we know. This book is also about remembering.

When a friend dies it is life changing. There is something significant about losing a peer. This is a type of loss that strikes close, much like lightening striking the tree next to you. It is shocking; because we, in part, survive by thinking our age group is not yet that vulnerable.

When adolescents lose a friend through death they are extremely vulnerable and need support. Death that strikes during the age of omnipotence moves the ground these young adults stand upon. Mortality is a concept that becomes real during adolescence. It is new and delicate as a concept, because it hasn't typically been tested much. Most teens have not lost parents or even grandparents, although many have. Teenagers generally do not lose friends to accidents or illness, but it does happen. As with all of childhood, *first-time* experiences are unique—scary or wonderful. First-time experiences encompass the first time a child eats solid food or drinks from a grown-up glass. It will also include the first movie and the first kiss. Death is the same in that there will be a first time remembered where death is concerned. Death is not easily understood by children or by teenagers. Teens will struggle with their feelings about death. They look to their parents and peers for support. They will tell stories about the person and they will write in their journals about the unfairness of death. They are afraid of death and at the same time intrigued by its power. Death has the power to bring adults to their knees, to bring forth confessions, to change lives and lifestyles, and to fill churches and synagogues with mourners. The teen will look to his or her adult models for the appropriate behavior to use, but silently they will ponder thoughts on the meaning of life. This can make things more dangerous for teens and for adults as well. The death of a friend or loved one breaks a taboo. If death occurs near to us it changes how we feel about death. It is no longer exotic, foreign, or something that happens to others. It is therefore no longer taboo. This is why we see mass suicides and local epidemics of suicide. If Johnny can die perhaps death isn't that bad, may be one teen's sentiment. Another teen may say, "What's the point, you live and then you die, why bother?" It is actually very common to hear these words in counseling .

Death and teens: the two words placed together create tension in a sentence just as they create tension in life. Teens need stable adults, counseling, group support, school support, and avenues to dialogue on the meaning of death and life. Counseling is very popular with teenagers. I have seldom met a teen who didn't like coming to counseling. In counseling they talk about all things, including coming to terms with what it means to live, to suffer, to die, and to understand their unique life purpose.

We may not think of young adults as being unhealthy, but illness and disease is common enough among young adults. And the loss of good health is no less significant for younger sufferers. In a study of adolescents with multiple sclerosis (MS), a grounded-theory research design looked at how teens addressed being ill, being terminally ill, and their secondary losses and grief process surrounding social, emotional, and cognitive grieving.[1] Loss of health was the primary loss, but losses in terms of one's social group, emotional connections, and the ability to cognitively express oneself were equally as significant where grieving was concerned. It is one thing to be an adolescent and have MS and quite another thing to lose functions, peers, and emotional support all at the same time. This study suggested, "Dynamic relationships either facilitated or impeded this process (of grieving)." What this means is that important and significant relationships had the power to positively or negatively impact the adolescent with MS.

One tool young adults can use to help them with their grieving, be it the loss of a friend or family member, or the loss of good health or something else, is books. Many people have written memoirs about their own losses that explore grief and the grieving process and shed light on what we feel when we can't put it into words ourselves. Such books help us understand new ways to view the grief process. Journaling is another important tool. Often teen clients keep journals and read from them during sessions. These journals could someday become best-selling books. A form of journaling known as auto-ethnographies provides detailed firsthand accounts of grief. This has become a research tool used by behavioral scientists to study the grief process. Other tools such as art therapy and music therapy will be discussed in upcoming chapters.

SEPTEMBER 11, 2001

No matter how you refer to it, September 11 or 9/11 or 9-11 all mean the same thing. By now most people remember the day when terrorists used aircraft to fly into the World Trade Center's North and South Towers in New York City, to crash into the Pentagon causing partial collapse on the western side of the building, and to crash into a field near Shanksville, Pennsylvania, following passengers' attempt to wrest control of the plane from the terrorists onboard.

This event was one heard the world over. It was shocking due to its suddenness. It was beyond belief due to the coordinated attack involving multiple planes and locations. It was dizzying because it was not expected. Close to three thousand people would die as a result of the September 11 attacks.

The world was shocked, America and Americans were shocked, and a ripple effect spread across our country following these attacks. It was as though the whole country became New Yorkers on that day and for many days following. We still feel the effects. Fear became a staple of modern life, the economy recoiled, and almost every teenager and many young children now have a cell phone. I asked one mother why she bought a cell phone for her eleven-year-old daughter. She said, "How else will I know where she is?" September 11 had an effect on adults, but also on young children. I see many of them, who are now young adults, in therapy. They suffer from anxiety, depression, fears of failure, and uncertainty about taking risks and moving into the future. I haven't conducted a study, but it does come up in counseling that they saw the terrorist attacks replayed on television and no one really explained what it all meant. Families were fearful of flying, vacations were cancelled, people spoke in fearful ways, or they spoke in anger and in a discriminatory manner. Children do not understand all these things. What they did understand was that things felt unsafe, because mom and dad and school and even the news said it was unsafe. Anxiety is fear about something that hasn't happened. Many children developed anxiety as a result of seeing and hearing all the 9/11 reports without fully understanding their impact. Parents kept them closer, by way of electronic tethers (cell phones), but gave them freedom because who knows how long anyone will really live given the terror threats.

One little boy said to me, "Ms. Nanette? I saw this newspaper at Ben's Market. There was a picture on the front of it of that Osama man. What I don't understand is why someone drew an X through his face and it said under the picture, Wanted Dead or Alive. Who would write those words, Ms. Nanette?"

Children don't understand hatred. Hatred is learned.

All of us were made more vulnerable by the September 11 attacks and hopefully we have used the losses and our grief process to make things better within ourselves, with our families, and in the world. The best use of loss and grief is to create something new and good with the change that was forced upon all of us.

New York City took the brunt of the terrorist attacks. Economic and health issues surfaced, and grief was palpable. When a city is hurt it is akin to a person being harmed. The person may be angry, vengeful, depressed, in shock, or enter acceptance. When a person is hurt they can develop posttraumatic stress disorder and many people did following 9/11. Is it possible for a city to develop PTSD as well? Sometimes by posing the question, the point is not that of being insulting, but of wanting to add a dimension of understanding so that assistance can be offered, so that compassion becomes palpable, and so that people and their city can heal.

SCHOOL SHOOTINGS

The most recent school shooting as of the writing of this book was in Newtown, Connecticut, at the Sandy Hook Elementary School. Adam Lanza murdered twenty children and six adults on December 14, 2012. Adam shot and killed his mother before going to the elementary school that morning. Adam was twenty years old. He committed suicide, by shooting himself in the head, following the rampage.

Mass shootings, and in particular school mass shootings, are deeply disturbing. Children killing other children is beyond our understanding.

School shootings are not common, but nor are they entirely uncommon.[2] In February 2010 there was a shooting at the University of Alabama-Huntsville, where a professor killed three people. In January 2011 at the Millard South High School in Omaha, Nebraska, a student killed one person. In Ohio, the Chardon High School shooting took place in February 2012 where a juvenile shot and killed three students. In April 2012 a forty-three-year-old former student of Oikos University in Oakland, California, shot and killed seven individuals.

In the years from 2000 through 2009 there were nineteen school shootings, with the deadliest being the Virginia Tech shooting where thirty-two people were shot and killed in Blacksburg, Virginia, by Seung-Hui Cho, a student at the university.

In the 1990s there were seventeen school shootings, including the Columbine School shooting in Columbine, Colorado, where Eric Harris and Dylan Klebold murdered twelve students and one teacher.

In the 1980s there were three school shootings. In the 1970s there were five school shootings, including the Kent State University school shooting where the National Guard opened fire on students protesting the Cambodian Campaign. Four students were killed and nine injured. There was one school shooting in the 1960s.

Mass killings that were not school shootings total thirty-three from the 1700s through 2012. The most known are likely the Beltway sniper attacks, the Waco siege, and the 2011 Tucson shooting of congresswoman Gabrielle Gifford and six others. Congresswoman Gifford survived.

We all experience loss and we all grieve when we hear of innocent children and adults becoming victims of someone's anger, revenge, or unresolved issues of another kind. Striking out instead of working things through has a devastating effect on everyone. It promotes more anger and anguish.

Why these murders happen and why they take place in public places with the victims largely being unknown to the killers is not entirely understood. Perhaps there is no way to make sense of something senseless. When these shootings occur there is a need for understanding, and government officials as well as thinkers and analysts try to find a way to curb or limit these events. You have heard about the measures to enact stricter gun-control laws. We know that mental health has entered into the discussions as well. It is safe to say that mass shootings and school shootings are the result of a complex series of factors, variables not known at the time of the events in the shooter's lives, and risk factors that outweigh protective factors in the mental health and personal/social life of the shooters. Can we come to know the people who live in our neighborhoods, on our block, and those who may, for whatever reason, feel they have become marginalized or pushed away from mainstream acceptance? If we truly want to stop killings we need to return to a time of knowing one another, intervening on one another's behalf, and have programs in place to assist people in need.

CRIMES AGAINST HUMANITY

Another type of loss is the loss that takes place when crimes are committed on a large scale against groups of people. These stories are covered extensively in the media. Our history books recount crimes against others and our children will learn about these crimes and wonder how such things could have happened.

Some of the most horrifying events are actions taken against people by other people. Some part of us understands that nature is outside of our control. We view storms and earthquakes as horrible but a part of living in the natural world. Actions by people against people are a very different story. We hold expectations about humanity and what is prudent, proper, and humane. When these rules are broken and people do unthinkable things to others, the loss explodes and can get stuck in anger and revenge for generations. "Immanuel Kant had written of the two things which fill the mind with admiration and awe, 'the starry heavens above me and the moral law within me.'"[3]

Where does morality go when women are raped in Bosnia, when human blood stains walkways and roads in Bangladesh, when six million Jews are exterminated in Germany, Poland, and elsewhere, when torture is customary, or when people are routinely "disappeared" for disapproving comments about the government?

The Rome Statute of the International Criminal Court Explanatory Memorandum defines crimes against humanity as "particularly odious offenses in that they constitute a serious attack on human dignity or grave humiliation or a degradation of human beings. They are not isolated or sporadic events, but are part of either a government policy (although the perpetrators need not identify themselves with this policy) or of a wide practice of atrocities tolerated or condoned by a government or a de facto authority."[4] Crimes against humanity can include murder, extermination, torture, rape, political, racial or religious persecution, and numerous other inhumane acts. Crimes against humanity that take place during a war are often referred to as war crimes. Many crimes against humanity take place outside of war settings. Examples of crimes against humanity outside a war setting include honor killings, mass murders (such as those described in the previous chapter of this book), school shootings, bullying, homophobia and resultant murder or torture of a homosexual, torture, isolation and long-term solitary confinement in prisons and jails, mistreatment of prisoners in prisons, jails, and detainment centers, ethnic cleansing.

Marc Pilisuk writes, "Violence is evident where any life is harmed or ended through the behavior or negligence of other people. It takes many forms. We will concentrate on two of these: military violence (or war) and economic violence in which the requirements for life and livelihood are taken away or destroyed. Violence may be direct, as when one uses a gun or bomb to destroy others, or structural, as when patterns of land ownership and land use by distant corporate entities result in the starvation of children who live on that land."[5]

Torture is defined by the United Nations Convention against Torture, as follows:

> For the purposes of this Convention, the term "torture" means any act by which severe pain or suffering, whether physical or mental, is intentionally inflicted on a person for such purposes as obtaining from him or a third person information or a confession, punishing him for an act he or a third person has committed or is suspected of having committed, or intimidating or coercing him or a third person, or for any reason based on discrimination of any kind, when such pain or suffering is inflicted by or at the instigation of or with the consent or acquiescence of a public official or other person acting in an official capacity.[6]

Violence, torture, and crimes against humanity may not be as rare as we are led to believe. When crimes against humanity take place we all suffer, we all lose, and we will all experience a deep sense of grief, while we mourn the injustice in the world, and more, we mourn what has happened to the sense of morality in our world.

Jonathan Glover writes of the My Lai massacre in Vietnam where U.S. troops led by Lieutenant William Calley acted out a crime against humanity:

Early in the morning the soldiers were landed in the village by helicopter. Many were firing as they spread out, killing both people and animals. There was no sign of the Vietcong battalion and no shot was fired at Charlie Company all day, but they carried on. They burnt down every house. They raped women and girls and then killed them. They stabbed some women in the vagina and disemboweled others, or cut off their hands or scalps. Pregnant women had their stomachs slashed open and were left to die. There were gang rapes and killings by shooting or with bayonets. There were mass executions. Dozens of people at a time, including old men, women and children, were machine-gunned in a ditch. In four hours nearly 500 villagers were killed.[7]

We grieve as human beings for other human beings who had to endure unthinkable acts perpetrated by others. I have worked with children of Holocaust survivors and they grew up hearing their parents speak of being in concentration camps and the death that surrounded them. The adult children of these survivors remember the solemnity of their childhood. One generation placed on the next generation an inevitable influence. These adults are careful how they tell their stories to their children for fear of robbing them of the joy of life.

Crimes against humanity and hate crimes can create a sense of powerlessness about the state of the world. Children and teens often comment on these things in therapy. I don't know how much they share with their parents, but I know in therapy it weighs heavy on their hearts. This is their world too and they wonder if things like this can happen to others, what is in store for the future, for them, or for their children.

The best way to honor the grief we feel for what happens throughout the world is to educate ourselves about those things and be able to respond with informed understanding when the occasion presents. We can be involved with many organizations that exist to raise public awareness and give grief the power to change things to something better. Amnesty International, Physicians for Human Rights, Doctors without Borders, Psychologists for Social Responsibility, United to End Genocide, the Southern Poverty Law Center, and many other organizations exist where help and input is appreciated. This is an avenue for expression of loss, grief, and a way to turn powerlessness into power.

NOTES

1. Thannhauser, "Grief-Peer Dynamics," 766–777.
2. Wikipedia, "List of School Shootings."
3. Glover, *Humanity*, 1.
4. Wikipedia, Rome Statute.
5. Pilisuk and Rountree, *Who Benefits from Global Violence*, x.
6. Crelinsten and Schmid, *The Politics of Pain*, 20.
7. Glover, *Humanity*, 58.

Chapter Nine

Global, Environmental, and Geographical Loss

Destroying rainforests for economic gain is like burning a Renaissance painting to cook a meal. —Edward O. Wilson

THE RAINFORESTS OF THE WORLD

The name rainforest comes from the amount of rain that falls on a heavily forested area. An annual rainfall in excess of sixty-five inches characterizes a rainforest. Rainforests are ecosystems that contain enormous biological diversity. It is estimated that more than 50 percent of all life on the earth is contained within the rainforests. It is further estimated that more than fifty million species live within the rainforests. Rainforests contain unique medicinal plants, from which many of our modern medicines have been derived. Many of the world's largest rivers are found within rainforests and the amount of oxygen turnover produced by rainforests is over 28 percent. Why then are rainforests destroyed, plowed down, and burned?

Rainforests are prime real estate, exquisite sites for timber harvesting, areas providing superb hunting and species collection, and areas that provide homes to many native peoples of the world. All of these factors have come into conflict over the years.

Deforestation is a process by which heavy logging and clearing takes place in the rainforests. Unique varieties of wood are sold and a profit is realized. It is hard to convince companies to look to the future when a profit can be made in the present. This is not a unique problem, but rather one that has plagued the world for some time.

As our natural world is destroyed, along with many unique species of plants and animals, we cannot help but feel a sense of loss, powerlessness, and grief. Who is it that decides on actions that affect so many? The answer to this question is involved but wraps around special interest groups, politics, corporations, and those who would choose a profit today over long-term world stability.

People can and do grieve environmental loss. I have visited places twenty or thirty years ago only to return and find forests gone, replaced by homes. A sense of loss and loss of control is palpable. The environment cannot be replaced. The damage done cannot be reversed. It is as though a disease was infecting our natural world and we are not using the medicines we know would address the problem.

Forest conservation is important for the control of global warming. Global warming is changing the world as we know it. Increased awareness is the key to controlling irreversible changes in the quality of our atmosphere and planet.[1]

FUKUSHIMA NUCLEAR REACTOR INCIDENT

It was March 11, 2011, when the Tohoku earthquake and the tsunami to follow would result in a perfect storm of events that led to the Fukushima Daiichi nuclear disaster in Japan.[2] Equipment failures, nuclear meltdowns, and release of radioactive materials would send a wave of fear throughout Japan and the world. There was fear of radiation levels, death, generations of people dealing with genetic changes resulting from radiation, and the poisoning of the waters around Japan. Further fear mounted due to the movement of water and the large fish industry for which Japan is known. Would the fish contain high levels of radiation and could people in California or New York find themselves eating toxic fish? There were no deaths as a result of this nuclear accident or any cases of radiation sickness. The event could be controlled in a short amount of time. But we were reminded of our global vulnerability: what happens in one part of the world in terms of loss and grief can and does affect the entire world.

Fear leads to anxiety and anxiety can be a part of a loss reaction. We lose our sense of safety when there is a nuclear accident. We don't imagine perfect storms that result in accidents that could destroy our world. People who were in Japan at the time of the incident openly grieved their loss of home and safety. I live in a town that is health conscious. Many people were openly worried about fish and the long-term supplies, as radiation contamination is long lasting. Fish caught anytime after the incident could be harmful to health. Local sushi restaurants were concerned, as many of their ingredients came directly from Japan. Many of the sushi restaurant owners were from Japan. There is a trickle-down effect where loss and grief is concerned.

CHERNOBYL

The Chernobyl disaster occurred in April 1986 in the Ukraine. This nuclear disaster is considered the worst ever nuclear power plant accident. There were numerous deaths, and long-term effects such as cancer and radiation-related deformities are still being counted and attributed to the Chernobyl incident. After exhaustive investigations, the cause of the incident would be blamed on human error (operator error), design defects, and operation malfunction.

Following the incident more than two hundred people would become ill due to radiation sickness and thirty-one died within three months of the disaster. Most of the victims were firefighters and rescue workers attempting to control the incident. Rivers, lakes, reservoirs, animal and plant life, and people were affected by the Chernobyl disaster. More than four thousand cases of thyroid cancer were tied to Chernobyl. The mental health of residents in the area and surrounding areas is still a concern more than twenty years later. People still fear the long-term effects of radiation, and this fear creates a sense of insecurity and results in anxiety as well as other mental health concerns.

Fred Mettler is a radiation specialist at the University of New Mexico. He commented, "The population remains largely unsure of what the effects of radiation actually are and retain a sense of foreboding. A number of adolescents and young adults who have been exposed to modest or small amounts of radiation feel that they are somehow fatally flawed and there is no downside to using illicit drugs or having unprotected sex. To reverse such attitudes and behaviors will likely take years although some youth groups have begun programs that have promise."[3]

When accidents happen and there is the potential for long-lasting harm to the environment, humans, and future generations, there is a sense of betrayal. Things changed from what was to a new construct of what is. Change is about loss. Some changes we actively seek whereas others are thrust upon us. We grieve as a world for those who will suffer from cancer due to these accidents and for future generations and their families. It is a painful enterprise.

HURRICANE KATRINA

Hurricanes and other types of natural disasters are devastating. Hurricane Katrina was the deadliest and most destructive of all hurricanes in the 2005 hurricane season. It was estimated that 1,833 people died in Hurricane Katrina. The only hurricane to have a larger death count was the 1928 Okeechobee hurricane.

In addition to deaths, injuries, lost homes and other properties, a disfigured coastline, fear and panic, and dislocation of people, Hurricane Katrina had far-reaching effects on the economy in the Southern states and inland. The oil industry was affected. The forestry industry was impacted. The insurance industry was impacted. People left the affected areas and relocated to other states thereby further influencing the economics of the areas hit by the hurricane as well as the areas receiving the unemployed, injured, and post-traumatically impacted individuals and families.

People were in fear for days waiting for help. People lost their people. They lost a connection to the land, their communities, and their homes. Many thousands of people had to begin again. There are levels of being harmed. Physical, emotional, psychological, and spiritual safety all had to be addressed in the early days, weeks, months, and years following Katrina.

Environmental influences continue to be an issue as beach erosion has occurred. Breeding grounds for marine mammals such as turtles, pelicans, fish, and migratory species were altered, lost, and changed.

When disaster strikes it can bring out the best or worst in people. Looting and violence was rampant following Hurricane Katrina. There was looting of stores for goods and water, carjacking, rape, assault, and murder. A bad situation was made worse.

There was considerable criticism of the government's response and the Federal Emergency Management Agency (FEMA) during and after Hurricane Katrina.[4] Issues such as response time and the pace of mortuary team efforts raised more concerns about human vulnerability and human rights. Disasters are not planned events, but plans do exist for disasters. It is hoped that much was learned from the mistakes made and future disasters will not include the type of trauma for which Hurricane Katrina has become known.

EPIDEMICS

"In 1976, when Ebola broke out in Yambuku that first time, there was a nun, Sister Beata, who died of Ebola," Close recalled (William T. Close). "There was a priest, Father Germain Lootens, who gave her the last rites as she died. She had a terrible fever, sweat was pouring down her face, and bloodstained tears were running down her face. Father Lootens took out his handkerchief and wiped the sweat from her forehead and the bloody tears from her face. Then, unthinkingly, he took the tearstained handkerchief and wiped the tears from his own face with it—he had been crying, too." A week later, he came down with Ebola, and a week after that he was dead."[5]

Epidemics are a scary fact of life. Microorganisms, invisible to the eye, are capable of killing, without mercy, millions of people within weeks. There are two sources of outbreaks, the propagated source or the common source outbreak. A common source outbreak occurs when individuals are exposed to a common agent. A propagated outbreak is one that is spread from individual to individual with each person becoming the source from which it can be spread again. There are many ways that agents, such as viruses, can be transmitted. Some transmission routes include: airborne transmission, arthropod transmission (by insect), biological transmission (the agent undergoes changes while in the host), colostral transmission (vertical transmission that occurs over generations), contact transmission (by biting, sucking, chewing, drinking), and fecal-oral transmission.

Regardless of how an agent is contracted and spread, it is scary and dangerous. Some commonly known epidemics/pandemics have included: smallpox, Black Death, typhus, Spanish flu, influenza, and tuberculosis. Plagues such as the bubonic (Black Death) were caused by bacterial infections originating from the fleas of rodents.

Loss takes place on multiple levels. There is physical loss, loss due to death, loss of safety, loss of comfort, loss of the way things were, and great psychological upheaval creating ancillary mental health problems including depression, anxiety, posttraumatic stress disorder, adjustment disorders, obsessive-compulsive disorders, and substance-abuse disorders to name only a few. The people we love and care about will suffer and so will we. The towns and communities will mourn and stories will be told for generations of the suffering. We are affected by what goes on in the world. Things that seem to come out of nowhere and decimate populations especially frighten us. Loss and grief have an intimate relationship with epidemics.

YOUR HOME TOWN

The place we call home is sacred. This includes the town and its geography. Pat Conroy, in *The Prince of Tides* states, "My wound is geography . . . it is also my anchorage, my port of call."[6] Geography speaks to us, supports us, and provides an anchor, a base, and a point of reflection. Have you ever been away from home only to return and have a surge of emotion upon seeing the Main Street grocery store or the movie theatre now boarded up and closed? We form relationships with places as well as with people. When these places are destroyed, altered, maimed, or mistreated we experience loss and we are asked to participate in grief and grieving.

Hometowns can be harmed by the people who live there, by outsiders who do not, and by nature or the passage of time. Much like people, towns require upkeep and care or they start to wither and die. It is sad to watch this happen to people and it is sad to watch this happen to towns. Although people may not think it is the same, our towns embody a part of us. We created these towns and the collective known as the townspeople maintain the town. If the town takes a downward turn it hurts the people. Did they do their part? Did they contribute to the downturn? Could they have done something to help?

When Disaster Strikes Your Community

There are disasters caused by people and those caused by nature. We know the devastating effect of wild fires, hurricanes, tornados, tsunamis, and earthquakes. Nature can explode in a fury and people, along with their geography and towns will be harmed. Change will occur and change takes us back to our discussion of loss and grieving those losses.

Let's talk a bit about wild fires.

Fire is about destruction, loss, grief, dismantling, decomposing, fragmenting, things falling apart and then somehow putting things back together again, but not in an identical way, because that is not possible.

We feel passionate about our geography. Our sense of place in our world is tied to our geography. One of the most immediate losses for individuals who live in the communities affected by fires is the loss of their geography. It changed; it is now charred and darkened. It is disfigured. It is barely recognizable. It is not the place of solace, nurturance, and dependence. It has been harmed and cannot now care for you. You have to care for it, while also attending to your other wounds.

There is a link between people and land. The people who live on the land in question are the insiders; it is their land and they have a relationship with the land. People who visit the land from elsewhere are outsiders. They do not have the same relationship with the land. This may, for some, complicate the grief process, as many of the helpers have come from elsewhere.

Wild fires can be natural disasters, but they are also often started by humans, whether on purpose or by accident. Other natural disasters, like hurricanes and earthquakes, cannot be prevented. In all such instances, however, there is not much we can do to prevent the loss of home and land. The pain that comes from sitting and watching, or running to save one's life as weather encroaches, can be confusing and contradictory. On the one hand, a person might feel grateful to have survived, on the other she may be mourning the loss of a well-loved home and its contents. Rebuilding is one way to repair such loss, but some things can't be replaced: the spot where little Nicky took his first steps, the wall where the chidren's heights had been recorded, the photo albums reflecting years in this home. Reflecting on such losses can be painful, but it can also be cathartic. When such contradictory feelings exist, it's important to honor the good ("I'm alive") alongside the bad ("I've lost all my precious belongings") and to start from a place of grieving that allows for growth in the direction of creating new memories.

Wild fires are life events. All disasters are life events. Life events include all of our combined experiences that lead us from birth through death. Life events carry a responsibility known as loss. All life events are characterized by loss, because unless we are suspended somehow in time, we must move from an event to the next event awaiting our attention.

We are accustomed to loss and we grieve those losses. We do this naturally. Judith Viorst talks about loss in her book, *Necessary Losses.* She says, "For we lose not only through death, but also by leaving and being left, by changing and letting go and moving on. And our losses include not only our separations and departures from those we love, but our conscious and unconscious losses of romantic dreams, impossible expectations, illusion of freedom and power, illusions of safety—and the loss of our own younger self, the self that thought it always would be unwrinkled and invulnerable and immortal."[7]

We can lose many things in a fire or a storm, but recovering what we can from the ashes and moving forward with feelings of a new beginning can help us heal from those wounds that come with material losses.

Things You Lost In The Fire, The Flood, the Storm

Physical Impact

You may have lost your health or physical well-being. Were you hurt, harmed, injured? Was someone close to you injured? There are many physical repercussions including blood pressure, heart rate, respiratory issues, and the release of adrenaline and norepinephrine. Adrenaline and norepinephrine allow us to cope with overwhelming stress. What was your physical health before the disaster, before the fires? What is it now? Recovering physical health is imperative to moving beyond this kind of loss. If damage is permanent, learning to live with new limitations can bring a sense of accomplishment. This will take time and it is important to give yourself the time you need.

Psychological Impact

You may have lost your psychological balance. What pre-existing mental health issues existed before this event? Did you have depression, anxiety, posttraumatic stress disorder, obsessive-compulsive disorder, or another mental health concern? Often after a devastating loss people will develop trauma-related disorders. Seek out help from others about the warning signs of trauma. There is a tendency to freeze up and become unable to act on your own behalf. Others can do this for you and they are willing to help.

Intellectual Impact

You may be challenged by what a disaster has brought to bear in terms of decision-making and cognitive functioning. Sometimes just the shock of an incident may result in limitations you didn't anticipate

Did you suffer from smoke inhalation? Smoke inhalation can cause cognitive ability impairment. You may have trouble thinking clearly and concentration may be significantly impaired. Is decision making more difficult? Are you having trouble remembering things? How is your short-term memory? All of these things are connected to smoke inhalation.

Emotional Impact

You may have lost your emotional equilibrium. Are you more emotional or less emotional? Have your emotions fled? Are you feeling too much or not enough? Do you feel you could explode? Are you angry? It is important to survey where you are emotionally as this will be the first step to deciding what you need to help begin the healing process. Shock takes away our balance and the flood of emotions to follow differs greatly from person to person.

Social Support Issues

You may have lost your social safety net, especially if the disaster requires you to move to a new location, even temporarily. We all need a social net to catch us if we start to fall. Who is there for you, family, friends, neighbors, co-workers, your pastor, priest, and rabbi, your therapist? There is community loss. With everyone struggling to pull their life together, the sense of community is loss, at least temporarily.

Occupational Impact

You may have lost your job or had to leave your job or your job was destroyed as a result of a disaster. One of the dimensions of wellness addresses our occupational wellness. When we lose our connection to how we interface with the world through our employment there is unsteadiness. Finding new employment brings on its own stressors and the loss of income may be devastating. Support systems are often put in place to find victims new jobs or to supplement their income until they do.

Financial Impact

You may have lost your ability to produce income or your losses are more than your finances can handle. You may have repair bills, health bills, and additional things the disaster brought to you that require financial expenditure. This is the time to find out what resources are available to you, and if you are unable to access these resources, it may be time to solicit someone to do so on your behalf—an adult child, a trusted friend, a lawyer, or family doctor. Reaching out in times of need may open some doors so your loss does not seem as great.

Spiritual Impact

You may have lost your spiritual or religious bearings. You may ask why me? You may feel forsaken by God. When life is more or less predictable people take comfort in feeling they must be doing the right things, because all is well. When things don't go well or when disaster strikes it is not unusual for people to question themselves and wonder if they are being punished. Everyone is impacted spiritually following a disaster.

Environmental Impact

You lost your land, your physical surrounding, and your geography. We depend on our physical surroundings to reflect back something beautiful about who we are. If the reflection we see is disfigured and blackened we are reminded about the loss, death, destruction, and we can do nothing but grieve. The environment gives to us and we are stewards of the land. Some people may feel they failed their land.

After a disaster or stressful event people feel they "should" be able to just *move on* and return to life as they knew it. Some experiences are so stressful that we refer to them as traumatic experiences. You may have trouble returning to your daily life. You may have trouble coping and functioning physically, psychologically, emotionally, socially, interpersonally, and in every other sphere of your life.

Posttraumatic stress disorder is the development of characteristic symptoms that last for more than one month, along with difficulty functioning after exposure to a life-threatening experience. Owning the loss, considering its full impact, and then addressing the practical issues may be a start to healing. Long-term emotional and psychological issues may take longer to fully heal

Global, environmental, and geographical loss takes a toll on the planet, our towns, the environment that surrounds us personally, and on animals, plant life, and humans. We discussed the impact of manmade and natural disasters. These are losses for the obvious reasons including displacement of people and animals and loss of plant life and species that were unique and one of a kind. People die, become disabled, and often suffer physical and emotional challenges as a result of disasters. People need to adapt to these changes, and part of that adaptation comes from acknowledging what has been lost in terms of material, personal, emotional, financial, and other losses. The first step toward healing, following the initial impact of trauma and shock is accepting what is. There is life on the other side of loss and grief. The new life will be different and yet change can be a good thing. Most humans resist change because they are holding on to something not yet resolved that is typically emotional in nature. When our hurt, anger, suffering, and sadness are allowed to move we too move to a new place. We often follow the clues and cues of our emotions, but our emotions want to hear from our rational cognitive mind. A little nudging and change is initiated and eventually accepted. This does not mean we forget or even forgive, but acceptance allows our life to continue on with an appreciation for what we do have.

NOTES

1. Gore, *An Inconvenient Truth*.
2. World Nuclear Association, "Fukushima Accident 2011."
3. Mettler, "Chernobyl's Living Legacy."
4. Much of the information on Hurricane Katrina was obtained by news accounts, and especially Wikipedia, "Hurricane Katrina."
5. Preston, *Panic in Level 4*, 81, 82.
6. Pat Conroy, *The Prince of Tides* (New York: Bantam, 1987), p 1.
7. Judith Viorst, *Necessary Losses: The loves, illusions, dependencies and impossible expectations that all of us have to give up in order to grow* (New York: Simon & Schuster, 1986) p 15.

Chapter Ten

The Physiology of Loss and Grief

All of the famous moralists of olden days drew attention to the way in which certain events would leave indelible and distressing memories—memories to which the sufferer was continually returning, and by which he was tormented by day and by night. —Janet (1919/1925, p. 589)[1]

THE BRAIN ON GRIEF

Where does grief originate? How is it made? What is its mechanism of delivery to the human heart and our feelings? Is grief related to our brain, and if so, where does grief live?

Researchers have been studying emotions for some time. We have come a long way in terms of understanding that our emotions have a place in our relationships and in our brains. In a recent study of emotion and the role of the amygdala, Jorge Armony found that the amygdala might be responsible for processing emotions other than only fear and anger.[2]

Years ago Bessel van der Kolk, Alexander McFarlane, and Lars Weisaeth edited a book on traumatic stress. The book, *Traumatic Stress: The Effects of Overwhelming Experience on Mind, Body, and Society*, has become a seminal work for understanding posttraumatic stress and its implications.[3] They posit the notion that we underestimate the role of trauma and traumatic stress in everyday life. It was a widely held notion that only things defined as unique in their catastrophic presentation qualify as a unique stressor necessary to arrive at a posttraumatic stress disorder diagnosis. This included war, dismemberment, rape, extreme domestic violence, and violent assaults. The authors raised the question of whether trauma and posttraumatic stress reside in our everyday lives. An experience of loss and the resultant grief response may indeed qualify as traumatic for many, but not for everyone.

Trauma is an emotional experience and the amygdala is one of the limbic structures studied extensively where emotions are concerned. The limbic system of the brain is where structures such as the hippocampus, amygdalae, anterior thalamic nuclei, septum, limbic cortex, and fornix reside.

Loss is an event and grief is the emotion we assign to that event. Grief is an emotional process. Emotions are tied to the brain. A brief trip through some neurophysiology is in order. The brainstem and hypothalamus are associated with regulation of internal homeostasis. The limbic structures are primarily in charge of maintenance of the balance between the internal world and the external presentation of reality. The neocortex works at analyzing and interacting with the external world. Many parts of the brain are important to emotional processing, however the amygdala has been studied considerably due to a number of controversies about its function where emotion is concerned.

We know the amygdala is connected to the prefrontal cortex of the brain.[4] This is the part of the brain almost directly behind the forehead. The prefrontal cortex can be seen as the thinker or decision maker who has the ability to mediate with the limbic structures and the amygdala on emotional matters. Jorge Armony notes that "Amygdala cells behave as novelty detectors: They respond quickly and strongly to new stimuli in the environment, but learn to ignore them if these have no biologically relevant consequences."[5] We know from studies on posttraumatic stress disorder and fear conditioning that exposure to extreme stress or trauma can result in amygdala hypersensitivity and a hyporesponsive ventromedial prefrontal cortex.[6] Human studies show amygdala activation following exposure to fear. However, studies have also shown that the amygdala is not only activated by fear but by other emotions, including sadness. Furthermore, the amygdala was shown to be active with facial and body recognition of emotion as well as detection of emotion in music. The amygdala is connected to our social processing. We learn about how others feel through their body language, vocalizations, and facial expressions. The amygdala is active in these areas of social-cue processing.

Let's return to our discussion of loss and grief. A loss can be simply a life event from which we quickly recover, such as a visit to the dentist for a tooth extraction. Or, it can be complex and extreme as in the case of a rape, child abuse, torture, death, witnessing death in war or school shootings, and other events that are catastrophic in scope and effect. When a person is grieving it will depend on how much grief has been a part of their limbic and prefrontal cortex processing. Generally speaking, by the time we are adults in our forties or beyond we have experienced considerable loss and learned to grieve emotionally. Our brains have become accustomed to how to work with grief. This is where terms such as resilience enter into the discussion. Some people have resilience, and no matter what life throws their way they seem able to recover and keep going. Other people struggle with what life tosses in their direction. They may manifest anxiety, depression, or other mental health symptoms and disorders. Resilience isn't about how much a person has experienced in their life that was grievous. Rather, it is about how their brain, neurochemistry, and adaptive skills for coping have all become uniquely arranged in a positive coping manner. It is about recovery time and about having a personal narrative about grief that works.

We want to remember that the brain has a role in grief, but what we do with grief will mediate with the amygdala and other brain structures. The prefrontal cortex gives us the reasoning ability, the ability to look at reality and horror, and know that coping is possible. When a person has been traumatized over and over and the amygdala has become oversensitized, there may be a tendency for some people to react to every life event as traumatic or to react to significant traumas in a repetitive, catastrophic way. This is not a conscious choice of the person, but rather a complex dance of life events, life history, trauma and grief history, neurochemical balance, and many other factors.

THE BODY'S RESPONSE TO LOSS AND GRIEF

Emotions are made up of physiological responses, subjective interpretations, consciousness, and mental states. Emotions are influenced by our past life experiences growing up, our culture, our personality, and our overall temperament. Chemicals are a part of a functioning body and our body produces many chemicals for varied reasons, including management of and expression of emotion. Hormones and neurotransmitters such as cortisol, oxytocin, serotonin, and dopamine are some that can help in emotional management. You have heard that good serotonin levels help stave off depression. Cortisol helps to regulate stress. And dopamine levels are related to rewards and drive. Drugs such as cocaine and methamphetamine act on the dopamine system. All in all, emotions are complex and there is no exception when we speak of how an individual interprets loss. Events that are loss-related can produce a personal grief process, which is also based on emotion. When upset due to the loss of a loved one, cortisol levels, serotonin levels, and dopamine levels will all be affected. Oxytocin is best known as the drug the body produces after childbirth. It is however involved in bonding of couples, anxiety, and orgasm. In turn, all of the drugs our bodies produce have an effect on our nervous system. The nervous system is responsible for things such as heartbeat, respiratory rate, muscle tension, sweating, and other functions.

When in a state of grief, we experience emotions, which are tied to hormones or neurotransmitters, which are further tied to the nervous system.

This is why grief is not only an emotional experience, but a physical experience as well.

THE LIMBIC SYSTEM OF THE BRAIN

Emotions are believed to be related to the structures located in the limbic system of the brain. We discussed the limbic system earlier as being responsible for maintaining a balance of the internal and external world of experience. The limbic system is often referred to as the premammalian or reptilian part of the brain. Its job is most closely related to instincts. It functions as a twenty-four-hour surveillance system recording audio, cooperating in video capture, and in recording smell, taste, and touch. It is watching even if you aren't. Its job is to keep you safe and regulate the necessary internal signals in response to what it has recorded and what, if anything, it hears from you on the matter by way of your prefrontal cortex.

When something awful, traumatic, or significant happens the limbic structures, likely the amygdala, pay attention and try to decide whether it is important or not. When many bad things happen the limbic structures are kept busy and the amygdala may become oversensitized. Hyperarousal may occur. Things that happened long ago may be awakened in memory because of something that just happened. The events are not the same, but the emotional response may be similar due to the way the limbic system has organized the events. If the smell of jasmine was in the air when you were struck by a car at age eleven and at age twenty you are walking down a dark street in Yonkers, New York, and smell jasmine, you might find your heart is pounding, your respiration or breathing rate is increased, and you may sweat and feel nervous. Your mind may race and you cannot be sure if you are picking up on danger lurking in the shadows or something else. These are the limbic system structures at work.

The limbic system, in part, is interested in making a record of what an event felt like in terms of the sensory experience of the event. The purpose of this function is self-protection. The limbic system will remind you if something takes place that is similar to a past significant, traumatic, or fear-related event. The limbic system, unless mediated by the prefrontal cortex, will place you in the alert mode. This is why a person might feel upset, tense, fearful, or reactive, and not understand why.

Let's assume that a tiger is chasing you through the jungle. You run as fast as you can. You dart through thickets and undergrowth. The damp leaves moisten your skin as you pass by. The smell of wood resin, plant aromas, and damp soil penetrate your nostrils. The sun is high above the jungle canopy and streams of light form iridescent laser tails through the thick growth thirty feet above. Birds call out. Monkeys howl. Sweat is pouring from your hair and you smell your own body scent. You cut your arm on a razor-sharp leaf and note the mimosa flowers throwing up their tiny arms as you pass. Shadows are everywhere and you think you see eyes in the shadows watching you as you run. You manage to make it to safety. The trauma is over. But is it really? What happens the next time you cut your finger on a knife? Or see a mimosa flower in your girlfriend's backyard? Or smell the damp soil in the neighborhood plant nursery? I think you see the potential here for what we call triggers. Triggers are not the cause of the emotion or trauma; rather, they are reminders of something of like kind.

ILLNESS, LOSS, GRIEF, AND TRAUMA

Being ill or dealing with a disease is far from a benign experience. Outside of colds and the flu when they present in a predictable fashion, many types of illnesses can be disturbing and the interventions may be traumatic.

Kathy was a fifty-eight-year-old woman who was athletic and the mother of two grown children. She lived alone and worked running two small businesses that catered to tourists. One day she was outside her home changing the filters out on her evaporative air-conditioning unit, readying it for use in the warm summer months that were approaching. She had worked up a sweat, but was drinking plenty of fluids. She went in the house to urinate. She took some toilet paper and wiped herself. She noticed blood. She had been postmenopausal for about eight years. She looked in the toilet bowl and noticed considerable blood along with fragments of small clot-like structures. She felt fear. She flushed the toilet and paced through her living room and kitchen. She returned outside to finish the work she had begun and came in and drank two large glasses of water. The next time she urinated, the toilet bowl water was red from an even heavier amount of discharge. She became very upset, but calmed herself and called a friend. Her friend told her it was probably no more than a urinary tract infection, common in women. She phoned her son who told her she should see a urologist, as there was no real way to tell unless a specialist was consulted. Her son indicated a primary care or urgent care physician would have no way to render an accurate diagnosis.

Kathy decided to go to the urgent care. They confirmed blood in her urine. After all, the entire urine cup looked like cherry Kool-Aid. The emergency room physician confirmed she needed an appointment with a urologist and follow-up with her primary care physician.

She went to her primary care provider and an ultrasound of the bladder was ordered. The results confirmed a suspicious mass. Next stop was the urologist who performed a cystoscopy. If you have ever had a cystoscopy you know this is not for the weak of heart. There is no anesthetic given and a tube is inserted inside the urethral opening into the bladder. It is more painful in men because the tubing or solid rod must pass through the penis and the distance to the bladder is far. In women the distance is shorter, but unless the practitioner is artful it will likely be quite uncomfortable.

Kathy's urologist confirmed bladder cancer. Tiny clumps of sea anemone-looking growths covered the top of her bladder. She was devastated. She was aghast. She laughed, "Bladder cancer, you've got to be kidding!"

The doctor wasn't kidding.

Since the original diagnosis over ten years ago, Kathy has had five surgeries to remove cancer from her bladder. She has had a bladder instillation of chemotherapy two times and BCG (Bacillus Calmette-Guerin) treatment twice, where a live attenuated form of *mycobacterium bovis* is given by instillation into the bladder.

Kathy felt traumatized every time she had to go for a three-month cystoscopy to check for cancer reoccurrence. It hurt. Many times her urethral opening clamped closed and the doctor had to dilate the urethra so that the tubing could be inserted. She had panic attacks and anxiety ran rampant. She was terrified of the cancer, its reoccurrence, of her body, and of the treatment necessary to keep her alive.

Kathy developed a form of posttraumatic stress disorder. She dreamt of the invasive procedure. She would have flashbacks and nightmares. She made a concerted effort to avoid talking about the cancer, urine, or anything like a bladder. She avoided going to the side of town where the urologist's office was located. For Kathy, medical interventions necessary to keep her alive and help her were also making her sick.

It is not unusual for people who are being treated in a hospital or for cancer to feel traumatized by the treatment, procedures, setting, or personnel. Most providers are kind and mindful that the patient is having a hard enough time, and they strive to make the treatments professional and compassionate. There are always exceptions, such as the occasional nurse or physician who is having a bad day on the day you arrive for chemotherapy. They may be preoccupied, short, noninteractive, or appear uncaring. It adds to the stress levels.

In Kathy's case she felt the nurse in the urologist's office was cruel. The nurse never made eye contact and would ignore her questions unless they were asked two or even three times. Eventually the nurse left the practice and her replacement was positive and cheerful. This made a big difference for Kathy.

We experience loss when something goes wrong with our body. We will grieve the loss of an arm, leg, or a functioning bladder. Kathy longed for the bladder that was full and the relief that followed an emptying of a full bladder. When hobbling around with a catheter she felt deprived of her beautiful bladder. She was in grief. The treatment, which she knew she needed and wanted, was traumatic, invasive, embarrassing, and painful. It takes time to come to terms with a medical loss, the grief that will follow, and often the traumas that will produce more grief and suffering.

THE BODY REMEMBERS TRAUMA AND LOSS

Every time we experience something significant our body will remember what happened long after our conscious mind has stored the item away. This is the basis of posttraumatic stress disorder, where triggers such as sounds, a touch, an expression, or an accidental shove can send a person with PTSD into an emotional avalanche of reactivity and hyperarousal. It can be thought of as a type of conditioned response. If one becomes oversensitized to being yelled at, the mere raising of another's voice will be interpreted as yelling, when to someone else it is simply a raised or passionate voice. "The organism receives information from the environment via its sensory input. After analyzing this input, it responds with movement either of the whole body or of parts of the body, such as limbs or vocal cords."[7] The body is never separate from our experience of events, emotions, traumas, or interactions. We may not be aware of how the body is cueing in on what is happening, but it is. It is in this way that the "body keeps score"[8] of everything we experience from birth through the experience of death.

NOTES

1. van der Kolk, McFarlane, and Weisaeth, *Traumatic Stress*, 47.
2. Armony, "Current Emotion Research."
3. van der Kolk, McFarlane, and Weisaeth, *Traumatic Stress.*
4. Armony, "Current Emotion Research," 5.
5. Ibid.
6. Rauch, Shin, and Phelps, "Neurocircuitry Models," 376–382.
7. van der Kolk, McFarlane, and Weisaeth, *Traumatic Stress*, 216.
8. Ibid., 214.

Chapter Eleven

Grieving Styles

Witnessing means both being present at an event and taking it in. It means having a responsibility to it, the obligation of telling the tale. It means conveying an event, through one's own experience, to the outside world. Witnessing becomes invaluable for significant events: life-affirming events such as birth and marriage, or events of death, loss, and suffering. —Robert Jay Lifton

UNDERSTANDING CULTURE TO UNDERSTAND GRIEF

Culture surrounds each of us. Whether we ascribe to all of the tenets of our culture is not the point. We are surrounded by its influence. Additionally we are influenced by the cultures of others. Culture plays a role in how we experience loss and the ways in which we will grieve. Culture offers some guidance around prescribed rituals, beliefs, and influence of religions infused with culture. The many cultures throughout the world handle loss, death, tragedy, and the process by which these things are internally and externally addressed in different ways.

If we look at American culture we quickly see that it is infused with many cultures. It is one of the hallmarks of the United States. Immigrants from many parts of the world have come here and made this country their home. They brought with them their culture of origin and with that the delights of customs, recipes, foods, medicinal practices and beliefs, and customs concerning grief and grieving. These cultures are at times blended and at other times stand as distinct and separate. We have examples of Chinatown, Japan Town, Little Italy, and other ethnic neighborhoods in many cities throughout the United States.

I grew up in the inner city of Chicago during the 1950s. We lived in a Jewish neighborhood that bordered a Greek neighborhood, which was three blocks from an Italian neighborhood, and one mile from a Puerto Rican neighborhood. As a child I remember the foods, the street smells, open-air produce markets, and rich diversity.

As a child, grief appeared governed by faith and religion. People followed their religious beliefs, which in turn offered rituals around grief, bereavement, and how long mourning should take place. It seemed to add some order to the disordered world of death, dying, suffering, and the bad things in the world. Religion still influences the grief process. Most memorials take place at a church or place of worship. We let our religious guides assist us because religion or faith speaks about an afterlife. Death, as one form of loss, is the bridge to an afterlife. Those who are agnostic or atheist also have the influence of their beliefs to guide them through a grief process. Sometimes it is a personal narrative that has been handed down from ancestors.

I live in Sedona, Arizona. This town is often considered a little subculture of its own. There are many mainstream beliefs in the town and dozens of traditional places of worship. There is also an active and thriving New Age community. The New Age community, as a subculture, espouses beliefs about life and death that vary widely. For example, many in the New Age community believe in past lives, Karma, punishment from past lives, blending Buddhism with New Age beliefs and Quantum Physics, and some unusual and interesting ideas about loss, suffering, and grief. Ceremonies, rituals, cremations, and all manner of prayer to the red rocks and Hopi ancestors of this region come together when tragedy presents. People rely on their culture to assist them at times of loss and transition.

I did my doctoral dissertation in central Mexico working with the elderly women beggars of a small colonial town in the state of Guanajuato. One of the remarkable things I learned during three years of talking to the beggars was how the words "death" and "dying" were inserted into their vernacular. It was a though they were never more than a few words away from death at any moment. The culture of this area is rich. Most people, and all of the beggars I interviewed, were Catholic. The area bore historical evidence of the Spanish Inquisition and the Spanish Conquest. Many of the elderly women recalled growing up on *ejidios* or *haciendas*. One woman recalled Pancho Villa roaming the countryside when she was a small girl. Oral history is rich in these areas as the indigenous population often lacks formal education. History is recorded and shared by way of verbal exchange.

The elderly women beggars I interviewed spoke intimately about death as though it was a friend or foe down the street. Death is a form of separation and abandonment. In the act of death we do take our final leave from life. It was interesting to observe that Mexico has a tradition of a "joking familiarity"[1] with death. These themes have their roots in Mexico's pre-Columbian past. "The ideas of earth and death are intimately intertwined in the religion of the ancient Aztecs. This is not surprising, since the earth envelopes the dead, receives them in her lap just as a mother might hold her children in a fond embrace."[2] According to Frank Gonzalez-Crussi, the Aztec were fatalist and saw humanity as existing for the appeasement of many gods. The sacrifices for which the Aztec are known had less to do with torture and barbarism than with the fertilization of the earth with blood so more crops could be produced. Blood is still used as fertilizer and can be obtained at local nurseries under the name of blood meal. Fatalism found its way into the Mexican culture. For the Mexican, death is a time for merrymaking while at the same time representative of fatalistic impassiveness. In Spanish, dying is a form of being carried away. *Se lo llevo* means he or she was carried away (by something). To die is to be carried away by whatever agents are seen as responsible. This can be God but can, as easily be the devil, the horn, the trap, the big teeth, or the bald one. Death is giving up one's life, a departure, and an element of fatalism. Death is celebrated on *El Dia de Los Muertos* or The Day of the Dead. On November 1st and 2nd, Mexico prepares to welcome back the souls of the departed. Souls return for a few brief hours in order to enjoy some of the pleasures they knew in life. Death is not hidden in Mexico. As Octavio Paz stated:

> The Mexican frequents it, mocks it, caresses it, sleeps with it, entertains it; it is one of his favorite playthings and his most enduring love. . . . He does not hide from death; he contemplates her face to face with impatience, with contempt, with irony. "If they're going to kill me tomorrow let them kill me for once and for all."[3]

Within the Mexican culture death is inseparable from the experience of the soul. The soul has a place in everything from life to death and is inserted in most illnesses.

Culture will influence the grief process. The elderly women beggars spoke about their grief over children lost to death, missing children, alcoholic husbands, domestic violence, and all manner of physical and emotional abuses. Grief was paired with God, the saints, patron saints, and whether alms were received or not in a given day. Grief was a punishment for things, which the women did not fully understand and so they would pray on the steps of a church or in the church in the back, huddled low, in a discrete corner. They were sure they must have done something to deserve this pain. Why else would God make them suffer so? A common utterance by the women each day was, "Well, let's see what God has for me today." They would proceed to walk the town, begging for alms, praying, and seeing what the day would bring.

Ana (not her real name) was a beggar I knew for over three years. She reported feeling very close to God. She was raised Catholic and religion had played a role in her life throughout her lifetime. She held that God grants mercy and she speaks to him every day. God is also the punisher from Ana's perspective. Ana felt God was responsible for a person's suffering. She felt that God decides about her life. Her life is in God's hands, not hers. Ana, at times, appeared conflicted about the dual role of God in her life as the giver and the punisher. If she had a good day of receiving alms, it was because God brought this to her. If her sons were drunk and hit or beat her, God brought this as well. She felt there must be something she had done to offend God, to cause the suffering, and yet she had no idea what this might be. At times it felt like Ana experienced shame when speaking of the suffering and the implication that God created this for her.

Culture and religion coalesce to create a personal grief experience for many people. The beggars of Mexico were extremely candid about their losses, their suffering, and their grief. It didn't fit neatly into five stages or a comfortable linear progression. One problem with loss is that the losses keep coming.

WHAT IS TABOO AND WHAT IS ACCEPTABLE?

Most taboos are cultural and some are personal. Authors writing in the United States about loss and grief often assert that the subject itself is taboo. It seems that Americans shy away from the subject of grief, loss, bereavement, and all aspects of death and dying. That is the perspective of some authors. We are different from other cultures where grief and loss are concerned, but I'm not sure it makes the issues taboo. A taboo generally refers to something forbidden, prohibited, or discouraged.

In American culture, being a developed country, we have access to ways of making illness, disease, death, dying, recovery, surgery, and trauma addressable. We address problems and have both the means and resources to offer people a different way of dealing with loss and grief. It isn't perfect, but is the American way uncaring or protective? We have hospitals, nursing homes, a hospice system that is incredible, social service resources, intervention specialist, protection for children and elders, a mental health system, and ways the poor can access most services. Some criticisms of the American way of grief speaks to Americans sending their ill and wounded away, rather than keeping them home and being more intimately involved in the illness, recovery, or death. Being a new country, comparatively, our way is ever evolving and changing where grief is concerned. The development of the hospice system speaks to the evolving changes.

Pamela Boker wrote *Grief Taboo in American Literature: Loss and Prolonged Adolescence in Twain, Melville, and Hemingway.* She takes the position, through a psychoanalytic assessment, that grief is repressed in both the authors and main characters she examines in her book. She notes the psychological wounds result in a failure to mature, and this observation is further tied to the failure to mourn losses and grow from the pain. Sigmund Freud speaks of grief in his book *Totem and Taboo*. Here he explores a fear of spirits of the dead among traditional societies. In *Mourning and Melancholia*, he takes the position that psychiatric illnesses were an expression of grief that became pathological or complicated. In these and other of his writings, Freud was trying to explain how loss and grief must include a dimension of breaking the attachment to the one we have lost and now grieve. This detachment and distance is necessary, and may account for a certain amount of taboo around death, as taboo suggests creation of distance.

Due to the connection of grief to mental health issues many authors have sought to distinguish between normal grieving and pathological grief. This distinction is important, as there is considerable difference in the path each will follow.

Ruth Konigsberg states, "As British sociologist Tony Walter has pointed out, when something is repeatedly characterized as taboo, as grief has been for the last fifty-odd years, that is a good indication that it is actually anything but."[4] Konigsberg makes a fine argument against the stages of death and shows the evolution of thought regarding how doctors, journalists, and thinkers have portrayed Americans' attitudes to death as taboo.

There may be a cultural taboo about talking about death and dying, but as a psychotherapist, this has not been my experience. Often clients report that their doctors, families, friends, and colleagues view death as a failure. Or death is viewed as something that happens to those who made a mistake or misstep of some kind. When an acquaintance of mine was diagnosed with cancer he was very angry initially and condemned everyone he knew who smoked, drank excessively, or didn't go to church. He felt they were the ones who deserved cancer. He felt he had led an exemplary life and his reward should be to not have cancer. We spoke about how cancer does not choose its victims on the basis of any determination of right or wrong. He had trouble with this until many months into his illness. It was reminiscent of the way children view death at different ages.

Maria Nagy describes three stages of how children view death.[5] Children under the age of five view it as reversible, sleep, separation, a change of environment, a departure, or a form of limited life. The child in the age range of five to nine views death as personified and contingent. Existence and definitiveness of death is accepted but death is remote and cast away. It is not inevitable. People who die "are those who got caught and do not get away." After age nine, death is understood as inevitable, the end of life for the body, universal, and caused by an internal process that results in an end to the body.

Death, dying, illness, and loss are not easy issues to address. Each loss experience is capable of ripping a person from their known universe and transporting them to an unreal place characterized by any number of reactions. These reactions can include a flood of emotions, uncharacteristic cognitions, physiological responses, and either avoidance of or immersion into the topic of the loss. For some they will drown in the literature of death and others will run from it. Perhaps this is what is meant by taboo.

If we look at taboo through custom we see that there are many things that are discouraged, prohibited, and forbidden where death, dying, and the dead are concerned. Every state has laws about where the dead can be buried. There are laws about how long a body can be kept prior to burial if embalming does not take place. Some states require a funeral director to "certify" the death of an individual. If a loved one dies in a hospital, their body will not be released directly to the family but rather to a funeral director or agency. This is true in the United States, but not true in other countries. Embalming (removal of visceral organs and draining of blood) is required in some states, but can be avoided if cremation is chosen or if burial takes place within twenty-four or forty-eight hours, depending on the state where one dies. A variety of states require cooling of the dead body prior to final burial if embalming is not to take place.

A friend of mine lost her father-in-law to cancer. The father-in-law wished to be buried in Mexico but died in a U.S. hospital. His body was released to a funeral director. The family wanted to use their truck to transport the body to the border, where a Mexican funeral director would then take the body to the funeral home in Mexico. The cost for transportation to the border (some three hours) would be over eight thousand dollars if done by the funeral home and the family felt this was inflated. Laws, custom, and perhaps taboo intersect in how a body can be dealt with following death. In the end a compromise was achieved where pricing was concerned. In addition to death certificates there are burial-transit permits and a host of other requirements related to dealing with death.

In Judaism, embalming is forbidden (unless unavoidable due to health or sanitation concerns) as it is seen as a form of disrespect and desecration of the body. In this sense embalming is taboo.

Some states forbid burial on private property unless the property has been licensed as a "cemetery." In Washington state a fetus less than twenty weeks old can be buried on private property.

Green burial is becoming more and more common. Green burial refers to a burial in the ground, in a biodegradable container, without embalming. Natural burial is actually an old custom that is seeing resurgence in popularity. For some years there was a trend toward vaults, embalming, crypts, mausoleums, and embalming. Preservation of the body for as long as possible has been in vogue until recent years. We are now seeing a return to more natural methods, with the goal of just preserving the body long enough to make it to burial.

One conflict observed in my counseling practice is the amount of time people are expected to grieve. There appears to be impatience around grief. Many clients present with stories of their friends, coworkers, and even family who urge them to let go and get on with their life. The person may have lost a child to death or a partner. Grief is a personal journey. Some people will take a little time overtly and grieve silently for much longer. Others take a long time to grieve openly. Most therapists that I know feel it takes at least one year to grieve the loss of a loved one, as it is necessary to experience the annual holidays, celebrations, and seasons without the loved one.

We look to ritual to assist in grief. Death involves considerable ritual. Religions throughout the world offer rituals at the time of death. Some utilize cremation and others wash and anoint the body. It can be a healing part of the grief process as it allows time to enter the painful process with support of faith, friends, and family. In North America certain rituals that aid the grief process include wakes, visitations, memorials, flowers, music, the burial service, and private services. Typically, following the rituals that involve family and community, the people most intimately involved with the grief will take some time to be alone or with close family or friends. Anything outside of one's belief system would be taboo. For some, cremation is taboo. For others, burial is forbidden.

INDIVIDUAL RESPONSES TO GRIEF

Throughout this book we have looked at the highly individualized nature of grief and grieving. A number of theories of grief were presented earlier in the book, but each person finds their own way through loss.

In 1996 the Melbourne Family Grief Study was published in the *American Journal of Psychiatry*. The purpose of the study was to identify grieving styles following the death of a parent. Some of the grief-style clusters identified in this study included those that were: supportive, sullen, conflict resolving, hostile, and intermediate (a blend of dysfunction and cohesive/supportive). The authors of the study offered, "In adaptive grief, family members rally together, share distress openly, and support one another through mutual consolation and care. Avoidant responses involve poor communication, little exchange of feelings, and a lack of intimacy. A distorted pattern includes excessive guilt, anger, blame, or idealization. Inflexible families have difficulty coping with change, insisting that life continue as before. Amplification arises from complex combinations of avoidance, distortion, and inflexibility and is associated with chronic grief."[6]

Kathleen Gilbert identified grief through the lens of families as well. She concluded that family members all have different roles through the grief process. She adds that during the grief process different styles of grieving are evident among family members. The goal of grief for the family and its members is preservation of the family after the loss, rather than a more individualized investment in grief. She raises the point that family members with the same loss do not grieve over that loss in the same way.[7] This may create conflict in families when there is the expectation that they all grieve similarly since they are experiencing the same loss.

Peggy MacGregor looked at parental responses to grief concerning a child with mental illness. She concluded that parents who have a mentally ill child are engaged in a grief response not unlike the grief we see with parents who have lost a child to death. The main difference is that if the grief is not recognized or validated by mental health professionals, there is an overall failure for the parental grief to be addressed. Instead, parents may be pathologized, which in turn exacerbates their bereavement.[8]

Grief is a part of the process of coping and loving someone with Alzheimer's disease. A 2007 study found that caregiver grief increased as the severity of the disease progressed and worsened. "When the spouse with Alzheimer's disease lived out of the home, spouse caregivers experienced more sadness and longing, worry and isolation, and personal sacrifice burden than did adult children caregivers."[9] Personal growth was a part of the grief process, especially among adult children caregivers.

When children experience a traumatic death of a loved one or someone close they can develop Childhood Traumatic Grief (CTG). This is a condition where trauma symptoms act to interfere with the normal grieving process. A 2011 study identified the importance of educators in assisting children with CTG.[10] It was identified that educators can learn to recognize the symptoms of CTG as they manifest in the school setting. Additionally, by teaching stress-management skills, children can be supported in addressing triggers and management of the trigger response to trauma. By staying on top of the trauma the normal grief process is allowed to better run its course.

An area of research neglected in the literature is research on grief and bereavement as it relates to same-sex partnership. A 2008 study looked at some of the mainstream psychological theories of bereavement and found them flawed when it came to helping to understand grief for individuals within same-sex relationships. They found that bereaved gay people were at a higher risk for both disenfranchised grief and stigmatized grief.[11]

Individual grief responses have been applied to the study of the self-employed. In a 2003 study grief and business failure were explored.[12] The author takes the position that grief over a failed business involves negative emotional responses, which can prevent the griever from learning from the events that surround the loss. He offers suggestions on how to incorporate grief recovery into business recovery where learning from the loss helps in both healing and rebuilding.

Do people prefer to grieve alone, with family, or with friends? And does whom we choose to grieve with change as time extends away from the moment of the loss? David Pressman and George Bonanno studied grief preferences using participants from the United States and China.[13] The results indicate people prefer to grieve with family or alone. As time went on, this was even more pronounced as a preference.

How do people deal with the death of a celebrity or fan? Celebrities and their families are often able to create considerable distance between themselves and their fans especially at times of loss. A study in 2012 looked at the death of Dale Earnhart Sr. and how his fans coped with his loss and engaged the grief process by "consumption-related emotions."[14] The fans reached out for things that were representative of the celebrity in order to help them cope with their loss.

There are many individual and group responses to loss. We have looked at a few of these in this section. Let's take a look at grief throughout the world.

NOTES

1. Gonzalez-Crussi, *The Day of the Dead.*
2. Ibid., 45.
3. Paz, *The Labyrinth of Solitude*, 58.
4. Konigsberg, *The Truth about Grief*, 23.
5. Nagy, "The Child's View of Death."
6. Kissane et al., "The Melbourne Family Grief Study," 650.
7. Gilbert, "We've Had the Same Loss."
8. MacGregor, "Grief: The Unrecognized Parental Response."
9. Ott, Sanders, and Kelber, "Grief and Personal Growth Experience," 798–809.
10. Cohen and Mannarino, "Supporting Children with Traumatic Grief," 117–131.
11. Green and Grant, "Gagged Grief and Beleaguered Bereavements?" 275–300.
12. Shepherd, "Learning from Business Failure," 318–328.
13. Pressman and Bonanno, "With Whom Do We Grieve?" 729–746.
14. Radford, "Grief, Commiseration, and Consumption," 137–155.

Chapter Twelve

Across the Globe: Multicultural Understanding of Grief

Loss is nothing else but change, and change is Nature's delight. —Marcus Aurelius, *Meditations*

KEY FACTORS AFFECTING A GRIEF RESPONSE

There are a number of factors that come into consideration when looking at the grief process. Much of what we know about grief comes from studies conducted on a specific type of grief known as complicated grief. Researchers are always looking for better ways to predict complicated grief. The National Cancer Institute offers a comprehensive array of assistance through their website which addresses grief and loss.[1] Some of the areas that have been researched include the following:

• Whether the death is expected or unexpected.
• The personality of the bereaved.
• The amount of social support available to the bereaved.
• The age of the bereaved.
• The religious background and beliefs of the bereaved.

According to studies, it is less difficult to deal with an unexpected loss, than one that was anticipated or expected. The variable appears to be self-esteem. If an individual has high self-esteem, a sudden loss can be dealt with within the normal grieving process. When there is low self-esteem, grief may leave the individual feeling out of control and this increases the likelihood they will develop complicated grief.

Individuals who were highly dependent on a loved one and cope with distress by thinking about the problem are more likely to have problems with complicated grief.

The lack of social support is linked with many mental health problems and with developing problems with grief. When friends, family, community, neighbors, and coworkers are available to help with psychological support or financial assistance or with strategizing about the future, a person tends to cope much better. People who are isolated and alone often suffer from complicated grief.

Research indicates that the younger the bereaved, the more problems they will have coping. However, they do tend to recover more readily. Age tends to be a protective factor where loss and grief is concerned. Living a lifetime has prepared people for loss and individualized grieving styles have developed. A young person does not have the history of loss and likely has an immature grief style.

Some studies show that people cope better with grief if they are religious and attend church regularly. Other studies raise the question that this may also be due to the fact that church is also a part of the social support system.

Children also grieve and there are factors that influence how well a child will cope with loss and grief. Some of these include

- The age of the child.
- The stage of development of the child.
- Prior experiences with death.
- The child's relationship to the deceased.
- How well the child's parent copes with loss and grief.
- The cause of death of the deceased.
- The child's personality.
- The family's openness to communication.
- The family's level of stability.
- The child's basic needs and care being continued.
- The avenues open to the child to discuss the death and openly grieve.

Throughout the world different cultures address mental health, loss, grief, and trauma in their own unique ways. Let's look at some of the cross-cultural considerations of mental health, loss, and grief.

SUSTO AND *ESPANTO*

In Mexico, parts of the Caribbean, and Latin America, there is a folk illness known as *susto*. *Susto* is also included in the DSM IV (*Diagnostic and Statistical Manual of Mental Disorders*, 4th ed.) as a culture-bound syndrome. *Susto* is related to the verb *asustarse,* which means to startle or frighten. Someone who has been frightened might say *"me asustaste"* (you scared me). We might say this when someone comes up behind us and catches us off guard. Someone who is said to be living is a state of sustained fright is said to be *asustado* (suffering *susto*). *Susto* viewed this way, as *asustado,* refers to more than just a startle reflex. It refers to experiences that were deeply affecting and frightening but not necessarily startling. [2]

Susto refers to a sudden fright, but also to soul loss. (Recent literature has brought into question whether respondents to questions about *susto* are referring to soul loss or death.) *Susto* is an illness or condition attributed to a frightening event that can cause the soul to temporarily leave the body. Symptoms can appear any time from days to years after the fright is experienced. Symptoms include loss of appetite, insomnia or hypersomnia, troubled sleep or dreams, feelings of sadness, lack of motivation, feelings of low self-esteem or dirtiness, and somatic complaints which may include muscle aches and pains, headache, stomachache, and diarrhea. [3] The DSM IV–TR states that *susto* may be related to major depressive disorder, PTSD, and somatoform disorders. *Susto* is also known as *perdida de la sombra* (loss of the shadow).

Elena Avila offers the following definition of *susto.*

> A soul that is off balance is said to be suffering from susto, and the treatment involves a "soul retrieval." If one's spirit has lost faith in God or the divine, one suffers an illness as real as a physical or mental illness. All aspects of the self suffer, and one will experience diseases that affect one's body, mind, emotions, spirits, soul, family community, and nature. [4]

Arthur Kleinman mentioned *susto* in his book *The Illness Narratives.* He notes that "soul loss" resulting from "fright" is common in Mexico as well as in various Asian societies. He explains,

> Culture fills the space between the immediate embodiment of sickness as physiological process and its mediated (therefore meaning-laden) experience as human phenomenon for example, as an alienated part of body-self, as a vehicle for transcendence, or as a source of embarrassment or grief. Illness takes on meaning as suffering because of the way this relationship between body and self is mediated by cultural symbols of a religious, moral, or spiritual kind. [5]

Kleinman further notes,

> When we meet up with the resistance offered by profound life experience—the death of a child or parent or spouse, the loss of a job or home, serious illness, substantial disability—we are shocked out of our common-sensical perspec-

tive on the world. We are then in a transitional situation in which we must adopt some other perspective on our experience.[6]

Susto for many is a way to deal with suffering and a way to speak of it. It is a way to grieve loss. However, it is more complicated than even that. The existence of *susto* may well speak of certain social contradictions, harm inflicted by ones we love and trust, and the inability of a culture to support profound loss among its members. As Robert Edgerton observes,

> It is likely that the ethnographic record substantially underreports the amount and kind of human suffering and discontent that has actually existed in small societies, just as it underrepresents the various things people believe and practice that do not contribute to their well-being.[7]

Susto is often used interchangeably with the word *espanto*. *Espanto* is similar to *susto* in that it too involves the soul leaving the body. How the two conditions appear to differ is that *espanto* is considered life threatening as the soul not only leaves the body, but it may wander far from the body, thereby creating a situation such that the individual could die or be seen as already dead. However, authors have documented the morbidity and mortality rates of those suffering from *susto* as higher than those not claiming the condition. The most comprehensive study to date on *susto* states,

> The relationship between *susto* and death falls into two parts. The first is the statistical correlation between *susto* and the likelihood of death, which is far higher than in the absence of *susto*. The second shows the effect of *susto* on the death rate from disease from which the patient is suffering simultaneously. Inclusion of *susto* in a patient's medical history tips the balance towards death.[8]

Susto is generally understood to cause physical illness. Some authors have focused on understanding the social function involved in such "fright illnesses" in an attempt to understand whether the illness of *susto* is a way to avoid culturally expected behavior and responsibilities. Fright-related illnesses are more common in women and children than in men, a finding noted by Rubel et al. and in the DSM IV–TR. In Kroesen's study of emotions in Mexico, he noted that three conditions are seen to be present with the existence of fright illnesses. These include: (1) People believe they can become ill if they are frightened; (2) Emotions such as fright are "hypercognized"; and (3) An explicit cultural desire exists to avoid the appearance of overt hostilities and to present a serene and tranquil exterior in social encounters.[9]

When I worked with the elderly women beggars of Mexico I found *susto* was a part of every participant's story. Life events coupled with the social contradictions concerning domestic violence, elder abuse, family closeness and family care, and shunning of widows all make for impossible situations. How does one grieve these losses in a culture that will not accept them as losses or necessarily as traumatic events?

Susto, like posttraumatic stress disorder, can have a delayed onset. This is referred to as *susto pasado*. Causes of *susto* can include seeing someone get killed, seeing or being in an accident, a sudden shock or surprise, a fall, fear of animals, loud noises, nerves, the devil, and abuse, domestic violence, rape, murder, and children or family becoming "disappeared."

When looking at loss and grief it is important to note that some cultures do not separate the mind from the body. In Latin countries the body and mind are seen as interconnected. Physical and psychological illnesses are often thought to be the result of conflicts within the family, community, or other interpersonal relationships. In Mexico and in Latin communities in the United States, people are less apt to seek out mental health services in favor of seeking remedies for physical complaints that are often highly infused with emotional meaning.

In the Mexican culture, there is no clear separation of physical and mental illnesses. It is believed that there must be a balance between the individual and environment, otherwise one may get a disease. Emotional, spiritual, social and physical factors are major contributing forces to illness, in addition to the humoral theory, God, spirituality, and interpersonal relationships. The causes are God's will or unacceptable behavior. Shame may be associated with genetic defects. Physical disability is usually more accepted than mental disabilities. Furthermore, illnesses are seen as a social crisis and are experienced by the entire group.[10]

ATAQUE DE NERVIOS

This is another Latin American, Caribbean, and Mexican disorder found in the DSM IV–TR as a culture-bound syndrome. It is also referred to in some Latin communities as simply *nervios*. The symptoms here include episodes of shouting, crying, trembling, anger and aggression, a feeling of heat in the body (in particular in the chest and head), dissociative-like features, fainting episodes, seizure-like episodes, and suicidal gestures or impulses. It is, simply put, an attack of nerves. The main feature reported with this culture-bound disorder is the feeling of being out-of-control. It is often brought on by a stressful event such as an argument in the family, hospitalization of a family member, death of a close friend or relative, a separation or divorce, witnessing a traumatic event regarding another, conflicts with children or spouse, or other types of loss.

We can see that in this culture-bound syndrome, as well as in *susto*, there are elements of loss and grief in the trigger events. We want to be mindful of the fact that the DSM IV–TR is not universal. Many countries have never heard of the DSM and many countries have limited access to mental health services or services that would directly address grief and loss. The culture has taken care of the grief expression when there is no formal avenue for which to engage these topics.

CORAJE

Coraje was a word heard frequently in my studies of the elderly women beggars of Mexico. It is not considered a diagnostic category or a culture-bound syndrome. Rather, it is a word used to describe anxiety-like emotions. It means intense anger. In some instances it also refers to courage. Of interest is the origin of the word. *Coraje* comes from the word *corazon* or heart. Kroesen described *coraje* as "a kind of bitter anger which was felt profoundly by the body but which normally did not produce outward retaliation against those who made someone angry. It was more of a suffering of the heart than a triumph of the heart."[11]

Coraje is an emotion that is felt to contribute to both physical and emotional illness. The state can last for years or "as long as the causal event was remembered."[12] *Coraje* can be caused by life events, interactions with people with whom one is close, and frustration that is not given alternative means for expression. Often the events responsible for the emotion are related to loss, change, or grief.

BILIS AND COLERA

These are culture-bound syndromes also known by the word *muina.* The underlying cause of these syndromes is intense anger or rage. Anger is a powerful emotion in any culture. In the Latin cultures it is considered especially powerful, with direct influences on the body. Symptoms can include hot and cold sensations, nervous tension, headaches, stomach problems, screaming, trembling, and in some case a loss of consciousness may occur. Chronic fatigue has been associated with these episodes. In short, anger held for a time without the ability to transform it to something healthier results in the tension finding its expression through the body. The anger may result from conflicts with loved ones or others.

In Western culture this condition would be comparable to what is called a "rage-aholic." It is believed that people who carry the condition of rage or *bilis* are at risk for acting out in ways that may harm others such as through child abuse or domestic violence. Elena Avila speaks about how when her father would drink, her mother would go into rages and violent fights would be the result.[13] The destructive effects on children in the family are palpable.

We can see that conditions such as *bilis* are connected to loss and grief. It is a maladaptive way of navigating through losses, grief, and feelings of being out of control.

HMONG DEATH CUSTOMS

The Hmong are an Asian ethnic group found in Thailand, China, Laos, Vietnam, and in immigrant populations in the United States. Anne Fadiman wrote the best-selling book *The Spirit Catches You and You Fall Down*.[14] It is about the Hmong people in the United States and their struggle to blend their own beliefs with Western culture and medicine. Fadiman writes, "A life-soul can become separated from its body through anger, grief, fear, curiosity, or wanderlust." The Hmong group is unique in its appreciation for the blend of the physical with emotional and spiritual. This is evident, in particular, in their death customs.

Many Hmong moved to the United States following the Vietnam War. They were largely refugees in Thailand who were granted asylum under the Indochina Migration and Refugee Assistance Act of 1975.

They believe in reincarnation, and their culture has a strong foundation in animism or the belief in the spiritual essence of plants, animals, inanimate objects, and all things including human beings. Souls or spirits embody all living and nonliving objects. This belief influences their death customs as the goal of the death rituals is oriented around guiding the soul back to the afterlife.

When a person dies his body is washed by his daughters and sons. Hemp shoes are made for the occasion, as these are necessary for the journey. Specific music is played to assist in the journey. Nicholas Tapp studied the Hmong and lived among them in China. He observes that after the body is washed and prepared, it is placed on a table. Certain items are placed near the body, including a bottle of alcohol, a cooked chicken in two halves of a gourd, a hard-boiled egg, a crossbow, a knife and a paper umbrella are then placed by the head of the deceased.[15] Incense is used to mask the smell of the body and as an offering for the ceremony. Tapp notes that funerals can last from three days to as long as twelve days. Status determines the length of the funeral. Part of the ceremonial process involves the men preparing three meals a day. Each meal will have a ceremonial dish, which is composed of pork and rice.

It is considered taboo to show sadness or distress at a Hmong funeral. Due to the belief in reincarnation, distress would be considered a failure of faith. Funerals do not mourn the loss, but celebrate a rebirth.

Burial follows the rituals of the funeral. Here oxen are sacrificed. A female will lead the funeral procession from the home, where the deceased is carried by a stretcher to the burial site. A number of maneuvers take place en route to the burial site. Directions may change or the procession may stop entirely and regroup. This is to confuse evil spirits who may be lurking. The burial site is typically on a mountainside. Bodies are placed facing west. A fence is constructed around the grave site to protect it from harm.

Following the burial, a thirteen-day mourning takes place where family members offer some sacrifice in memory of the deceased. Due to the belief in reincarnation, a soul can return as a child in the family of one of the relatives. According to Tapp, males in the family of the deceased may not have intercourse for two years for fear of pregnancy. Souls return by way of the males impregnating females.[16]

The Hmong funeral and death customs are extensive. Only a small amount of their ritual and belief has been presented here. There are excellent resources available for those wishing to learn more.

Throughout the world, death involves ritual, custom, beliefs, influence of religious beliefs, and involvement of people in accepting loss, engaging in grief, and letting go of their loved ones. All cultures speak to the importance of life and some ritual accompanies the final departure.

NOTES

1. National Cancer Institute, "Grief, Bereavement, and Coping with Loss (PDQ)."
2. Kroesen, "Es otra cosa."
3. Symptoms of *susto* have been reported in Baer et al., "A Cross-cultural Approach," 315–337; Davis and Low, *Gender, Health, and Illness*; Salgado de Snyder, Diaz-Perez, and Ojeda, "The Prevalence of Nervios," 453–470; Rubel, O'Nell, and Collado-Ardón, *Susto: A Folk Illness*; Mongelluzzo, "Street Stories."
4. Avila and Parker, *Woman Who Glows*, 19.
5. Kleinman, *The Illness Narratives*, 27.
6. Ibid.
7. Edgerton, *Sick Societies*, 5.
8. Rubel, O'Nell, and Collado-Ardón, *Susto: A Folk Illness*, 110.
9. Kroesen, "Es otra cosa,"198.
10. CIRRIE, "Mexican Culture and Illness," 15.
11. Kroesen, "Es otra cosa," 107.
12. Ibid., 108.
13. Avila and Parker, *Woman Who Glows*.
14. Fadiman, *The Spirit Catches You*.
15. Tapp, "Hmong Religion," 59–94.
16. Wikipedia, "Hmong Funeral."

Chapter Thirteen

Complicated Grief and Mourning

To spare oneself from grief at all cost can be achieved only at the price of total detachment, which excludes the ability to experience happiness. —Erich Fromm

WHEN GRIEF DOESN'T GO AWAY

It is one of the most excruciating and painful experiences to know what it is like to have grief last for a very long time. Grief can last in an acute fashion for weeks, months, and years. This type of grief is different from what is referred to as normal grief. Complicated is the word that took the place of pathological grieving. In the literature on grief, the words complicated, abnormal, and pathological are often used interchangeably. Let's look at what is meant by this type of grief.

Margaret was a seventy-six year-old woman. Her husband had died one year earlier from a long illness that primarily revolved around heart failure issues. Margaret and Jeffrey had been married for thirty years. This was the second marriage of both and they had no children by their union. They had a dozen or so children from their prior marriages. Margaret took care of Jeffrey in the last two years of his life when declining health limited his mobility and their choices as a couple. Jeffrey was a Vietnam War veteran and the president of a large corporation. Margaret had several college degrees, but had not worked much outside the home except in volunteer capacities. After Jeffrey's death Margaret was overwhelmed. She lost fifteen pounds in one month and started to develop problems with high blood pressure, neck and back pain, mood disturbances, and stomach issues that further limited what she could eat. Margaret began drinking excessively, especially at night alone in her living room sitting across from the chair where she and Jeffrey spent so many nights watching television. Jeffrey had left Margaret in pretty good shape financially. She would have to be mindful of her expenditures, but she would not sink into poverty. Margaret went to her primary care physician complaining of her physical problems, and he spoke to her about going to counseling.

Margaret remembers telling her doctor, "I have never been to counseling in my life and I am seventy-six. Why would I need it now?"

The doctor explained that Margaret's blood work and other test results showed her health steadily declining. Her symptoms were spreading like germs across a kitchen sink and her mood alternated between crisp and exacting, and angry. Margaret argued with the doctor who in turn told Margaret, "You will die if you don't deal with your anger and your grief."

The doctor now had Margaret's attention. Margaret said, "Die, from grief?"

The doctor said, "Indeed."

Margaret began counseling and soon discovered she had an enormous amount of pent up anger laced around her grief. She loved Jeffrey and yet Jeffrey had been a tyrant, verbally abusive, downright insulting, and limited what Margaret could do in her life. Indeed, Margaret was as angry as a hornet's nest disturbed by raccoons. Jeffrey was also an angry drunk and he smoked incessantly in the house where Margaret lived as a nonsmoker. But Jeffrey was her anchor and her mate. Without him she had trouble imagining life. She longed for him, she mourned his loss, and she felt guilty about her anger.

After about four months of counseling Margaret's blood pressure returned to normal. After six months of counseling Margaret's blood work was normal. After one year she was no longer angry. After two years she was employed and working in a field she had always dreamed about but never thought obtainable. At the three-year mark Margaret won an academic award and was busy helping one of her adult sons deal with cancer. She is happy, healthy, and actively engaged in her life. She is now eighty-four.

Margaret was, before her counseling and recovery, dealing with complicated grief.

Researchers do not agree on one definition for complicated grief. It is described as "an acute form (of grief) persisting more than six months, at least six months after a death. Its chief symptom is a yearning for the loved one so intense that it strips a person of other desires. Life has no meaning; joy is out of bounds. Other symptoms include intrusive thoughts about death; uncontrollable bouts of sadness, guilt, and other negative emotions; and a preoccupation with, or avoidance of, anything associated with the loss. Complicated grief has been linked to higher incidences of drinking, cancer and suicide attempts."[1]

Dr. M. Katherine Shear, in the article cited, notes that an estimated 15 percent of the population grieving the loss of a loved one (or more than one million people) suffer from complicated grief or "a loop of suffering."

Some authors note that complicated grief can take on multiple forms.[2] A grief can be said to be complicated if there is an absence or delay in grief or if grief becomes excessive in intensity and prolonged. If grief is associated with suicidal ideation or psychotic symptoms, it is also considered complicated.

The literature is conflicting when reporting about who is most at risk for complicated grief. Some sources note that individuals at greatest risk are those who suffer a sudden loss or a loss that occurs through traumatic and horrible circumstances. Those who are socially isolated or those who feel responsible for a person's death are also more likely to suffer from complicated grief. One's mental health or the existence of behavioral health problems can predispose an individual to a complicated grief. If a person has a heavily conflicted relationship with the deceased this too can account for complicated grief scenarios.

Other studies have found that sudden loss is easier to deal with for those who have healthy self-esteem and a positive outlook on life. These people would be less likely to develop complicated grief with a sudden loss. Still, loss connected to a sudden or extreme manner of death becomes a challenge even for people with high self-esteem. The unthinkable is often unmanageable.

Mardi Horowitz studies PTSD, trauma, grief, and adjustment disorders. He compares normal and pathological grief in his book *Stress Response Syndromes*. Dr. Horowitz identifies the following grief phases: Dying Phase, Death and Outcry, Warding Off (denial), Reexperience (intrusion), Working Through, and Completion.[3] The experiences of each phase are explained from the perspective of a normal grief course and one that is considered pathological. Pathological or complicated grief involves extremes. There may be panic, dissociative reaction, psychoses, flooding of emotions or negative images, intrusive anger, shame, hyperarousal, psychophysiological syndromes, compulsivity, maladaptive avoidance that may include drug or alcohol abuse, and feelings of derealization. Grief, in the complicated presentation, becomes an experience of trauma in both symptom presentation and emotional experience. As is the case with trauma and PTSD, complicated grief becomes extremely difficult to address with its wide range of signs, symptoms, behaviors, and emotionally tenuous points of interface with dangerous choices. This is one of the reasons we want to identify, address, and hopefully prevent the manifestation of complicated grief.

A clinical observation is that grief can become trauma if the grief lasts too long. An example is Jessica.

Jessica's best friend, Mindy, committed suicide her senior year in high school. Mindy and Jessica were very close. Mindy had asked Jessica to come over and Jessica forgot. She was engaged in the teenage whirlwind of things to do and places to go. That night Mindy ended her life. This was a terrible experience for Jessica. It was her best friend and she felt she could have stopped the suicide if only she had gone over to her house. She also started thinking and discovered how many hints had been left, like bread crumbs marking a trail.

Later, Jessica married a fine young man. He died in Iraq in the line of duty. It was another deep blow.

Jessica's childhood was filled with its own challenges. She grew up in a rough neighborhood in Los Angeles and was often bullied. She had started using drugs after the death of Mindy, got clean, and then after the death of her husband found herself anxious, panicky, and checked out. She alternated among these states.

She remarried and then became even more hypervigilant about where her husband was, what he was doing; she was seemingly jealous of his every move. But was it jealousy or something else? She had been to multiple therapists who misdiagnosed her with everything from an attachment disorder to jealousy to immature adult. The last two are not diagnostic categories and the first one pertains to children.

Jessica was dealing with complicated grief. The early grief regarding the suicide of her friend was not dealt with. She had no help. The second death superimposed on the first. She developed coping skills that were maladaptive, ranging from substance abuse to jealousy-like behavior. The jealousy-like behavior would be understood later as panic over loss, abandonment, and a failure to grieve in a normal fashion. Substance abuse early on stunted the movement from loss through grief. Her personality continued to develop around a loss-grief-panic continuum. She thought she was crazy and her partners were pulling their hair out. Jessica had, in effect, become traumatized by grief.

WHAT IS NORMAL GRIEF AND BEREAVEMENT?

After reading up to this point in this book, you are familiar with many types of loss. Perhaps you have found your loss among the pages. As has been stated throughout, we begin the experience of loss with the advent of life. It is my premise that we know a great deal more about loss than we might have thought. This includes having had experiences with what we refer to as normal grief and observing or experiencing grief that is either absent or complicated (complicated grief can be the absence of grief).

Normal grief is an individual matter. As Chapter 1 explained there are many theories on how we grieve. Most often grief can be broken down into phases a person goes through. These do not need to be viewed as stages and they are not linear. We will move through the phases we need, as we need them, while we come to terms with our loss and how to move on.

Clearly the loss of moving or changing a job is in a different category from the loss of a child, being diagnosed with a terminal illness, or being at Ground Zero on 9/11. However, in therapy with clients who often feel they are not entitled to their grief or sorrow because so many others in the world have suffered more, I tell them that pain is pain. Pain does not distinguish itself and say it is worse than someone else's pain. Pain hurts.

Loss involves acknowledgment of that which has changed and the pain that very often accompanies change. As humans we have a love-hate relationship with change. We see it as good and we dread it if it takes something away from us that we covet, hold as dear, or have come to attach significance.

Grief is the process we will choose to come to terms with that loss and change. Grief may include shock if the life event was not anticipated. Sudden events are more likely to produce shock and disbelief. We need time in order to take in the event and make it real. We all know the feeling when we were engaged in something and then out of nowhere something else happened. I have a couple of very different examples.

One late afternoon in the fall I was talking on my cell phone while taking a walk. I had decided to walk through the golf course, as it was near sunset and the golfers had all dispersed. I was having a pleasant conversation and was engrossed in the telephonic exchange. Suddenly I felt an intense pain in my right inner thigh. It took me about a minute to come to my senses. I told my friend on the phone that something just happened, but I didn't know what it was. I spoke in telegraphic phrases, "Hurt, thigh." "No, don't know." "Painful, a sting, deep." "Muscle, it hurts."

A stray golfer had hit a ball and did not see me. The golf ball had come through the air at a high speed, likely fifty miles per hour. It was a good thing that it didn't hit my head, face, or soft tissues surrounding vital organs. However, the inner thigh is tender. It was several minutes before I could put together what happened. And, then several more minutes to catch my breath. When the golfer came nearer he was unaware of what he had done. I explained his ball hit me. I saw his face turn to shock and disbelief. Then I saw worry, the lawsuit type of worry. He would neither confirm nor deny what he had done. As the minutes gathered momentum, the pain followed suit. By the time I arrived home in twenty or so minutes there was already a purplish red round mark somewhat larger than the golf ball.

My wound would eventually heal after several weeks of macabre color transformations of my inner thigh. I had about a dozen flashbacks of the event that focused on the initial strike by the ball and the look on the golfer's face. My feelings ranged from relief that I wasn't hurt more severely, to anger at the golfer's attitude, to worry that the bruise would result in a blood clot, to hesitancy at walking on the golf paths. Over the months I kept thinking about the golfer. I was angry at his not taking verbal responsibility for what he had done. It was past golfing hours and the course was closed. I was in no condition to ask for his name or photo ID so I could later report him. I tried to imagine how people feel following car accidents, hit-and-run accidents, and all of those sudden, unplanned events that change our life in less than one second. In the big picture of life my accident was small. If, however, we slow down the events and take a closer look, there are elements of the grief process in all events, even those that are minor such as the golf ball incident. In my example, the shock, the time it took to understand what had happened, the lack of caring from the one responsible, the physical wound itself, and a permanent change where the golf course paths are concerned. I cannot walk the path without a slight thought of what happened there.

Below, a young woman tells the story of her brother's death. This is an example of normal grief, although, it sounds anything but normal presented with all the details. Grief is detailed and exacting. It is a whisper, a shadow, a flinch or quiver, and we break grief down into minute parts and particles in order to better understand what happens to people and what happens to us. This does not make it pathological; rather, it makes it palpable and pliable enough for us to work with during weeks and months of working toward some acceptance.

> *My brother died. I usually tell people he died in a car accident. You have to be careful what you tell people because everyone makes assumptions based on the facts you provide. Do people ever completely tell the truth? Is it always necessary? People lie.*
>
> *Vince was twenty-two when I got the phone call that everyone dreads. My dad said, "Doll, something bad has happened." His voice was unusually unsteady.*

"Is it Mom?"

"No, it's your brother."

"Michael?"

"No, Vincent."

"Vince? What could have happened to Vince?"

"He's dead."

> *With all my fear of something happening to my mom or one of my other brothers, I never thought that Vince would die. The possibility made perfect*

clinical sense, but I was never clinical about my family. I was not paying attention to the fact that no one spoke about Vince. Everyone spoke of my other brothers and Mom, but never about Vince. There was no need to talk about him because he was fine. Everyone loved Vince. He was a charismatic, hippy kid who smoked pot and had a ton of friends. He worked, played in a rock band and was always happy. He made everyone laugh except Mom, but he could make her smile. He made my dad think twice about only one path in life. More than two hundred people attended his funeral; I knew virtually none of them.

I learned that he attempted suicide three times. The fourth time was a charm.

My dad painfully told the story of finding Vince in the utility room located on the bottom floor of the family home. Dad went to the utility room to retrieve something in the middle of the night. He said he wanted to find an instruction booklet he left there. Upon entering the room he saw Vince laying flat on the floor with the dryer hose taped to his face. Dad yelled. Vince opened his eyes. Dad pulled on the hose and Vince sat up.

Dad said, "What are you doing?"

Vince said, "What does it look like?"

Dad accused Vince of acting immature and stupid. Nothing more was said.

Vince was found two more times in the utility room performing the same ritual, which was intended to end his life.

Dad didn't tell Mom.

Dad didn't offer to send Vince to counseling.

I had been a psychotherapist for more than six years and Dad didn't tell me.

Someone knocked at my parent's door at 4:00 A.M. on December 15, 1981. My dad climbed out of bed. Mom lay awake but motionless. Dad walked slowly to the front door. The knocking continued. He switched on the porch lights, unlocked the deadbolt and reached for the doorknob. He paused and looked to the tiled entry as though there might be a comfort reflecting back at him. The floor offered him nothing but silence. He opened the door and through the security screen door, also double-bolted, he saw two uniformed police officers with a flashlight turned on.

"Mr. M.?"

"Yes?"

"Is your son Vincent M.?"

"Yes."

"We have some bad news. May we come in?"

"Yes."

They stood in the entryway. My dad leaned against the wall papered in shades of green with red roses strewn about. They were the color of spilled Chianti. His hands fumbled nervously looking for comfort and finding themselves naked, exposed and pale.

"We found your son behind the buildings of the Hoffman Estates shopping mall. The car was running. He had cut a hole in the bottom of the car and attached a hose from the exhaust. It appears he died from carbon monoxide poisoning. We need you to come down to the morgue to identify the body."

I don't know what my dad did then. I don't know how he worked the words into his brain and sifted among them, looking for something bright and shiny and finding only the approach of suffocation. He was a proud man. This was not a proud context. He said his heart was pounding. He said he had trouble breathing. He remembered being asked if he needed to sit down. He didn't sit. He told them he was fine. He had the officers write down the address of the morgue. He said he would tell his wife and then come to the morgue around 8:00 A.M.

The private agony of intimate moments resents being recorded. It is all ugly, distasteful and wretched.

Dad went to the bedroom where Mom lay on her back staring at the ceiling. She had already departed to a place of stoic solace. She said she learned how to disappear as a child when her brothers touched her private parts. She said she improved at the skill of leaving her body when she married my dad. He was hard to live with, she said. She said that Grandma J hated her and made her life miserable. She never wanted children; the diaphragm failed four times. She was an honest woman when she spoke. I appreciated that about her. Always honest. She had over twelve treatments at Mount Sinai. Each time they inserted the rubber ruler in her mouth so she wouldn't bite off her tongue. Each time they turned up the electricity she wondered why she had been convicted and sentenced without a trial. Each time she convulsed and convulsed some more, she fought with a tiny voice inside her head. "Don't give in to them. Don't. Hold on. Don't let them win."

Dad said, "Vincent is dead." He sat on the edge of the bed with one arm holding one of her shoulders.

Mom looked at my dad with contempt.

She climbed out of bed.

She went to the bathroom. She closed the door. She locked it. She turned on the shower.

This young woman would use her story to help herself with grief. She needed to record the moments and capture the way grief crawled throughout the house and across her parents' faces and through the doorway into the bathroom. Normal grief is very sad and not pretty. Loss is not pretty either. We do want to take care, especially in a book of this nature, to not become numb and academic. Stories help us to heal and help us identify how loss and grief work. This young woman would use the emotional landscape provided in her story to eventually have a dialogue of honesty with both of her parents. For her this was part of her healing process. This was her brother.

Grief is intimate. Grief is highly personal. Grief looks for words when words fail time and again. Yet, it is in the details that words provide some help for circling around, going inside, looking, touching, and feeling the loss.

Normal grief involves shock and disbelief if it is sudden and you were not prepared. It involves distance and closeness, depending on your role in your family and your relationship with the one whom you grieve. Grief has moments or long tirades of anger. It can also be silent and suffocating in its stillness. Grief moves one downward into something like depression, but not really depression. It is a confined hole where sadness mutates on itself. Happiness, smiles, joy are all acts of treason when in grief. Acceptance peeks around the corner and asks for an invite. It is like a neighbor you are not yet sure you trust. What are its intentions? Normal grief involves some or a lot of guilt. It depends on how *in the moment* you were with the one you have lost. It will also depend on whether you had ambivalence and conflict in the relationship with the one that died. The less ambivalence, the less anguish long term. Normal grief comes in waves and there are still moments when everything looks like it might be returning to normal. Then in comes another wave triggered by a memory, a smell, a person, or an event.

Normal grief is anything but normal because grief, in its pitched and piercing presentation, tears you away from normal. But in loss situations, people do experience grief, and that part of the process is normal. If a parent did not grieve the loss of a child, we might consider that reaction abnormal. Still, there is a difference between healthy, "normal" grieving, and the more complicated forms that trap people in a rut out of which they may not be able to climb.

Normal grief is preferable to complicated grief. Complicated grief is in a place of twilight where it is neither light nor dark, good or bad, but simply a state of betwixt and between. Complicated grief exists on the margins, whereas normal grief revolves around the center, erratic, but reasonably predictable.

WHAT IS THE DIFFERENCE BETWEEN DEPRESSION AND COMPLICATED GRIEF?

Depression is a mood disorder that may arise from a combination of factors including a medical condition (such as a thyroid disorder), genetics, personal history, history of traumatization, and a substance abuse or dependence history. Depression can also be a side effect of many drugs intended to treat physical problems. Depression is a common feature in many other behavioral health diagnostic categories.

Mood disorders can be viewed according to episodes, disorders, and specifiers that describe the recurrent episodes or the most recent episode.

There are several types of depression including: major depressive disorder, dysthymic disorder, depressive disorder not otherwise specified, bipolar I disorder, bipolar II disorder, cyclothymic disorder, bipolar disorder not otherwise specified, mood disorder due to a general medical condition, substance-induced mood disorder, and mood disorder not otherwise specified.

Mood episodes can include a major depressive episode, manic episode, mixed episode, and a hypomanic episode.

Specifiers that describe features of a current episode include terms such as chronic, with catatonic features, with melancholic features, with atypical features, and with postpartum onset. Specifiers that describe a course of recurrent episodes include terms such as: longitudinal course specifiers, with season pattern, or with rapid cycling.

As you can see, depression is complex in assessment and in treatment.

Grief is normal because it comes in reaction to something. One can be diagnosed with an adjustment disorder that includes features of depression, or depression and anxiety. An adjustment disorder is one where a person is in an adjustment phase for a period of time. Moving, going through a relationship breakup, or losing a job are all adjustment issues. If one adjusts with features of depression, we code it as an adjustment disorder with depression features. What we are saying is that the depression is a result of the adjustment and would not exist without the adjustment issue.

Grief is also an adjustment issue and often it is diagnosed as such. Or, bereavement is diagnosed with what we refer to as a V Code Diagnosis. V Codes refer to things that are in the normal range but still problematic in presentation and effect on the individual's functioning level. Of interest to note is that most insurance companies have denied claims that are V Codes as they are not considered "serious." There is no separate diagnosis for Complicated Grief. It has been suggested that the new DSM V, due out in 2013, include this as a diagnostic category.

Here is a short list of the symptoms of depression:

- negative or antisocial behavior
- feelings of not being understood or approved of
- restlessness, grouchiness, sulkiness, aggression
- unwillingness to cooperate in family projects
- withdrawal from social activities
- hiding out in one's room
- inattention to personal appearance
- extreme or sudden mood changes
- sensitivity to rejection, especially in love relationships
- abuse of alcohol or other drugs
- sexual promiscuity
- weight loss or weight gain

- sleeplessness or sleeping more than normal
- physical agitation or restlessness
- physical lethargy, dragging around, slowed physical responses

Clinical depression is different. In order to qualify as clinically depressed, at least four of the following symptoms need to be present nearly every day for a period of at least two weeks.

Symptoms of clinical depression:

- poor appetite, significant weight loss when not dieting
- increased appetite, significant weight gain
- insomnia or hypersomnia (inability to fall asleep or need for excessive amounts of sleep)
- physical agitation—a jumpy, nervous, twitching, restless body
- slowed physical body movements, no "spunk," dragging around
- loss of interest or pleasure in usual activities (not able to have fun)
- apathy (an "I-don't-care" attitude)
- loss of energy, fatigue
- feelings of worthlessness or excessive feelings of guilt and self-blame
- inability to think or concentrate, slowed thinking and/or inability to make decisions
- frequent thoughts of death or suicide, death wish, or suicide attempt

Just what causes depression?

There are many factors in depression, but feelings of loss play a major role, often evoking feelings of powerlessness or helplessness. When not dealt with, these feelings can lead to despair or to a type of trapped, unexpressed, immobilized anger, either of which can result in depression.

Key points about depression:

- Usually there is not just one cause of depression.
- Depression can be physical (organic), having its origin in the body's bio-chemistry; or it can be functional, having its origin in the individual's environment.
- Environmental factors include psychological stressors (e.g., divorce, major illness, alcoholism in family) and traumatic events (e.g., death of a loved one, incest, rape).
- Most often the first occurrence of a major depression takes place before age thirty, and depression may recur throughout one's life.
- Environmental factors, including psychological stressors and traumatic events, have one important element in common—the element of loss.
- Feelings of powerlessness or helplessness become more likely to occur as losses multiply.

- Feelings of powerlessness may lead to the trapped feeling of despair, which may result in depression.
- Often depression results from a type of trapped, unexpressed, immobilized anger. Without a way to release this anger, individuals may turn the anger that belongs outside on themselves.
- Even when available resources exist, most young people do not consider contacting a professional for help with depression.

Normal grief and pathological grief may initially feel like the same thing. The main difference rests with a couple of observations. Normal grief will begin to move although it may take time. Complicated or pathological grief is stuck and moves very little. They both have the same components where feelings are concerned, as well as many of the signs and symptoms. Complicated grief doesn't move much and it becomes darker due to the lack of movement. This is where we begin to see major depressive disorder symptoms, suicidal risk, risk taking, and even the use of substances such as alcohol, street drugs, or prescription drugs as a maladaptive coping mechanism. Depression is a normal reaction and it is a component of many mental health challenges. Depression is a mood disorder, but depression can be a normal feature of things such as adjustment-related problems. For example, a teenager moving to a new school will often go through some depression as part of the adjustment. This is not a major depressive illness, bipolar disorder, or dysthymic depression. Some depression is normal for the circumstances and life events we encounter. Depression is a normal part of the grief process for many people. Depression that gets stuck and translates into a major depressive disorder—where the person cannot function, cannot go to work, stays in bed for days or off and on for days, uses alcohol to cope, and any of the signs of depression we have already spoken about earlier—represents a problem such as complicated grief.

Depression is a normal reaction to loss. It is important to remember that everyone gets depressed sometimes. If the depressed mood feels connected to something in particular and it doesn't stay stuck for weeks, it is likely normal. If the depression began with a loss, carried into grief, and does not move, but rather becomes deeper and darker, it is likely complicated grief rearing its head.

Loss and depression go hand in hand for many people. We are uniquely different from one another. A teen I worked with experienced depression due to thinking about and planning his first year of college. The depression was real and it was related to loss (loss of predictable high school experiences, moving away from family, leaving a girlfriend behind). He was able to work through the depression by understanding where it was coming from and translating the powerlessness he felt about the losses into transitions rather than endings.

Let's now look at traumatic grief, posttraumatic stress disorder, and resiliency.

NOTES

1. Schumer, "After a Death."
2. Sadock, Sadock, and Kaplan, *Synopsis of Psychiatry*, 63.
3. Horowitz, *Stress Response Syndromes*, 115.

Chapter Fourteen

Traumatic Grief and Posttraumatic Stress Disorder

When all sides are assailed by prospects of disaster the soul of man never confronts the totality of its wretchedness. The bitter drug is divided into separate draughts for him; today he takes on part of his woe; tomorrow he takes more; and so on; till the last drop is drunk. —Herman Melville, *Pierre*

WHAT IS TRAUMATIC GRIEF?

Traumatic grief is a term most often used interchangeably with complicated grief, prolonged grief, or complex grief. However, there are many similarities between traumatic or complicated grief and posttraumatic stress disorder. Let's take a look at why this is an important point of clarification.

WHAT IS POSTTRAUMATIC STRESS DISORDER?

Posttraumatic stress disorder is considered an anxiety disorder. Unless changes are made in the 2013 edition of the DSM (*Diagnostic and Statistical Manual of Mental Disorders*), this is what we are currently using as a definition. If you look at anxiety as a large black umbrella under which reside different types of anxiety, we find: panic disorders with or without agoraphobia, agoraphobia without a history of panic disorder, specific phobias, social phobia (social anxiety disorder), obsessive-compulsive disorder, posttraumatic stress disorder, acute stress disorder, generalized anxiety disorder (includes overanxious disorder of childhood), anxiety disorder due to a general medical condition, substance-induced anxiety disorder, and anxiety disorder not otherwise specified.

Posttraumatic stress disorder is most associated with war and returning veterans. However, PTSD exists in the lives of many people who have never seen war combat. Car accidents, rape, childhood physical and sexual abuse, sudden deaths, bullying, plane crashes, terrorism, school shootings, and many unthinkable events can and do cause posttraumatic stress disorder.

Some authors have questioned whether anxiety is the best fit for a diagnosis such as PTSD. Elizabeth Brett notes that certain clinical features of PTSD, such as the recurrent and overlapping phases of reexperiencing and numbing, are actually closer diagnostically to mourning and bereavement.[1] She and other authors note that a new category in the new DSM may be helpful in terms of helping people better distinguish between trauma, grief, anxiety, complicated grief, and posttraumatic stress. They share many things in common.

Posttraumatic stress disorder, as a diagnosis, is arrived at by looking at several qualifiers that are listed below. These quantfiers were taken from the DSM IV-TR.

POSTTRAUMATIC STRESS DISORDER DIAGNOSIS AND CHARACTERISTICS

The person has been exposed to a traumatic event in which both of the following were present:

- The person experienced, witnessed, or was confronted with an event or events that involved actual or threatened death or serious injury, or a threat to the physical integrity of self or others.
- The person's response involved intense fear, helplessness, or horror.

The traumatic event is persistently reexperienced in one (or more) of the following ways:

- Recurrent and intrusive distressing recollections of the event, including images, thoughts, or perceptions
- Recurring distressing dreams of the event
- Acting or feeling as if the traumatic event were recurring (includes a sense of reliving the experience, illusions, hallucinations, and dissociative flashback episodes, including those that occur on awakening or when intoxicated)
- Intense psychological distress at exposure to internal or external cues that symbolize or resemble an aspect of the traumatic event

Persistent avoidance of stimuli associated with the trauma and numbing of general responsiveness (not present before the trauma), as indicated by three (or more) of the following:

- Efforts to avoid thoughts, feelings, or conversations associated with the trauma
- Efforts to avoid activities, places, or people that arouse recollections of the trauma
- Inability to recall an important aspect of the trauma
- Markedly diminished interest or participation in significant activities
- Feeling of detachment or estrangement from others
- Restricted range of affect (e.g., does not expect to have a career, marriage, children, or a normal lifespan)

Persistent symptoms of increased arousal (not present before the trauma), as indicated by two (or more) of the following:

- Difficulty falling or staying asleep
- Irritability or outbursts of anger
- Difficulty concentrating
- Hypervigilance
- Exaggerated startle response

As you can see, some of these specifiers also go hand in hand with grief, as it has been discussed throughout this book. Many losses and therefore grief have to do with traumas. It is a trauma when a sudden death takes place. Assault and rape are traumas, but they are also losses and events we must grieve. It is traumatic to have and to love someone with a substance abuse/dependence issue especially when that person takes risks. Many parents I work with have posttraumatic stress symptomology as a result of loving an adult child who uses substances and ends up arrested, assaulted, or being in harm's way.

When traumatic grief blends with posttraumatic stress disorder it is a difficult situation, to say the least. The person who suffers from these conditions will often be incorrectly diagnosed. Furthermore, the treatment options are generally longer term and require a triage or team approach to really get a significant reduction in symptoms and potential for self-harm. When substance dependence and abuse are superimposed on the traumatic grief and PTSD, it is an unthinkable diagnostic cocktail. Yet, this happens more often than people think. Our prisons are filled with men and women who got into trouble and yet underneath their substance issues was a history of trauma, complicated grief, and PTSD.

WHO IS VULNERABLE TO PTSD?

When we work with clients in the field of mental health we are thinking, as professionals, of many things at the same time. In addition to striving to establish a relationship of trust, we are also assessing the protective factors and risk factors of each client. Risk factors are those things that place a person at risk. They may have to do with personal decisions, family, the general environment, economics, employment, and many other factors. Protective factors are those things in a person's life that act directly or indirectly to protect them. This includes the same things listed under risk factors, but turned in a positive fashion. A protective factor might be faith or religion for one person. Another protective factor might be a large social network. Still another protective factor might be a history of compliance with medications and psychotherapy recommendations. Risk factors and protective factors need to be assessed when looking at posttraumatic stress disorder and who is vulnerable, as well as who might evidence resiliency.

Approximately one in twelve individuals will develop posttraumatic stress disorder in their lifetime. Women are considered more vulnerable to developing posttraumatic stress disorder. In fact, they are twice as likely to develop PTSD. In a 2004 study of women veterans, it was concluded that women in military service were more likely to develop military PTSD if they had a history of military sexual assault, childhood sexual assault, or civilian sexual assault.[2] Many studies have shown the connection of prior traumatization to risk for developing PTSD as well as for revictimization. It is not that women or men who have been victimized and traumatized choose to have a repeat of these circumstances. As we discussed in earlier chapters, the brain is affected by trauma. If the limbic system structures are oversensitized it places individuals at greater risk due to the inability to correctly ascertain or discern safe from unsafe in the environment and in interpersonal relating.

Research has indicated childhood exposure to violence can result in negative mental health repercussions in childhood and later adulthood. A 2011 study attempted to determine if there was a difference between childhood exposure to violence and PTSD by looking at two different violence exposures.[3] The study looked at children who witnessed violence (domestic violence) and those who experienced violence (child abuse). This study found a correlation between later development of PTSD or current PTSD as related to child abuse only or a combination of child abuse and witnessing abuse, but not to witnessing abuse only.

Anyone can develop posttraumatic stress disorder. Not everyone exposed to traumatic events will.

Specific risk factors include the following:

- Anyone who has witnessed a violent act or has been repeatedly exposed to life-threatening situations. If you feared harm could come to yourself or another or the threat of death was imminent, this is understood to mean life threatening.
- Victim survivors of domestic violence or intimate partner violence.
- Victim survivors of rape, sexual assault and sexual abuse.
- Victims of physical assault.
- Victims of other violent acts at work, in school, or in the public.
- History of being physically, sexually, or verbally bullied.
- Survivors of car accidents or other accidents involving public transportation.
- Survivors of natural disasters such as hurricanes, tornados, earthquakes, wildfires, avalanches, and tsunamis.
- Survivors of major disasters or events such as terrorist attacks, nuclear reactor accidents, and industrial accidents affecting the populace.
- Combat veterans.
- Civilian victims of war.
- Childhood history of physical abuse, sexual abuse, emotional abuse, and neglect.
- Professionals who work with victims of trauma and posttraumatic stress disorder.
- Individuals who are diagnosed with a life-threatening or terminal illness.
- Individuals who must undergo a major medical procedure.
- Anyone who learns of the sudden death, kidnapping, or grave harm coming to a close relative or friend.

Risk factor and protective factor variables affecting posttraumatic stress vulnerability include:

- History of trauma; prior trauma increases vulnerability.
- Life stressors; the existence of life stressors such as a divorce, job change, or loss at the time of the trauma increases vulnerability.
- Coping-skill breakdown; low self-esteem is associated with increased vulnerability.
- Personality characteristics; persons who are more pessimistic or withdraw may be more vulnerable to the development of posttraumatic stress disorder.
- Genetic factors; some studies have shown there is a familial predisposition to vulnerability under stressful conditions such as those that exist at the time of a trauma.
- Brain structure changes; this was discussed in an earlier chapter.
- The severity of the trauma.

- The proximity to the trauma; the closer one is to the trauma, the more likely there will be a stressful reaction of an enduring nature.
- The type of trauma.
- The nature of the trauma; when a trauma is sudden, repetitive, enduring, or unpredictable, it can increase the probability for PTSD.
- Existence of social support network.
- Existence of personal support.
- Existence of secondary victimization.
- Existence of treatment soon after the event.

WHAT IS RESILIENCY?

Resiliency is viewed as the ability to regain, or return to, a normal balance following a trauma, traumatic life event, disaster, or other significant experience. Resilience refers to something being able to regain its shape even after being stretched or repositioned. Interest in this subject has emerged largely due to studies that show not everyone who experiences trauma will develop PTSD. So, researchers asked, why is that?

George Bonanno states, "The good news is that for most of us, grief is not overwhelming or unending. As frightening as the pain of loss can be most of us are resilient. Some of us cope so effectively, in fact, we hardly seem to miss a beat in our day-to-day lives."[4] Resilience is not a personality trait, but rather something that can develop in all of us over time. In this way development of resilience is seen as a process.

The American Psychological Association formed a task force on resilience in African American children and adolescents. What they found was that these youth had special assets that helped them cope with racial prejudice.

There are a number of factors identified that increase resilience. These include things like strong social connections or networks, family connections, faith-based connections, and friendships. Attitude also influences resiliency. When we view the cup as half full rather than half empty, it is a statement of resilience and positivity. Attitude has been associated with building resilience. When things seem overwhelming, break them into doable parts. The parts come together to create the project or goal. The ability to set realistic goals helps build resiliency. Good self-esteem has much to do with setting realistic goals, following through and actualizing dreams, hopes, and desires. Low self-esteem can prevent goal setting and movement toward life's joys.[5] Resiliency is further enhanced by understanding that change is a part of life, as are losses along the way. People who are proactive, as opposed to burying their head in the sand, build resiliency by nature of taking action. Resiliency is enhanced by way of positive coping skills, stress management skills, and learning how to cope with distress in positive ways. Avoiding maladaptive coping skills is key to the building of a strong, resilient platform. Resiliency is about being present, taking positive action, holding a healthy image of yourself, staying connected, and gifting yourself all the joys this life has to offer.

THE KINDLING EFFECT

The term the *kindling effect* has been used to describe the neurological tendency of the brain to become oversensitized following exposure to trauma.[6] This results in the lowering of the individual's threshold to trauma, making him both more susceptible to retraumatization as well as revictimization. The individual is more likely to suffer the biological effects of trauma as evidenced by mood disturbances, personality disorder, anxiety states, as well as classic DSM IV symptoms of PTSD. Contemporary authors such as van der Kolk, McFarlane, and Weisaeth have referred to this composite of posttrauma symptomology categorically as Disorders of Extreme Stress. Revictimization becomes more likely because of this sustained condition of arousal. Sustained arousal does not sharpen an individual's intuitive, intellectual, emotional, and physical protective mechanisms but dims them. The individual loses the ability to discern safe from unsafe due to the lowered thresholds and increased arousal states. The individual becomes accustomed to arousal states and these states become associated with normalcy. Everyday decision making becomes a dangerous enterprise.

Here is an illustrative vignette, with some details changed and combined, that shows how past trauma can become retraumatization. The girl in this story has a history of abuse and is unable to discern safe from unsafe. Her limbic system has been overchallenged. She is suffering from PTSD and is unable to take a stand in her own defense. She keeps finding herself harmed by others. She has not connected her past trauma to her inability to say no. This will change once she enters therapy.

> *Jen was sixteen and asked her mom for an appointment to speak to a therapist. When her mom asked why, Jen said she just needed someone to talk to. Jen was a shy, tall girl with long, blond hair and radiant, naturally rouged skin. Her eyes were brown; she had an awkward way about her. Her response times were too slow; they created dangerous pauses of nothingness. It took us months to develop a spontaneous exchange. Mother was not happy about Jen seeing me because therapy cost money and she wanted results. Since the girl wasn't doing anything "wrong" her mom wasn't sure what kind of results to look for.*
>
> *Jen had been having sexual intercourse with many boys and young men. She was writing to a man who was in prison and due to be released in about six months. It was beginning to be apparent that Jen had been added to the list*

that guys pass around to one another. This is the list of little deer in the headlights. These girls don't say yes, but they don't say no. They don't fight back, but they don't really engage. They will do what they are asked and they are beautiful. Guys know these girls and tell other guys these girls are "easy."

They're easy because they're suffering from posttraumatic stress disorder. You have easy PTSD and hard PTSD. Those aren't clinical terms, but they accurately describe what happens when a person is traumatized. Easy PTSD is the deer in the headlights. She freezes, goes numb, and waits for "it" to be over. Hard PTSD is the shotgun aimed at the headlights. The girl with hard PTSD will blow a man's head off and cut off his penis to spite his manhood. She is characterized by fight, react, hair-trigger animal instinct. Everyone is the enemy. She uses machine-gun communication skills.

Jen described one encounter with a boy.

He said, "Do you want to do it?"

She was silent.

"Is it OK that I take your clothes off?"

Silence.

"If you don't say no I am going to assume it's OK."

Silence.

He undressed her and rolled her over like a fifty-pound sack of grain and viewed her young and toned buttocks.

"Can I give it to you up the ass?"

Silence.

"OK then."

When he was done he rolled her back over. "That was so fine, Jen."

Silence.

I asked Jen where she was when this was happening. I told her that I doubted she was in the room.

"I don't know where I went. I know what he did. I just waited for it to be over."

"Did you think about yelling, saying stop?"

"At first, but I was afraid to say stop."

"How come?"

She was silent for a long time.

"This has happened to you before, hasn't it?"

"Yes."

"When you were little?"

"My brother."

"You didn't tell?"

"No."

"Did it make you angry?"

"Yes."

"Are you angry now?"

"Yes."

"I can't see your anger, Jen. Can you try to show it?"

She looked embarrassed.

We began the practice of affect management. I taught Jen how to make her facial expressions match her feelings. We needed to change her from a deer in the headlights to a deer in the headlights with a stop sign. She needed a look that would stop any car.

After a couple of months of practice we decided to test drive her new affect. We decided mutually that we would visit a construction site. Construction sites are sociologically interesting because they are largely male compounds where dominant male behavior is rampant. She was being pursued by an older guy and was trying to get rid of him. He worked at a nearby site. She had managed to avoid him and felt proud of herself that he hadn 't been able to fuck her yet. She wasn 't sure how long she could keep ducking him.

The guy said, " It 's only a matter of time, Jen, and I will fuck you too. Everyone does it to you. You know you like it. "

With her mom 's permission, we planned our strategy. The guy would be at the worksite all afternoon on the day of our next appointment. We would drive to the site and park about two blocks away. The site was located in a heavily treed area and our approach by foot would not be seen. Once at the site I planned to hang back behind the stacks of lumber and other building materials. She would proceed without me. If I sensed difficulties I would intervene. We did a test run on a rainy afternoon when no one was at the site. Everything went according to plan.

On the day of the for-real experiment Jen and I paused before she went on without me. Jen wore what she said she wore when out with friends. She poured herself into black, straight-leg jeans and a halter top that made it just to her belly button. Her hair was down, flowing and thickened by the humidity of the damp air. She wore a stroke of blush across her high cheekbones. Two strokes of mascara lifted her lush eyelashes into a butterfly effect. She was ready.

Jen walked slowly from the street to the construction site. Two men were installing Spanish tiles on the roof; one man was working on a scaffold with an automatic spray gun, painting the side of the house; and another man was walking to a lumber pile to gather materials to take inside the home. This lumber-gatherer was our target. His appearance surprised me. There was nothing outstanding about him. He was skinny, his dark-brown hair ungroomed. He seemed unsure of himself as he tripped, collected himself, started to go in the house, stopped and returned to the lumber pile. He didn 't see Jen 's approach. Jen walked slowly, paused and turned in my direction; then she carried on.

Suddenly he turned and saw her there. He became flustered but squared himself to stand tall and confident.

" Jen, what are you doing here? "

Silence.

" I bet you had a change of mind, didn 't you? "

" Yes, Bob, I did. "

" I knew you would. Let me take this shit inside and I will take a break. There are trees out behind the porta-potty and we can do it there. "

Bob walked away.

Jen turned and surveyed the street, looking for me. I waved and started walking to her.

Bob was leaving the doorway of the new house. He was smiling and was saying something to a coworker in the house. He gestured by grabbing his groin.

I was just a few feet from Jen and her eyes said she needed a little help.

Bob looked up. I imagined he had been watching the swelling of his groin.

He stopped, but only momentarily, when he saw me. He must have felt compelled not to back down, run or hide. He came to where Jen and I stood. I looked into his eyes and remained silent.

Jen said, "I have wanted to tell you how angry I am for your insulting behavior and assumptions that I would even consider having sex with you. I am sixteen years old and you are twenty-something? Who are you? What are you thinking? I could have you arrested."

Bob recoiled. He looked like a five-year-old with his hand caught in the cookie jar. His head drooped from his spinal cord and his right foot smashed imaginary bugs in the soil.

Jen added, "Don't you ever approach me again. If you do I will call the police immediately."

He said, "OK."

Jen looked at me with moistened eyes and she sighed. We walked away to my car leaving Bob standing there alone.

This is one example of how it is that trauma can work its way into daily decision making. Life becomes dangerous for the person who doesn't understand or seek help for what is taking place. There are plenty of people out there willing to rationalize that silence means yes and that a young girl wants something because she didn't have a voice to say she didn't want it.

Jen was traumatized by the incest of her childhood. Her brother touched her private areas, he had intercourse with her, and he did what he wanted to her body. He instructed her on what he wanted her to do to him. This is trauma. This created PTSD. If a child does not get help when these things happen, many scenarios are possible, but the usual scenario is that of growing up feeling helpless and powerless. You do as you are told. You do what others want and you silence your own sense of what is right or wrong. Someone with PTSD can freeze or become numb, flee, or react. Jen froze. When frozen, anyone can do anything they want to you. Anyone who has ever survived PTSD understands what this means. Anyone with a history of trauma also knows what this means. The prefrontal cortex of the brain is not communicating with the limbic system and the limbic system is telling Jen to stay silent and wait till it is over because this was the strategy for survival she employed when her brother sexually violated her years earlier. Jen's therapy would show her what was happening to her and why. The therapy would employ greater use of her prefrontal cognitive skills. We worked on building self-esteem and on placing the original blame on the inappropriate and illegal actions of her brother. She found her voice and began saying no to things that she did not want in her life. Most children who have a history of sexual abuse do not have an opportunity to go to therapy. Not all teens that go to therapy will be able to connect the dots of understanding. Jen's current promiscuity was related to earlier child abuse. Trauma becomes PTSD, and revictimization will keep happening until these connections are understood.

In terms of American culture, one wonders about our emotional societal landscape especially when it comes to our mixed messages about violence. There is considerable violence on the news, Internet, in movies, and in video games. There is violence heard in the ways people speak to each other and the ways in which they interact. There are obvious indicators such as yelling and screaming. There are less obvious forms of violence such as infidelity and workplace meanness. Teachers say inappropriate things to students and peers berate one another. Politicians on the news set a poor example for our youth and this does filter down into the psyche of young people. There are school shootings, angry kids, families in crisis, and a welling of emotion all around.

Is it possible that a *kindling effect* applies to the whole of a society or culture?

Can societies become traumatized and experience the same lowering of thresholds and increased states of arousal as individuals?

Hyperarousal creates a desensitization and unaware state in response to violence. Traumatized individuals can suffer from an inability to self-regulate. Can society and does society suffer from the same posttraumatic impairment in self-regulation? Has society lost its ability to discern safe from unsafe? Perhaps an individual mirrors the illnesses embedded in society. Can individuals with PTSD exist unless the society they live in also has societal PTSD? I call this the *kindling effect*, a term I coined by borrowing from biological studies in neurology.

The identification of an outsider (i.e., anyone different) is the beginning point of human violence. The identification of an outsider is the origin of all hate crimes, the Holocaust, genocide, and war. In his 1989 book *The Roots of Evil: The Origins of Genocide and Other Group Violence*, Ervin Staub commented on certain psychological tendencies common to all humans. He noted that, early on, humans learn to distinguish between "us" and "them." As this process begins, it is closely followed by a tendency to devalue anyone in the "outgroup."

Blaming others, scapegoating, and marginalizing others diminishes our own responsibility. Through scapegoating a false understanding is achieved which temporarily reduces unease for those who scapegoat. The action of scapegoating offers understanding, false as it is, and provides psychological usefulness. It promises a solution to problems by action against the scapegoat. It allows people to feel connected as they join to scapegoat others. Devaluation of a subgroup helps to raise low self-esteem. Joining a group enables people to give up a burdensome self, adopt a new social identity, and gain a connection to other people. This requires action, but it is frequently not constructive action. These psychological tendencies have violent potentials.[7]

The effects of family, culture, children, and conflicting allegiances at too young an age, mixed messages about violence, intermittent reinforcement in areas of depersonalization and derealization, and the identification of outsiders provide the kindling that begins to smolder in childhood and continues to burn throughout a lifetime.

In their book *The Politics of Pain*, Crelinsten and Schmid reported on torture and arrived at social-oriented conclusions similar to Staub's:

> We need to work with the media, politicians and opinion makers who influence the public and the political process. We ourselves need to become writers, develop educational programs and exert influence on our governments to become active. A basic long-term goal is to humanize groups of people in each other's eyes. People need identification with their group. Maybe someday we can all be only humanists and internationalists, and will not need this. But while we do, identification need not take the form of devaluation of others. We can identify with us without devaluing them.[8]

Otto Rank, in his posthumously published collection of essays, discussed separation and the concept of being different. Khamsi summarized Rank's *Psychology of Difference* with the following passage:

> Difference is the dim awareness of our momentary and meaningless lives, and the source of our deepest pain. The perception of difference is a painful awareness of separation. In every case of suffering is the feeling of being different. The universal human search for the beloved is an attempt to project one's own will onto another in order to unburden existential guilt, to transform our painful difference into likeness.[9]

If we begin with culture and families within that culture we might explore the *kindling effect* of violence from a socially applied perspective on cultural posttraumatic stress. Let's look at the symptoms of posttraumatic stress as applied to an individual.

POSTTRAUMATIC STRESS DISORDER DIAGNOSIS AND CHARACTERISTICS

The person has been exposed to a traumatic event in which both of the following were present:

- The person experienced, witnessed, or was confronted with an event or events that involved actual or threatened death or serious injury, or a threat to the physical integrity of self or others.
- The person's response involved intense fear, helplessness, or horror.

The traumatic event is persistently reexperienced in one (or more) of the following ways:

- Recurrent and intrusive distressing recollections of the event, including images, thoughts, or perceptions
- Recurring distressing dreams of the event
- Acting or feeling as if the traumatic event were recurring (includes a sense of reliving the experience, illusions, hallucinations, and dissociative flashback episodes, including those that occur on awakening or when intoxicated)
- Intense psychological distress at exposure to internal or external cues that symbolize or resemble an aspect of the traumatic event

Persistent avoidance of stimuli associated with the trauma and numbing of general responsiveness (not present before the trauma), as indicated by three (or more) of the following:

- Efforts to avoid thoughts, feelings, or conversations associated with the trauma
- Efforts to avoid activities, places, or people that arouse recollections of the trauma
- Inability to recall an important aspect of the trauma
- Markedly diminished interest or participation in significant activities
- Feeling of detachment or estrangement from others
- Restricted range of affect (e.g., does not expect to have a career, marriage, children, or a normal lifespan)

Persistent symptoms of increased arousal (not present before the trauma), as indicated by two (or more) of the following:

- Difficulty falling or staying asleep
- Irritability or outbursts of anger
- Difficulty concentrating
- Hypervigilance
- Exaggerated startle response

It is an interesting experiment to apply the DSM IV criteria to cultures. Replace the word *person* with *culture* throughout the diagnostic criteria for posttraumatic stress disorder. When this is done it is easy to see how culture has collectively experienced traumatic events throughout history. American culture has in its origin a violent beginning. All of our wars with other countries and our own civil wars, racial violence, hate crimes, terrorist acts, and personal violence add up and take a toll on the collective experience of being an American.

American culture has experienced deep traumatization. There are human rights disasters and atrocities such as the terrorist attacks of September 11, 2001, the Iraq and Afghanistan wars, news of Third World atrocities, the Gulf War, the Vietnam War, the race riots, hate crimes, neo-Nazi demonstrations, child abuse, murders in communities, school shootings, child abductions, more murders, robberies, assaults, and all manner of human-generated violence. It is my premise that *we* (the many cultures of the world) suffer from collective posttraumatic stress disorder. One could say that our culture and many countries of the world have become "posttraumatically correct."

In this chapter we have moved from the individual to the culture and now back to the individual. We want to keep in mind that culture is made up of individuals and it is important to shift our focus from ourselves to our town, community, culture, nation, and world. What happens on an individual level in families and homes takes place on a larger scale throughout the world.

When in the thick of one's own trauma it is not the time to reflect on the state of culture or of the world. Once healed, perhaps one can turn that trauma into a helpful understanding to be shared with the world. When we are able to take our own pain, loss, grief, trauma, and suffering, and personally attend to healing, this is a wonderful experience and quite empowering. If we then can take what we learned from that pain and look differently at larger problems in our families, communities, culture, country, and world, we have experienced the ultimate transformation of negative into positive or what Sigmund Freud would term as sublimation. Sublimation is a form of displacement of the negative into a positive. When we hear of someone who may have been hurtful to animals as a child becoming a physician or veterinarian as an adult, this would be a form of sublimation. John Edward Walsh, who lost his son by way of abduction and murder, would turn his grief into one of television's most popular shows, *America's Most Wanted*. He would be responsible for the passage of the *Adam Walsh Child Protection and Safety Act*, which was made a law by President George W. Bush in 2006.

We feel the insult of trauma and PTSD as individuals. We can use what we learn from our own process to make contributions to others.

NOTES

1. Brett, "The Classification of PTSD," 117–128.
2. Suris et al., "Sexual Assault in Women Veterans." 749–756.

3. Kulkarni et al., "Violence in Childhood," 1264.
4. Bonanno, *The Other Side of Sadness*, 7.
5. Mongelluzzo, *The Everything Guide to Self-Esteem*.
6. van der Kolk, McFarlane, and Weisaeth, *Traumatic Stress.*
7. Staub, *The Roots of Evil*.
8. Crelinsten and Schmid, *The Politics of Pain*, 122.
9. Khamsi, "Healing of Pre and Perinatal Trauma."

Chapter Fifteen

Coping Strategies for Loss and Grief

Health is a state of complete physical, mental and social well-being, and not merely the absence of disease or infirmity. —World Health Organization, 1948

A sad soul can kill you quicker than a germ. —John Steinbeck

We have reached the part of this book that addresses coping and general ways that loss and grief may be addressed. Let's begin by looking at some of the myths and facts about loss and grief.

MYTHS AND FACTS ABOUT LOSS AND GRIEF

The Hospice Foundation is an organization that many of you are familiar with. As an organization they locate themselves in communities throughout the United States and offer assistance to people who are dying, to family members of the dying, to individuals who are aged and require monitoring or support, and to people with a terminal illness who may die quickly or not for some time. They also assist in the care of people who are seriously ill, but not necessarily terminally ill. They are a compassionate organization of people who choose their workers carefully. They contribute to our community, neighbors, and personal well-being. Hospice works in nursing homes, private homes, hospital settings, and other institutions where people with incurable diseases reside while in transition from life. Hospice centers are located throughout the world.

The Hospice Foundation has published extensive literature on death, dying, grief, and the myths about loss and grief. Here is the foundation's Eight Myths about Grief:[1]

Myth #1: We Only Grieve Death
Reality: We Grieve All Losses
Myth #2: Only Family Members Grieve
Reality: All Who Are Attached Grieve
Myth #3: Grief Is An Emotional Reaction
Reality: Grief Is Manifested In Many Ways
Myth #4: Individuals Should Leave Grieving At Home
Reality: We Cannot Control Where We Grieve
Myth #5: We Slowly And Predictably Recover From Grief
Reality: Grief Is An Uneven Process, A Roller Coaster With No Timeline
Myth #6: Grieving Means Letting Go Of The Person Who Died
Reality: We Never Fully Detach From Those Who Have Died
Myth #7: Grief Finally Ends
Reality: Over Time Most People Learn To Live With Loss
Myth #8: Grievers Are Best Left Alone
Reality: Grievers Need Opportunities To Share Their Memories And Grief, And To Receive Support

The Hospice Foundation has also published a list of Eight Myths about Children and Loss.[2]

Myth #1: **Children do not grieve.**
Children of all ages grieve. The child's development and experiences affects the grieving process.
Myth #2: **The death of a loved one is the only major loss children and adolescents experience.**
Young people experience a variety of losses. These include losses of pets, separations caused by divorce or relocations, losses of friends and relationships, as well as losses due to illness or death. All of these losses generate grief.
Myth #3: **Children should be shielded from loss.**
It's impossible to protect children from loss. Adults can teach ways of adapting to loss by including young people in the grieving process.
Myth #4: **Children should not go to funerals. Children should always attend funerals.**
Allow young people to make their own choice. They should decide how they wish to participate in funerals or other services. Adults must provide information, options and support.
Myth #5: **Children get over loss quickly.**
No one gets over significant loss. Children, like adults, will learn to live with the loss. They may revisit that loss at different points in their lives and experience grief again.
Myth #6: **Children are permanently scarred by loss.**

Children are resilient. By providing solid support and strong consistent care, adults can help children cope with loss.

Myth #7: **Talking with children and adolescents is the most effective approach in dealing with loss.**

Different approaches are helpful to young people. It's important to talk openly with children and adolescents; it's also helpful to let young people use creative approaches. Play, art, dance, music, and ritual are all valuable modes of expression that allow them to say what words cannot.

Myth #8: **Helping children and adolescents deal with loss is the family's responsibility.**

Other individuals and organizations can share this responsibility. Hospices, schools, and faith communities can all offer necessary support.

The National Funeral Directors Association deals with grief and the support of those who are grieving as well as those who will assist the bereaved in planning for and being part of a funeral.[3] They have also published a set of myths and realities about death, dying, grief, and grieving. I have summarized some of their thoughts below:

Myth #1: After a year of following the death of a spouse you should be dating.

Every relationship is unique. Some people will never date again and others will date when they are ready. Most people who have lost a loved one know they must have a sense of enough time to feel they could engage in a new relationship completely. If one moves too soon this isn't possible.

Myth #2: If you look well during bereavement and loss it means everything is going well.

People can look handsome or beautiful and refreshed or calm on the outside, but this is not always an accurate description of what is going on inside the person. Sometimes well-intentioned others associate outside appearances with inside process.

Myth #3: Avoid discussing the loss with the griever.

As was mentioned earlier in myths noted by Hospice, this is very far from accurate.

Myth #4: After six to twelve months the grief should be over.

Again, this is far from the reality that is associated with embracing individual grieving styles and the nature of the loss.

Myth #5: Getting out and becoming more active helps to cope.

Although encouragement to maintain relationships on the outside is healthy, one wants to avoid contributing to not addressing the loss by escaping in trips, people, places, and over activity.

Myth #6: Funerals are expensive and depressing.

Most funeral expenses can fit into the desired budget. They can range from very costly to several hundred dollars. Most often people need the funeral services to assist them in the process of mourning. It is, in most countries, part of a ritual associated with death.

Myth #7: Death is the will of God.

Faith is also a personal perspective. People can be offended or hurt when told that the death of someone important was the will of God. We want to be mindful of people's beliefs as well as one's own when inserting faith statements into a phrase of comfort.

Myth #8: Your loved one is no longer in pain. Be thankful for that.

Clichés are seldom individualized enough to have any meaningful impact. Rather, they tend to make people feel rather invisible and part of some recipe. People's pain and the offering of support can be individualized.

Myth #9: Crying excessively leads to a nervous breakdown.

Crying releases toxins from the body and it is an important stress and tension relief. Crying does not lead to a breakdown.

Myth #10: Grief support groups are too depressing.

Many people find support groups a safe and compassionate place to support others and find support.

Let's take a look at some of the dimensions of wellness that go hand in hand with coping well through life and when confronted with the losses that are a part of life. When in grief, these are things that help maintain a healthy focus.

PHYSICAL WELLNESS

Our bodies are the vessel that contain all of our emotions, our spirit, our memory, and knowledge about who and what matters most to us as we take this journey through life. Generally speaking we are born with health and healthy bodies. The trick throughout life is to maintain and foster that health. Things like illnesses and disease can offset the best of intentions, but a healthy body is more resistant to many illnesses and diseases, but not all.

We all know that a mild to moderate amount of exercise is good for you. It reduces blood pressure, stress, and changes the perspective when too many things are on one's mind. Adapting a lifelong exercise routine is important. Choosing things you like and then doing them on most days is the simplest way to incorporate health into a lifelong pattern. When grieving, maintaining some attention to exercise can be helpful, even if you can't keep up with your "normal" levels of activity.

What we want to avoid is becoming sedentary and assuming the posture of a couch potato. Housekeeping, gardening, working in the garage, cleaning out closets, and chopping or splitting wood are regular activities for many people. We have become used to having others do these things for us that fifty years ago would have been unthinkable. By trading off the physical aspects of life so as to have more time for work or leisure doesn't always make sense. Priorities do need to be set and a healthy body is an essential gift we can give ourselves.

Exercise routines can be as simple as walking five days out of seven for twenty or thirty minutes each day and building to forty or more minutes. Hiking is a great exercise and places you out in nature. Nature is healing and we are beings of nature; being outside for periods of the day can help with the grieving process. Tennis, volleyball, basketball, soccer, or any other team sport mixes exercise with socializing and this too is healthy. Swimming, aerobics classes, and weight training are other options. The point is to move. The body and all of its organs love movement. It need not be exotic or excessive and it is best if it is not. Things that resonate with you are going to be easier to maintain as a habit.

The other concern for the body is nutrition. Again, we all know the difference between healthy nutrition and junk food. We know a salad is better than a hamburger and vegetables and fruits need to be present at all meals. Sometimes stress, grief, loss, being overly busy, or just bad habits are some of the many reasons people have for why it doesn't matter. In times of great stress, when loss or grief is part of everyday life, eating can become an issue. Some people soothe their anxieties and fears and grief with overeating; others find it impossible to eat anything at all. But food is fuel, and it's important to try to eat, and to eat healthfully, even in times of grief. We wouldn't put dirt in our car engines, and we wouldn't let our tanks dry out either. That would be unthinkable. In no time the car would be sick.

Most nutritionists agree that smaller, more frequent meals are healthier. Often this is referred to as grazing. Birds, cattle, other livestock, reptiles, and many other beings graze throughout the day. They eat all day, but in small quantities. Humans can do the same thing. Grazing or smaller meals is healthier. When in a grief process this will usually help keep up energy levels and not overwhelm the body. Large meals use more energy. Portions are the issue most likely to throw folks off. A big plate at breakfast, lunch, or dinner is deadly. It is best to have a small plate. In many parts of the world meals are served on what we refer to as a desert plate. When I lived in Mexico for a time, I noticed the tradition. If you ordered fish tacos, what came on the plate was two fish tacos. No beans, rice, or anything else. If you ordered beans and rice you received a small scoop of rice and a ladle of beans. Small plates are the rule not the exception. In North America, big plates rule and it has made people unable to discern correctly the portions necessary to sustain good health.

Physical well-being and health is also maintained and nurtured by being mindful about wellness. It's easy to forget about yourself if you're caring for a loved one during times of illness or imminent death. It's also difficult to care for your own health when you've suffered some other loss that preoccupies your time and your mind. But you can continue to care for yourself in the routine ways even while experiencing grief and loss. Some questions to ask yourself include:

> When was the last time you had a physical exam?
> Are you current with all of your immunizations, including tetanus?
> When was the last time you had a dental exam?
> How about a vision exam?
> When did you last check your cholesterol? If it was not normal did you follow up on this?
> When did you ladies last have a gynecological exam?
> Ladies, how about your mammogram?
> Have all of you been screened for sexually transmitted diseases?
> For you guys, have you been informed about prostate and testicular cancer?
> In the last five years have you had your hemoglobin and blood-sugar levels checked?
> Do you sleep seven to eight hours a night at least five nights a week?
> Do you smoke? Have you tried to quit?
> Do you drink alcohol? Has it become a problem?
> Do you use street drugs such as marijuana, cocaine, crack, or heroin?
> Do you know your BMI (Body Mass Index) and is it normal for your height and weight?
> Do you practice safe sex always?
> Have you been tested for HIV?
> Do you use or overuse prescription drugs such as painkillers, anxiety medications, or other drugs? Has it become a problem?

It is important to your physical well-being to be mindful about all aspects of your health and your body. There are many risks in life, along with innumerable losses. We can avoid some suffering by taking a personal inventory of what is going on and what needs to change.

When addressing issues of loss and grief you will be able to deal more effectively with what life has for you if your body is well, nurtured, and as finely honed as possible. The stress of loss and grief can take a terrible toll on a body, so it's important to try to tune in to your body and help it through the very difficult period of change it may be experiencing.

EMOTIONAL AND PSYCHOLOGICAL WELLNESS

Our emotions are a part of our everyday life experience. We are feeling beings and we will feel our own pain as well as the pain of others. We need not even know the others for whom we feel pain. Often clients tell me about how they cried or couldn't sleep because of a news story or a very sad account that they heard. Emotions go with being a human being and we must learn how to balance our emotions.

Grief, loss, grieving, and eventual acceptance of the losses we will encounter require emotional well-being. Emotional well-being is accomplished through a balance of the past, present, and our future dreams. We need to accept who we are, what our life has been about, accept our limitations, embrace our strengths, and hopefully strive to create a life that serves as a blessing in terms of a legacy. Sherwin Nuland stated,

> Rabbis often end a memorial service with the sentence, "May his memory be for a blessing." It is a specific formula of words that is not familiar to the non-Jews who are present when it is said, and I have listened in vain for it in churches. Though it expresses what is obviously a universal wish, this simple thought deserves more frequent pondering by all of us, and not only in houses of worship. . . . The greatest dignity to be found in death is the dignity of the life that preceded it. This is a form of hope we can all achieve, and it is the most abiding of all. Hope resides in the meaning of what our lives have been.[4]

Emotional wellness is a combination of psychological, behavioral, and emotional wellness.[5]

The psychological part of our emotional wellness addresses our mental health. It is here that we look at how healthy we are from a mental health perspective. If you suffer from depression, anxiety, adjustment disorders, relational disorders, substance dependence, or more serious diagnostic categories, then you have some mental health challenges affecting your emotional psychological wellness. We don't always get to choose what life will give us, only what we do with what we have. This holds true for psychological challenges as well. You are worth the challenge to address the issues you have. All mental health problems can be addressed in some way and improvement is possible with most issues. In many cases spectacular results can and do occur. Sometimes just reaching out for help can alleviate some feelings of loss. It can often be the first step on a road to healing that may be short, or long, or ongoing for a lifetime. But taking action is a good start.

The emotional part of emotional wellness addresses our feeling. Think of all the feelings you have. You have feelings of love, joy, anger, sadness, and fear. These are the primary emotions, just like we have primary colors. Secondary emotions branch off from the primary emotions. Compassion is a branch of love; excitement branches off of joy, irritation comes from anger, grief comes from sadness, and worry comes from fear. Feelings are a subjective experience and yet throughout the world the primary emotions are recognizable in facial expressions and body language. Feelings do not always define reality. Just because we feel it, it doesn't mean the same as reality. For example, if you feel your boyfriend is a jerk and you feel angry with him, it doesn't mean he is a jerk. We can feel our feelings, but it stops with us. We don't define another by way of our feelings. Sometimes feelings, like many things in life, are learned. We saw our parents handle anger, frustration, loss, or even love in certain ways and we often emulate what we witnessed growing up.

Behavioral emotional wellness is how we act to others and to our self. Some people lash out at others when they are disappointed, frustrated, afraid, or angry. Some people take on the feelings of others when people lash out at them. People can become anxious and depressed by way of the manner they are treated by others. We can also harm our self when we feel bad and then take risks with our health, safety, or future. The way in which we handle the balance of our emotions and psychological makeup in terms of behavior is extremely important.

Where loss and grief are concerned, you can see how psychological, emotional, and behavioral wellness come together and easily influence how one will deal with loss and how they may grieve.

SPIRITUAL WELLNESS

When we speak of spiritual wellness we are speaking of something that is highly personal to most people. Spirituality and religion are personal choices that involve emotion, our past, our beliefs about the future, and our beliefs about death, dying, loss, grief, and even suffering. People need to propose their own spiritual wellness plan. Whatever your beliefs, there are guidelines within those beliefs that encourage wellness, care of the body, care of the soul, and the regard for others. All the world's main religions are a lot more similar in their primary tenets than they are dissimilar.

For our purposes regarding loss and grief, spiritual wellness is about acknowledgment of your spirituality, learning to listen for the wisdom within yourself, and developing a language of understanding between your body and your mind by way of your spiritual body. Spiritual wellness is about acceptance and, at times, forgiveness. It is about the cultivation of gratitude in your daily life and appreciation for all things that grace your life. Perhaps it is even for accepting and having gratitude for challenges such as loss and grief present. We learn a great deal by engaging in challenges. We are brought to our knees and then stand again with losses we never thought we could endure. We rise up and celebrate surviving and loving and becoming better people by finding the strength to turn tragedy into triumph or grace. Spiritual wellness is about living in grace.[6]

SOCIAL AND INTERPERSONAL CONNECTIONS

We are not islands and we all need connection. It is true that some people thrive with more connections with people, whereas others do best with fewer connections. Most people would not fare well with no connections at all.

We need people, we need one another, and we need community and a sense of belonging to something outside of ourselves. Family and friends can provide this, towns may nurture this, and organizations make an effort to find a bond that can be shared. Wellness extends into our connections with one another. In fact, longevity studies often point out connection as one of the key ingredients to living a long and healthy life. Evidence-based studies suggest genetics and lifestyle choices influence longevity. Included in lifestyle choices are things such as family and social-life connections. It goes without saying that diet and moderate exercise are a part of this equation and contribute to living a very long life.

Family is our first social connection. It is here that we love and learn to love. If we have siblings we learn to share. If we don't have siblings we learn to share with parents and peers who will become an important part of our social network. Family provides a base. It is here that we hopefully trust we will be cared for, fed, housed, and taught how to live as adults. We will take on our parents' value systems until we form our own. Very often our own values will reflect what we learned in our families. When we experience loss or grief, it is often our families we turn to first for solace. But that is not always the case. Some families are not close, and then a person may turn to his or her friends for comfort and help.

School is a significant social connection. Children begin socializing with other children outside the family at younger and younger ages. Play dates, preschool, kindergarten, and elementary school are the beginning points for children learning about connections with others and learning interpersonal skills necessary for community living. Later in middle school and high school the relationship tools are more finely honed. As most parents know, these are also critical times in a child's life. Although we encourage and want to foster peer relationships, it is a double-edged sword. We might liken it to different tribes coming together to learn, play, and socialize. Sometimes the belief systems, values, ethics, and perspectives vary widely from tribe to tribe. It is the perfect recipe for a potential disaster as often happens in the case of school-related violence, bullying, cliques, and the tendency to marginalize certain individuals or groups.

Homeschooling as an educational choice has been around for years, but has increased in popularity over the last ten years. This coincides with the increase in bullying awareness and also with the 9/11 terrorist attacks. The Home School Legal Defense Association (HSLDA) notes that an estimated 1.7 million to 2.1 million children in kindergarten through twelfth grade are homeschooled in the United States.[7] The National Center for Education Statistics notes that in 2007 1.5 million students were being homeschooled. This represents an increase from 850,000 in 1999 and 1.1 million in 2003. They note a 74 percent relative increase over an eight-year period (1999–2007) and a 36 percent relative increase since 2003.[8]

The reasons given for why parents chose homeschooling over public or private schooling were: (1) To provide religious or moral instruction (36 percent); (2) Concerns about the school environment (drugs, safety, peer issues) (21 percent); (3) Dissatisfaction with academic instruction (17 percent); (4) Other reasons, which included travel, finances, distance, and family time (14 percent); (5) The remainder of those polled cited special needs, a child's health problems, or the desire for a nontraditional education approach.[9]

Community is an important outlet and resource for increased socialization and forming connections. There are numerous civic organizations including the Humane Society, Big Brothers/Big Sisters, teen centers, The Boys and Girls Club, and specialty groups such as the Audubon Society, the Sierra Club, and AARP (American Association of Retired Persons). In addition, many communities have adult community centers, Meals on Wheels programs, CASA child programs (Court Appointed Special Advocate), and Volunteers in Victims Assistance (VIVA) programs. There are many ways to become involved in your community. You can volunteer or just participate in the things that go on in your hometown. Grief and loss assumes a two-way design. When we have our own grief we need others, and programs are there to help. We can also donate our time in these programs and give back to those who are experiencing loss and grief.

There are people all around us grieving. Sometimes it takes just making a connection for them to let you in on what their grief is about. On occasion, I have been hiking in the woods and stopped to rest when other hikers emerge from another trail. We all sat and spoke for a while and shared information about where the natural springs were to fill water bottles. In these conversations people have shared they were hiking because a wife recently died or because a parent died from cancer or because they just went through a loss in a love relationship. Loss is everywhere. Grieving people do not wear a sign; it is our job to show up and open the conversation. Likewise, it is important to know that people usually do want to help you.

Getting to know your neighbors is another form of connection. Make it a goal to know everyone on your block by his or her first names. It is surprising how many people don't know who lives next door. And you never know what really happens in the lives of others if you don't know them. Having a neighborhood security net can help you through times of grief, and helping others with their own losses can help you work through your own.

Shop in your community whenever possible and support the local economy. It is a convenience to shop on the Internet, but it is a gesture of community support to order your books from the local bookstore, and your clothing, hardware, and other items from local stores. Eating foods grown in your area not only supports your local economy, it is also better for you. When foods travel from other countries, it may be weeks from harvest to the table. When you buy local produce, it was usually harvested a day or two previously and retains most of its vitamin content. Shopping at farmers' markets enables you to meet other people who may have similar interests and needs. Finding those people increases the support you have, and the support you're able to provide to others.

We need one another. It goes a long way to smile, assist, and to be cordial and friendly with those who work in our communities. Everyone likes a smile and no one gets tired of a helping hand. If we all do just a little it makes a big difference in how others feel, in how we feel about ourselves, and in how cohesive our community feels.

DOES TIME HEAL?

It depends on whom you ask. It is true that time helps take us out of the shock of a loss, and in doing so we are able to catch our breath and assume some sense of dignity in taking care of the other things in our life. It depends on the type of loss, but generally we become better skilled over time with dealing with loss and with becoming familiar with our own unique grieving style. However, this isn't always the case.

In a study of PTSD and non-Hodgkin lymphoma patients, it was found that the PTSD symptoms persisted or worsened in more than one-third of the patients studied seven years after diagnosis.[10] The researchers conclude with a caution that there is enduring risk for PTSD even when patients are in recovery and long-term survivors.

In another study regarding divorce, researchers found that divorced people reported lower levels of life satisfaction than married people.[11] Satisfaction increased as years went by following a divorce, but a baseline of return to previous life satisfaction was never achieved. The study concluded that future life satisfaction was influenced by preexisting satisfaction with life (pre-divorce) and the lasting effect of the event of divorce. Divorce has long-term lasting effects especially when it comes to feeling satisfied with life. Some people will never feel quite the same even if they remarry.

Another study on spousal bereavement among the elderly raises interesting issues. We have heard about the phenomenon of an elderly spouse dying, only to be followed in death by the other spouse within months. Mortality among elderly widows and widowers has become a cause for concern. This study, published in 1986, concludes with the need for more proactive services being available to the surviving spouse.[12] This situation is one where time does not heal. A couple who has been together most of their lives often cannot imagine life without the one they have lost. A curious biological, emotional, and spiritual dance begins to take place and the surviving spouse may begin his or her own death process.

A 2007 study examined what is known as the Set-Point Model.[13] This model looks at individuals as having a set point where adaptation is concerned. Basically it proposes that people can adapt to any life event, and any fluctuation is around an already determined biological set point. Researchers decided to study what happens to happiness after changes involving loss occur. What they found was that, although some adaptation to loss takes place, certain losses such as divorce, death of a spouse, unemployment, and disability were associated with lasting changes in what is referred to as subjective well-being. Subjective well-being is a measurement of happiness. What this study illustrates is that time does not heal all losses, and a return to a state of happiness may not always be possible.

Does time heal? Time will help but it is not clear if people actually ever fully heal from certain losses. People have found eventual strength, inspiration, purpose, and grace following loss. People have discovered they are more than their anger, sadness, anxiety, or grief. They have also found that certain losses simply change who we are, and some of these changes will be good whereas other changes may be less than favorable. What we do know is that loss is about change.

NOTES

1. Hospice Foundation, "Shattering Eight Myths about Grief."
2. Hospice Foundation, "Eight Myths about Children and Loss."
3. National Funeral Directors Association, "Ten Common Myths-Realities."
4. Nuland, *How We Die*, 242.
5. Mongelluzzo, *The Everything Guide to Self-Esteem.*
6. Ibid.
7. Home School Legal Defense Association, "Homeschooling Research."
8. National Center for Education Statistics, "Fast Facts Homeschooling."
9. Ibid.
10. Smith et al., "Post-Traumatic Stress Symptoms."
11. Lucas, "Time Does Not Heal All Wounds."
12. Baro, Keirse, and Wouters, "Spousal Bereavement in the Elderly."
13. Lucas, "Adaptation and the Set-Point Model," 75–79.

Chapter Sixteen

Therapy, Counseling, Psychiatry, and Medication

Therapy is too good to be limited to the sick.
—Erving Polster

I think therapy is a helpful thing. I think everyone knows it. You do it for your life, you do it for yourself, because you want to explore some things, and get at the bottom of some things. It's about your life, the quality of your life. — Phillip Seymour Hoffman

Loss involves change and change is often difficult. Sometimes we need help with change. We need help with allowing it, embracing it, defining it, and working with what it means in our life. Life events are striking in their ability to impact us in both positive as well as negative ways. Death, divorce, domestic violence, or marriage, birth, and harmony with others are all life events.

People seldom seek out assistance for the wonderful events in life, but sometimes they do. I frequently have young couples make an appointment for premarital counseling. They want to explore who they are as individuals coming together as a couple. They want a place to highlight the potential triggers that can lie in wait for future eruption. They want to practice and hone their communication skills preventatively before any real issues arise. I really enjoy such couples.

Sometimes adolescents come in for counseling during their senior year in high school. They are in the middle of some significant angst. They are eighteen and lost. They feel like imposters in the play of life. They are afraid of the future and feel ill-equipped to manage adult life. So, many come to counseling to start sorting it out. They look at school, their relationships, college or work choices, and they look at their families. They try to make sense of what has taken place so that when they move onward they will have a better template of understanding. I really enjoy this work as well.

Occasionally, I see children who are eight, nine, or ten, who ask their parents to send them to counseling. Perhaps they heard from friends or a teacher about the advantages of having someone outside family and friends with whom to discuss the things of life. One little guy told his mother, "I need an appointment to talk to a therapist."

Mother asked, "For what?"

The boy responded, "I have things on my mind that are confusing."

Mother said, "But you can talk to me."

The boy implored, "But you are my mother and I love you."

The mother queried, "I love you too and that's what I'm here for, to listen."

The boy added, "No, you are here to love me and I need someone I don't love to talk to about things."

Mother said, "Well, then, Ok."

The boy began counseling and after several visits, his mother came in one day to pick him up. In front of the therapist, mother said to the boy, "So how did it go today? Did you talk about what you needed to?" The boy responded, "What goes on in counseling, stays in counseling." His take on the What Happens in Vegas, Stays in Vegas commercial. We all smiled.

Counseling is best used when one isn't in the middle of a crisis. It is also used for things of great crisis proportions. When one works in counseling before big problems arise, the work can be more carefully honed to fit the needs and goals of the client. In crisis work the client is typically busy putting out fires and then rebuilding their emotional life.

Kate Scharff is a social worker who published a useful book titled *Therapy Demystified*.[1] It is a good read for anyone embarking on choosing a therapist. In her book she has a chapter on the top ten misguided reasons for avoiding therapy. Here she lists things such as not having the financial resources, not having time, worrying about making matters worse by talking about things, a belief that people who go to therapy are whiners, a belief that family and friends are those who should provide the help, a fear therapy will last into eternity, a belief therapy is for crazy people, a fear of needing to dredge up your entire life, fearing the use of therapy might be a future liability, and the belief that therapy is useless and doesn't work anyway. Ms. Scharff debunks all these beliefs and myths. You are worth the effort, and therapy has been proven time and again to help people. It frequently saves lives, it offers different perspectives, and it is actually an interesting and fulfilling process. The end result, when a correct match of client to therapist is made, is more joy, self-awareness, and new skills.

So, just who are the folks out there who are the helpers for all types of emotions, psychological issues, loss, grief, and matters of the mind?

TYPES OF COUNSELORS

Counseling is a general category that describes what we do. We counsel people on matters that are related to behavioral health. Behavioral health is another word for our mental health. Counselors can have a master's degree or a doctoral degree or both. Even medical doctors (MDs) can offer counseling if they work as psychiatrists. A psychiatrist is a medical doctor who specializes in behavioral health.

Psychotherapy and counseling are terms that are often used interchangeably. To some people, psychotherapy denotes a more in-depth process of exploration, whereas others align the word with psychologists who hold a PhD in the field. Most often psychotherapy is used to address diagnosable mental illnesses and more in-depth work. Typically psychotherapy and counseling mean the same thing. If in doubt, always know you can ask for a provider to distinguish how he or she uses the terms. Psychotherapeutic interventions may be based on a medical model where a diagnosis is rendered or may be based on a more educational/helper role. Insurance companies require psychotherapy to be coded in the medical model with a diagnosis if reimbursement is being sought.

Psychotherapy is a process that includes a range of techniques used to assist individuals, couples, and families. These techniques are designed to improve mental health, life skills, relationships, and other things such as self-esteem. Psychotherapy uses spoken communication although there are techniques that utilize other forms of communication such as the written word, artwork, or even music and dance. Psychotherapy with children can utilize play, games, and projective questions as well as techniques such as mutual storytelling. Psychotherapy takes place between a trained therapist and his or her client(s). Psychotherapy may be used to address mental illness or the everyday problems that are seen in career, relationships, goals, or the effects of illness and loss.

All individuals who work in the counseling, psychotherapy, or psychiatry fields are required to be licensed by the state they are practicing in. Below are the most common forms of psychotherapists and counselors:

Psychiatrist (MD or DO): Psychiatrists are physicians who specialize in psychiatry. They hold a medical degree. Psychiatrists can prescribe medications for mental health issues. Some psychiatrists use psychotherapy in their work in addition to evaluating the need for medication and monitoring its effectiveness with the client/patient. In medicine the term "patient" is most often used, whereas in counseling and psychotherapy "client" is used.

Psychiatric Nurse Practitioner (PNP, RN, PMHNP): A psychiatric nurse practitioner is a registered nurse who is licensed to work independently or under an MD physician. The PNP can prescribe medication and also engage in counseling or psychotherapy.

Psychologist (PhD, PsyD, EdD): There are three types of psychologists, depending on the state in which you live. A PhD is a doctoral degree in psychology and a dissertation is required to confirm this degree. A PsyD is a doctoral degree in psychology and emphasis is less on research and more on clinical practice. An EdD is a doctoral degree in which clinical emphasis can result in professional licensing as a psychologist in many states.

Psychologists may use testing as a part of their practice. Not all PhDs are in psychology. You can have a PhD in any subject. Ask your provider what their PhD is in.

Clinical Social Worker (LMSW, LCSW): Clinical social workers have a master's or doctoral degree (DSW, PhD) in clinical social work. LCSW professionals are licensed to practice independently. Social workers engage in the practice of counseling and many are also equipped to offer case management skills if your situation requires this.

Licensed Professional Counselor (LPC): Licensed professional counselors have completed a master's degree or doctoral degree in professional counseling. They engage in counseling, psychotherapy, and referral for medication-needs assessment.

Marriage and Family Therapist (LMFT): Marriage and family therapists have completed a master's program. Marriage and family therapist often do individual work as well as family counseling.

Licensed Independent Alcohol and Substance Abuse Counselor (LISAC): The licensed alcohol and substance abuse counselor holds a master's degree and specialization in the treatment of a specific area of mental health known as chemical dependency. Generally speaking, substance-abuse counselors do not receive training in psychotherapy with populations other than chemical dependency as the identified problem area.

Always remember to ask about your provider's licensing, training, education, and if they accept insurance or if they are in network or out of network with your specific insurance company. You can never ask too many questions. Determine your needs where finances are concerned and the specialty area you are seeking. For example, if you are seeking counseling for relationship issues, but you know you have a history of PTSD and you have in-network benefits for counseling with your insurance plan, then call your insurance and find out who is in your network in your geographic area. This is a good starting point. Then, call those people and find out if they specialize in relationships and PTSD. Next, confirm if they bill your insurance for you. Lastly, schedule an appointment to see if you feel comfortable with that person. The most important ingredient in counseling is the fit between client and therapist. The better the rapport, the better the outcome.

Loss and grief are specialty areas in the field of counseling and psychology. Many therapists have general or even specific training in loss and grief. Ask your provider if this is an area they have worked in.

Let's take a look at the types of therapy that are available that might be used with loss and grief issues as well as general mental health issues. This does not represent a complete list of all the therapies out there. That is worthy of a book in itself. The choices I have made for inclusion here are commonly accepted therapies that are often used in loss and grief work as well as to address other mental health issues or concerns.

COGNITIVE BEHAVIORAL THERAPY (CBT) APPROACH

The term cognitive behavioral therapy refers to two types of therapy, cognitive therapy and behavioral therapy. We often combine them because the therapies are commonly used in conjunction with one another. The focus of cognitive behavioral therapies is on your behavior and your cognitions or thought processes. This group of practitioners believes that changing your behavior and thoughts about things are the main goals or ways to assist people in crises or in different diagnostic categories.

Cognitive behavioral therapies have been studied the most extensively of perhaps all the forms of mental health treatment. One of the reasons for this is that the techniques are amenable to being studied. Another reason it has been studied is because it is viewed as shorter term, perhaps more cost effective, and it is heavily goal oriented. This makes it attractive in certain treatment settings as well as for reimbursement from insurance companies.

Cognitive behavioral approaches operate on the premise that a person's beliefs and attitudes influence their emotions and behavioral choices. CBT often takes an inventory of a person's beliefs about things such as self-worth, belief in affecting life changes, setting of long- and short-term goals, strengths, weaknesses, risk factors, and protective factors. A therapist may help a client with setting goals, with acquiring more "rational" thinking about problems, or with ways to improve self-esteem. The main problem areas are identified and the therapist works with the client on making a treatment plan that addresses each problem area and a strategy for addressing improvement or change in that area. Generally speaking CBT includes: problem assessment, conceptualizing the problem, learning skills, honing skills and applying them to problem areas, reinforcement and maintenance of the skill and problem resolution, and a post-treatment follow-up plan.

With grief and loss, we often see group therapy for specific losses or for assistance in the grief process. This may take many forms. One example might be group counseling for divorced parents. Another would be a psycho-educational group for victims of a hurricane disaster. Still another might be an adjustment group for rape survivors. There are also bereavement groups for parents who have lost a child and parents who have lost a child to murder. The cognitive behavioral approach would influence how the group is conducted with specific goals and assignments over a designated period of time. The exercises both in and outside of group would be oriented around achieving goals that the clients and the therapist have discussed or group members agreed were valuable goals for assisting them in their process.

EMDR (Eye Movement Desensitization and Reprocessing)

This is a form of cognitive behavioral therapy known as exposure therapy. It has been influenced by other theories such as systems theory, behavioral theory, and experiential and hypnotic theories. The premise behind this form of treatment is that people store painful and traumatic memories. The memories continue to impact the person, producing undesirable "psychopathology." Therefore this technique attempts to reduce the influence of the memories.

This is accomplished by participation in eight stages.[2]

The **first stage** gathers history and begins to look at a general treatment plan.

The **second stage** focuses on identifying the disturbing memory or memories. In the second stage the therapist will have the client focus on one of these memories while initiating lateral eye movement. The client focuses for up to thirty seconds and then the therapist asks the client if any other memory or thoughts emerged during the focus set. If so, then these memories will be used in a subsequent set of exposure and lateral eye movement.

In the **third stage** a memory will be elicited and the client will be asked to pair a negative and a positive thought with the memory as well as identifying any part of the body that feels uncomfortable.

The **fourth stage** involves the client focusing on the distressing memory and the negative thought associated with that memory at the same time. The therapist will then use bilateral gestures and ask the client to follow the therapist's gestures with their eyes. This continues until no negative thoughts remain associated with the particular memory.

In the **fifth stage** the client is asked to focus on the positive thought associated with the memory. The therapist will initiate the bilateral gestures and the client follows the gestures with his or her eyes. This continues until the positive thought is associated with the memory or memory image.

The **sixth stage** involves a body scan where the client attempts to identify any discomfort remaining in the physical body. The distressing memory is reintroduced to the client and the client scans his body for any areas of discomfort. If discomfort is noted, the bilateral gestures and eye movements are repeated until there is no discomfort. Completion of this stage is considered successful when the memory no longer elicits discomfort when spoken or thought about.

The **seventh stage** reinforces what has been learned. The client is taught relaxation and other techniques to help stave off unwanted thoughts, images, or memories. Any resurfacing of memories is addressed and journal work is asked of the client for recording anything that comes up outside of the session.

The final **eighth stage** assesses progress and makes plans for continuing with more EMDR or with termination.

Typically EMDR is used in conjunction with another form of therapy, rather than being a stand-alone therapy.

Exposure Therapy

Exposure therapy is another cognitive behavioral therapy. It is used primarily with disorders in the anxiety category, including generalized anxiety disorder, posttraumatic stress disorder, specific phobias, and also obsessive-compulsive disorder. The goal of exposure therapy, much like EMDR, is to expose the client to the trauma, event, situation, or item, and attempt to desensitize the person's response to it.

Some therapists consider exposure therapy controversial. By its nature it exposes people to the very thing that caused the trauma or problems in the beginning. Some clinicians are ethically opposed to doing that. However, studies show exposure therapy is effective in certain populations such as combat-related posttraumatic stress disorder.[3]

Exposure therapy has been effective in treating specific phobias such as those associated with things such as cockroaches or other insects, PTSD in male sexual assault,[4] posttraumatic nightmares,[5] trauma-related nightmares in children,[6] emotional distress associated with cancer diagnosis in adolescence,[7] and body dysmorphic disorder in adolescent females.[8] There are numerous other examples of success with this form of therapy being combined with other therapies. It is usually used in conjunction with another form of therapy.

Loss and grief that result from trauma, mental illness, cancer, and even body dysmorphic disorder may be helped through this form of therapy. Issues to do with loss and grief that are a result of death, dying, and divorce would likely not be treated with this form of therapy.

Dialectical Behavioral Therapy (DBT)

This is another of the many cognitive behavioral therapies. This, like many of the cognitive therapies, is a blended therapy incorporating mindfulness, reality testing, distress tolerance, and cognitive tools for emotional regulation. This form of therapy is considered effective in work with borderline personality disorder. It is also used with substance dependency, sexual abuse survivors, other traumatic assaults, and a variety of mood-related disorders.

DBT asks the client to make as strong a commitment to therapy as does the therapist. Although one would assume all clients make a commitment to treatment, for certain people treatment is difficult for both client and therapist due to the length of time adequate treatment might typically take. So, in this form of treatment, the client and therapist are seen as allies working conjointly on the therapeutic issues at hand.

DBT is typically used by combining individual and group treatment. Seldom will only one format take place.

There are four components to most DBT. These include: mindfulness, distress tolerance, emotion regulation, and interpersonal effectiveness. Each component or module includes subsets to be learned and practiced. For example, mindfulness involves the development of core skills that involve learning the "what skills." These teach you to observe, describe, and to participate. You then learn the "how skills," which involve practicing being nonjudgmental, mindful, and effective. Next you move on to distress tolerance, which includes learning to distract in meaningful ways, self-soothing skills, participation in improving the here and now moment, using pros and cons to understanding the inner debate about not letting go of distress, radical acceptance, and embracing willingness as opposed to willfulness.

DBT is a comprehensive therapeutic program and the scope of this book does not allow an entire presentation of what is involved in the therapy.

DBT does teach new skills, and encourages the client to meet their challenges head on. The motivational aspect does empower this technique.

The types of loss this technique might be useful for include childhood trauma that persists into adulthood, which is often the case with the borderline personality client. It is also useful in other traumas and in substance dependency. It likely doesn't apply to grief associated with death or dying unless the grief was complicated and traumatic grief. However, that said, DBT has been very useful in regulating emotions. As we know, grief is often characterized by extremes in emotions, moods, and behaviors.

PSYCHODYNAMIC PSYCHOTHERAPY

Psychodynamic psychotherapy represents a departure from cognitive behavioral approaches. Psychodynamic psychotherapy is a form of depth psychology. It has been around a very long time and is similar to psychoanalysis in the way the client and history is viewed. It is not psychoanalysis in other ways. The relationship between client and therapist is paramount in this form of therapy. Psychodynamic psychotherapy does look at the client's past, the patterns and themes therein, and what from the past might be present in the here and now. Developmental theory is woven into this form of therapy as a means of understanding the client as well as his or her interactions or dynamics with others. This form of therapy uses a variety of intervention styles such as family therapy, group therapy, individual therapy, and child and adolescent therapy. Psychodynamic psychotherapy is also referred to as insight-oriented therapy. It was influenced by Freudian psychology, ego psychology, self psychology, and object relations psychology.

This form of therapy looks at both the conscious and unconscious interplay that occurs in life. Often people will find themselves repeating maladaptive behaviors or they notice patterns that have been present throughout their lives. If they choose to understand these patterns or themes they will, in essence, be bringing unconscious material laid down from the past into consciousness. It is only when our "material" is conscious that we are actually empowered to make any changes.

Psychodynamic psychotherapy has several underlying tenets. These are:

- Self-reflection and self-examination;
- The client-therapist relationship is examined as a portal to understanding the client's difficulties in relationships or in identifying relationship patterns;
- An emphasis on unconscious conflicts and developmental stages;
- Defense mechanisms such as denial, projection, and others are viewed as ways to avoid consequences of conflict;
- Early childhood sets the stage for later psychopathology;
- Conflicts are organized around relationships with others and therefore relationships are examined in this form of therapy;
- Insights lead to awareness, which leads to the ability to make change.

Psychodynamic psychotherapy fell out of favor when cognitive approaches were seen as in vogue and a better fit for busy people. However, the American Psychological Association notes that psychodynamic psychotherapy is highly effective with lasting benefits obtained through self-knowledge.[9] "The American public has been told that only newer, symptom-focused treatments like cognitive behavior therapy or medication have scientific support.

The actual scientific evidence shows that psychodynamic therapy is highly effective. The benefits are at least as large as those of other psychotherapies and they last."[10]

GROUP THERAPY

Group therapy is therapy in a group setting. Typically there will be one or two therapists leading the group. Most groups are oriented around a topic or theme such as a divorce adjustment group, incest survivor group, adolescent support group, anger management, relaxation training, or groups for children of divorce.

Groups may be closed or open. A closed group starts and ends at a specified time. Once it begins no new members are added. An open group is ongoing and new members join continuously. Groups are also considered time limited (an eight-week group for example) or continuous (the group keeps running, sometimes for months or years).

One type of group model is the psychoeducational group, which imparts information in a teaching-processing model. For example, a divorce adjustment group might be psychoeducational if it has eight weeks of weekly meetings, with a different topic about divorce presented each week by the therapist for the purpose of learning. Then the group members discuss their feelings or observations about the topic. Support groups orient around a helping model. Here each group member might take ten minutes to describe their week and the things that were challenging. The other group members may chime in and offer support. The therapist may summarize the support offered.

Some groups are cognitive behavioral and others are based on psychodynamic principles.There are also group therapies utilizing art, music, dance, and other expressive therapies. Group therapy is viewed as a highly effective model for offering assistance. It is a way to share with others, build a therapeutic network, learn new information and skills, reduce isolation and stigma around mental illness or other issues. It offers a place for catharsis, and a way to take responsibility for your life and wellness.

There are a number of grief support groups throughout the United States. Larger cities have more options than do more rural settings. Some resources for finding a grief support group include the following:

- Grief Share—weekly support groups with groups throughout the United States and Canada. More information is found at www.griefshare.org.
- Hospice Foundation—a wide variety of support groups for grief. More information can be found at www.hospicefoundation.org.

- Many major hospitals have grief support groups on site. Call your local hospital for information on groups in your area.
- Guidance centers and community mental health centers offer grief support groups. Contact your local community mental health center.
- All major colleges and universities have access to grief support groups and lists of support groups in your geographic area.
- Compassionate Friends is a grief organization with chapters throughout the United States. Groups are located in small and large cities across the country. For more information look at www.compassionatefriends.org.

Many more resources exist. Ask your family physician, counselor, church minister, friends, priest, or rabbi about the resources they have recommended.

FAMILY THERAPY

Family therapy is also known as couple's therapy, marriage and family therapy, family counseling, family systems therapy, and conjoint therapy. In this form of therapy the entire family or a part of the family unit is involved in psychotherapy or counseling. Depending on the reason for referral, your therapist will look at this form of counseling as a primary or secondary resource for your treatment plan.

The premise behind family counseling is that entire families can become ill. Furthermore, if one member in the family is suffering from a mental health problem, it will affect the entire family. It differs from individual therapy in that the identified client is the family or the couple. The therapist's allegiance is to the family rather than to one member of the family.

There are many types of family therapy techniques available. There is a cognitive behavioral approach, a psychodynamic approach, a family systems approach, an intergenerational approach, Gestalt therapy model, an emotional focus model, and many other different approaches. The goal is to identify the family's strengths and weaknesses and to form goals. What would the family like to accomplish? Perhaps the family would like to communicate better. Or, the family may need to address a family member who is recovering from an addiction or concurrently being treated for an eating disorder.

Family therapy is useful in grief counseling. It is extremely powerful as a tool to help families heal and make them stronger. Families may not create the time to sit with one another outside of a clinical setting. It can be helpful to have a safe place to express feelings, to problem solve, to grieve together, and to enhance the existing strengths in the family.

INTEGRATIVE MEDICINE

According to WebMD, integrative medicine is a philosophy of treatment aimed at treating the whole person including the mind, body, and spirit. Dr. Andrew Weil is one of the best-known leaders in integrative medicine. He defines integrative medicine as follows, "Integrative medicine is healing-oriented medicine that takes account of the whole person (body, mind, and spirit), including all aspects of lifestyle. It emphasizes the therapeutic relationship and makes use of all appropriate therapies, both conventional and alternative."[11]

Integrative medicine incorporates aspects of conventional and alternative medicine. What this means is that a person may be treated in a conventional manner by a physician who also suggests other treatments to address the presenting complaint. The alternatives might include things such as acupuncture, medical massage therapy, herbal medicines, yoga, relaxation, stress-reduction techniques, chiropractic medicine, craniosacral therapy, myofascial therapy, nutritional counseling, biofeedback, Reiki, and other choices. The alternative approaches are not to take the place of a medical intervention, but rather, they are seen as complimentary to the medical intervention. Thus, integrative medicine is often called complimentary medicine.

Integrative medicine has enjoyed much recent mainstream awareness. Think of all the people you know, perhaps yourself included, who utilize massage, chiropractors, herbal medicines, acupuncture, physical therapy, and more specific techniques such as Reiki. The general population uses these techniques for healing. Integrative medicine incorporates them into the plan of health care because they have been shown to be of benefit. Many medical centers throughout the United States offer integrative medicine as a part of their treatment options. Integrative medical clinics can be found in most major cities and many smaller towns throughout the United States.

HOSPICE

We discussed hospice earlier in this book. A briefer summary will be included here. The Hospice Foundation is an organization that believes that the terminally ill, gravely ill, or the dying and their families are entitled to physical, emotional, and relational support in the days, weeks, or months preceding death. Hospice offers individualized care for all people who find themselves suffering or in transition from life into death. They operate in individual centers, in hospitals and clinic settings, and they work in people's homes or in institutional settings. Their goal is that their patients receive care, respect, support, and freedom from unnecessary suffering.

Hospice offers individual and family counseling or referrals for counseling, as well as grief support through grief groups.

MEDICATION

Sometimes people who are dealing with loss and grief do benefit from medication. As we discussed earlier in this book, complicated grief takes on a life of its own and can beset a person with anxiety symptoms, depression, posttraumatic stress disorder, adjustment disorders with anxiety, depression, or behavioral problems, and the body can become exhausted. Sometimes we simply run out of reserves and our natural resiliency to endure distress, stress, and stressors starts to break down. Therapy, group therapy, family therapy, alternative therapies, and medication can all have a place in helping individuals regain a balance and feel better.

Medications are prescribed by medical doctors, physician assistants, psychiatric nurse practitioners, and nurse practitioners. It is important for medications to be monitored. I have heard of many people who were prescribed an antidepressant twenty years ago, which they are still taking but no one is monitoring the continued need for the medication or the dosage. Medications for grief usually fall into the category of mood stabilizer, antidepressant, or antianxiety. Some people will need a combination of medications depending on the types of symptoms that have become troubling.

In the chapter to follow we will look at more of the alternative therapies that can assist during times of loss, grief, or for other conditions or situations for which a person might need support.

NOTES

1. Scharff, *Therapy Demystified.*
2. EMDR Institute, "What is EMDR?"
3. Wald, "Implementation and Outcome."
4. Abbas and Macfie, "Supportive and Insight-oriented."
5. Cavera, Jacobs, and Motta, "Experimental Exposure Therapy."
6. Fernandez et al., "A Case Series."
7. McNicol et al., "Alleviating Emotional Distress."
8. Burrows et al., "ERP, Medication."
9. Jonathon Shedler, "Psychodynamic Psychotherapy." American Psychological Association.
10. Ibid.
11. Weil, "What Is Integrative Medicine?"

Chapter Seventeen

Alternative Therapies

Volumes are now written and spoken upon the effect of the mind upon the body. Much of it is true. But I wish a little more was thought of the effect of the body on the mind. —Florence Nightingale, *Notes on Nursing*

Treatment originates outside you; healing comes from within. —Andrew Weil, MD, *Health and Healing*

MEDITATION AND GUIDED MEDITATION

I live and work in Sedona, Arizona. My town is considered a mecca of alternative therapies. People come from all over the world to explore the alternative healing practices found in this town. In addition to conventional medicine there are practices in acupuncture, homeopathy, herbal medicine, integrative medicine, Reiki, massage therapy, craniosacral therapy, physical therapy, chiropractics, myofascial release, drug and alcohol treatment programs, programs for treating mental illness and drug or alcohol problems without medication, art therapy, music therapy, sand tray therapy, many mental health mainstream therapists and techniques, and much more.

Meditation is common in Sedona and becoming increasingly common throughout the United States. Meditation is from the Latin verb *meditari,* which means to think, ponder, or contemplate. Sedona has a Buddhist center where one can go to meditate near or around the *Amitabha Stupa*. Spiritual seekers from around the globe come to Sedona for its spiritual inspiration. The *Stupa* is but one of dozens of sites dedicated to meditation and reflection. The Native American Hopi tribe considers a part of Sedona their sacred site for prayer.

Meditation is a practice that requires training in order to arrive at mastery. The techniques that are learned and practiced have the end goal of relaxation, training the mind to respond to stillness on command, inducing a state of consciousness, building up the life force or qi (also known as prana or ki). The further result of such mind training is that of increased awareness, compassion, forgiveness, patience, and gratitude. Meditation has been shown to improve many medical concerns such as high blood pressure, depression, anxiety, and other health issues. Meditation is often in use in major medical centers throughout the United States as an adjunctive therapy with chemotherapy, surgery, and serious illnesses.

Meditation can be done sitting. The eyes are usually closed. The point is that of single-mindedness. In order to remove thoughts, images, and the thinking process, the meditator focuses in on a single thought or image in an attempt to still the mind of all other thoughts. At times a mantra or saying is repeated in order to arrive at this state. Again, the goal is "being awake inside without being aware of anything except awareness itself."[1]

Medical research has shown that meditation can increase focus and attention span, diminish the perception of pain, and improve memory.[2] Meditation comes in many forms. Some types include attention meditation, mindfulness meditation, passage meditation, and benevolent meditation.

Guided meditation is a meditation guided by an instructor or by a voice on a tape or CD. One powerful meditation utilizing sound and guided meditation was recorded by Dr. Mitch Gaynor, an oncologist working in New York City at Weill-Cornell College of Cornell University.[3] Dr. Gaynor utilizes sound, chanting, meditation, and other supportive techniques for his cancer patients. Loss and grief, in addition to fear, are often a part of the cancer process and the treating of cancer.

ENERGY WORK AND CHAKRA BALANCING

For some these words may sound exotic and strange. As I mentioned, I live in Sedona, Arizona where everyone here knows about chakras and energy work. When I first moved to Sedona, over twenty years ago, I thought these words were mystical and strange. I would come to find that they speak to owning our health, wellness, and mindful responsibility for ourselves in our life. Many people address issues of loss and grief regarding those losses by way of energy work.

Chakras are centers of your vital life force within your body. Earlier we spoke about the ki or qi. Ki is the center of your energy. It is pronounced like "che." Our chakras are important centers. In the Western blend of understanding chakras there are seven main chakra sites.

The crown chakra is located at the top of the head or what we refer to as the crown. The brow chakra is between both eyebrows. It is often referred to as the third eye. The throat chakra is self-explanatory as is the heart chakra. The solar plexus chakra is located just below the rib cage, in the region of the solar plexus. The sacral chakra is also called the spleen chakra and extends from the rear sacral bone around in front of the body above the sexual organs. The root chakra is in your seat or lowest part of your body before your legs and includes the sexual organs. There are seven more chakras that extend down the legs.

So what does all this mean? Chakras can get out of balance. When there are physical, emotional, or spiritual challenges, it takes a toll on your entire body. In Chinese, Japanese, and other cultures, medicine is based on the chakras as seats of energy in your body that get disrupted and result in disease, illness, or an inability to heal from emotional challenges and trauma. If you get out of alignment, your chakras are out of order. Balancing of chakras restores body balance and harmony. Acupuncture is based on the chakra system. The points where acupuncture needles are inserted correspond to your chakras.

Energy work involves working with chakras. There are many kinds of energy therapies including Reiki, Qi Gong, vibrational medicine, prayer, and Tong Ren.[4]

Qi gong is base on traditional Chinese medicine. The Qi Gong practitioner uses his or her own energy to locate and stimulate acupuncture points. The point is to move "stuck" energy, which is believed responsible for disease and illness. This form of healing is used throughout the world.

Reiki is very popular as a form of energy medicine. It is often found in hospital settings and clinics throughout the United States and the world. It is based on the qi or ki energy earlier discussed. Reiki does not focus on specific acupuncture points. Rather, the practitioner has the ability to see into your body and psyche and assist you in healing blockages, especially those that are highly emotional or traumatic as might be associated with complicated or traumatic grief.

Tong Ren is similar to Qi Gong, adding Carl Jung's belief in the collective unconscious (the consciousness we have from life that has preceded us since the beginning of time). It was originally developed to assist patients who were dealing with cancer, but has since been used successfully with many other conditions such as rheumatoid arthritis, ALS, multiple sclerosis, and Parkinson's disease.

Vibrational medicine is a broad category of healing based on the use of sound, color, magnets, or crystals. It is believed that all of these send out vibrations which, when in touch with a disturbed part of the body, can induce healing or balance.

Prayer has long been used to heal disease, illness, and trauma of all kinds. Sometimes prayer is individual or it may take place in a large or small group setting for the purposes of sending the prayer to one or more persons. There has been research done on prayer groups, which concludes positive prayer does influence health. There are many well-known healers who heal solely through the use of prayer.

The point of any energy work is to understand and appreciate that our bodies and minds are made of energy. We influence others and are influenced by others by way of energy. Think of all the lore around things such as the evil eye, curses, and spells being put on people. The same holds true where positive energy is concerned. Love and compassion go far in terms of relaxing the spirit, and a relaxed spirit can contribute to physical and emotional healing.

SOUND AND MUSIC THERAPY

Sound therapy can be used to improve physical health and emotional well-being. Often times music and sound therapy are used interchangeably as terms, but not always. There are many forms of sound therapy ranging from those used to enhance educational performance such as the Tomatis Method[5] to those used for oncology patients in sound healing, as was described earlier as a method used by oncologists such as Mitchell Gaynor.

Music therapy is one of the evidence-based therapies used to treat emotional issues and to improve physical health. There is a credential available to professionals who have studied music therapy. Music therapists use their skills with all age groups, and they work in private settings, hospitals, psychiatric facilities, prisons, and substance-abuse treatment centers.

Music therapy employs many techniques, but underlying all music therapy is the belief that music is universally enjoyed and can influence the way people feel. Think of the last time a song came on the radio that was associated with a special time, a romance, or someone special. Your mood was instantly transformed. Likewise, harsh music or sound that is an irritant to you can have the effect of disrupting your sense of calm.

Music therapy has been used with stroke victims, heart patients, cancer patients, in the treatment of neurological disorders such as Parkinson's disease, in the treatment of emotional disorders such as depression, in treating Tourette's syndrome, and with Alzheimer patients, to name a few.

The different techniques utilized are too many to mention for our purposes here. Many good resources exist for those wishing to learn more, including Dr. Mitchell Gaynor's book *The Healing Power of Sound: Recovery from Life-Threatening Illness Using Sound, Voice, and Music.*[6] Another book, *The Tao of Music: Sound Psychology—Using Music to Change Your Life*[7] is also a good choice.

ART THERAPY

Art, like music, has been around since before the written word. It too is universal in its use and appeal. It has been used for centuries as a form of expression and a tool for healing. Anything that touches our senses, such as sight, sound, smell, touch, and taste, are capable of healing a part of us. It is through our senses that we meet the world. It is through our senses that our world comes to makes sense. It is in the world and how we sense it, that we learn discernment. We learn what is good, what is dangerous, and we learn how to express both on the outside and the inside.

Art therapy practitioners have obtained a master's degree in art therapy and often have many additional credentials. In many states they are required to hold a license. There is considerable research showing that art therapy is not only enjoyable, but also effective in treating many problems. Some of the many areas treated by art therapists include ADD, ADHD, autistic spectrum disorder including Asperger syndrome, substance abuse and dependency, sexual abuse, traumatic brain injury, posttraumatic stress disorder, and grief and bereavement. This is the short list.

Studies around grief and bereavement show art therapy to be useful with children and with children and their parents. Art is often used in clinical practice by mental health therapists who work with children. The old adage "a picture is worth a thousand words" is more than true when looking at how art informs. Art not only informs, but it sets up a communication that is nonthreatening. It allows for a discourse to take place and it allows for change by way of artistic representation of change.

Many techniques exist in the world of art. Art therapy is not limited to drawing. It can utilize any art medium. Art therapy is most often used in conjunction with another therapeutic approach such as psychodynamic psychotherapy. At times art therapy can be a stand-alone therapy.

In my clinical practice children draw for me their family, or their artistic rendering of their problem. In time they will also draw solutions.

BREATH WORK AND YOGA

Breathing and Yoga go together. Learning to breathe properly is at the core of what Yoga and all of its exercises are all about.

People often ask, "What is the correct way to breathe?"

Most often breathing that begins from the abdomen is ideal. A breath is initiated higher up in the rib cage diaphragm area. With practice we can exercise the diaphragm to pull from below for long breaths, rather than relying on the diaphragm or above to do the work. The farther down you can go with your breath, the better, as the inhalations and exhalations will be longer and steady in rhythm. Higher-up breathing tends to be short and shallow, as though you were trying to catch your breath.

Most relaxation breathing is known as belly breathing. In therapy with anxious children or adults I teach my clients how to do the seven-second exhale. I don't know whom to credit for this technique, but I have used it for many years. Here is how it works: you take a deep breath and relax, next begin the exhale in a controlled manner while counting one thousand, two thousand, three thousand, and so forth until you reach seven thousand, which is roughly seven seconds. Most people cannot make it to seven and they have to exhale around number four. With practice you can learn to control your breathing and with control comes relaxation. This is always good for the body.

Yoga is a discipline. Some people see it as a form of stretching or exercise. It is much more. It is an ancient form of breathing, movement, meditation, and centering of the body, mind, and spirit. It is a way to obtain a goal. Often the goal is relaxation. Other reasons that people engage in the practice of Yoga is for improvement of physical and mental health.

There are many forms of Yoga and the beginner needs to find a beginning form in order to not encounter discouragement at the difficulty. Yoga postures take some time to master. Different Yoga disciplines have at their center differing goals. Some of the types of Yoga include:[8]

- Anusara: a beginner's Yoga aimed at attempting positions and expression of self through positions.
- Ashtanga: a rapid flowing movement through six yoga postures. With movement from one posture to the next, an exhale is followed by an inhale.
- Bikram: Yoga postures done in heat such as a sauna room.
- Hatha: an all-around basic Yoga method with tried and true postures and balance of breathing.
- Iyengar: this form of Yoga incorporates the use of harnesses, incline boards, and blocks into the moves and breath work.
- Jivamukti: a high-energy, advanced form of Yoga that incorporates chanting and ancient scripture into the class.
- Kripalu: a self-empowerment type of Yoga where knowing, accepting, and learning from your body are the core components practiced.
- Kundalini: this is a high-energy and movement-intensive form of Yoga intended to enhance energy levels. It is a big workout geared to awaken your body.

- Power: the athlete's form of Yoga. Definitely not for beginners unless you are an athlete.
- Prenatal: this form of Yoga was designed to be a safe form of exercise for expectant moms. Pelvic floor muscles are strengthened and flexibility is enhanced.
- Restorative: a form of Yoga designed for relaxation. People recovering from illness or injuries can safely use this form of Yoga.
- Sivananda: a form of Yoga that focuses on chanting, meditation, breathing, relaxing, diet, exercise, and an intense experience all rolled into one.
- Viniyoga: in this form of Yoga you set individualized goals and the instructor works with you on designing poses, chants, meditations, and breath work to accomplish those goals.
- Yin: this is a quiet and relaxing form of Yoga intended to release tensions and practice quieting of the mind, body, and spirit.

Check out Yoga classes in your area and find out if one can be of assistance to you. Loss and grieving expends energy. Yoga is a renewing activity for your mind and body.

MEDICAL MASSAGE AND REFLEXOLOGY

Medical massage is used interchangeably with the words massage therapy. In recent years there has been a return to the term medical massage, which is what massage therapy was originally called.

Medical massage therapists are licensed professionals who work with specific parts of the body or with the whole body. There are many types of massage work that can be done, including: Swedish massage therapy, aromatherapy massage, hot stone massage, deep tissue massage, Shiatsu massage, Thai massage, reflexology, pregnancy massage, sports massage, and back massage. Most therapists are trained in all of the types of massage.

If you have ever had a massage by a professional you know how powerful it can be in working out all the kinks in the body, but also in working out the stresses and sorrow we carry. Many massage therapists are masters of intuitive awareness. They can tell where you are storing trauma, loss, hurt, anger, and sadness. Their job is to improve your body's flow so that you find both physical and emotional release.

When a person has a specific complaint such as an injury, pulled muscle, stiff neck, or lower-back pain, the medical massage professional will know how to provide release. They are masters of understanding how your muscles work and how to help them to relax. Most therapists I have known send you home with instructions on how to keep the tight areas loosened up. Many people believe that a massage every two weeks to once a month can keep a body in top working order. This is often preferred over presenting to the therapist with pain.

Many people who are dealing with grief find massage helpful. They feel the support of the therapist and touch is another one of our senses that needs attending if we want to be well. When thinking about ways to augment the healing process, massage is one that should be at the top of the list.

Reflexology is a type of massage that focuses on your feet. Our feet carry us through the days of our life and yet they are one of the most ignored parts of our body. Reflexology is based on the understanding that pressure points in the feet correspond to each of our vital body organs. When the pressure points are worked with, relief or assistance is channeled into those organs.

Reflexology is used for intestinal complaints, insomnia, stress reduction, tension headaches, arthritis, sports injuries, premenstrual issues, back pain, and hormonal imbalances. At the very least it feels good to have the feet receive some attention. It is an ancient form of therapy and a widely used alternative therapy.

CRANIOSACRAL THERAPY

According to the Stillpoint Center in Sedona, Arizona, craniosacral therapy or CST "is a healing modality that grew out of Osteopathy, the ancient art of bone setting. It dates back to 1970 when John Upledger, a doctor of osteopathy, first noticed rhythmic movement of the cranial sacral system during spinal surgery. CST is a gentle, hands-on method of evaluating and enhancing the functioning of a physiological body system, the craniosacral system. Usually craniosacral therapy is performed on a person fully clothed. Using a soft touch generally no greater than 5 grams, or about the weight of a nickel, practitioners release restrictions in the craniosacral system to improve the functioning of the central nervous system."[9]

Some of the issues this form of therapy can address include chronic pain, scoliosis, motor coordination problems, some learning disabilities, and eye difficulties. Where grief is concerned, this form of therapy might assist someone who has been in a state of chronic or complicated grief.

Craniosacral therapy can be powerful. I have a personal example. As I mentioned I live in Sedona, Arizona, a mecca of alternative therapies and spiritual awareness. I have tried most of the alternative therapies at one time or another over the twenty-plus years I have lived in this town. Two therapies stand out as particularly powerful from my perspective, and things that suggest but do not deliver do not easily sway me.

I had a problem with my neck that developed about twelve years ago. I would experience bouts of neck pain so severe that I couldn't move my head side to side. I went to a medical doctor who could find no reason for my pain.

I had not had a recent injury. I went to a physical therapist and obtained some relief. The physical therapist referred me to a craniosacral therapist. In Sedona craniosacral therapists are physical therapists who also do craniosacral work. The therapist was about half my age and a gorgeous blond. She worked on my neck for three sessions. She looked at how my body was aligned. She moved me like a human pretzel into positions I didn't know a body could assume. She also initiated conversation. She asked open-ended questions and listened intently. On the fourth session I was on the table on my back. She asked me to raise my arms. Then she asked me to bend them at the elbows. She grabbed my hands with hers as she leaned over me.

She said, "I want you to push me back."

I thought this was odd but I did as she said and pushed against the resistance she offered. She was strong.

She next said, "Push harder, push me back, fight back."

In her words "fight back," I felt a tinge of anger. I wondered why.

She added, "Fight back."

I pushed as hard as I could and sent her flying away from me. She looked at me satisfied and said, "Good."

The rest of the session we discussed the last time I felt that way. It was at the age of eight in the inner city of Chicago where I was born and raised. It was a hot summer evening and my brothers and I were out playing in the backyard and back alley. We had, as do most neighborhoods, a neighborhood psychopath. He was a sixteen-year-old whom I will call Robbie. Robbie had been arrested more times than he had years to show for his life. He had been in the mental ward of the Mt. Sinai Hospital a couple of times. He had decided to enact his pathology on my older brother. He shoved him, called him names, and was bullying him. I was so angry. Robbie had an ice cream bar in his hand, which he had just recently purchased from the Good Humor truck that came down the alley at the end of the long summer days. I went to slap Robbie's face and by accident knocked the ice cream bar from his hand, which went flying into the dirt and debris of the alley. He was enraged. He picked me up and hurled me to the ground. He sat on top of me. My heart was pounding hard within my chest. I screamed at him and I screamed for help. No help came and Robbie punched me and held me down by my neck.

So if we fast-forward, the point of craniosacral work is release. If there are stored body memories of trauma, then the body may just decide to activate the pain years later. I had recently gone through a scary incident that was not physical, but I imagine it triggered the neck problem. I have never had a recurrence of the neck pain since that session.

MYOFASCIAL RELEASE THERAPY

This is a form of soft-tissue therapy, which came out of osteopathic medicine. The fascia is the soft-tissue part of our connective tissue. It is fibrous and surrounds muscles, groups of muscles, blood vessels, and the nerves. Its function is protective in nature. There are several types of fascia including superficial fascia, deep fascia, and visceral fascia. Fascia surround muscles whereas tendons and ligaments serve as joining structures holding things in place.

Myofascial release therapy works with relaxing contracted muscles and by increasing the circulation to areas that may be injured. The lymphatic system can also be drained using this form of therapy. When muscles are relaxed, circulation is improved, and the lymph system is drained, the body operates in a healthy fashion, thereby increasing resiliency and the ability to bounce back from trauma.

Myofascial therapy has been used for people with chronic pain when even narcotics offered no relief. I have had many clients report the benefits of this form of therapy. People who struggled with walking returned to normal following only a couple of sessions. Of course, maintenance is often required because the body has a way of returning to the old state of tension.

HOMEOPATHIC MEDICINE

Homeopathic medicine is sometimes used in integrative medicine practices. It is controversial and utilized by an estimated 3.9 million people in the United States.[10] The controversial aspect rests with the fact that the FDA regulates it now and only three states have licensing boards that oversee the administration of homeopathic medicines. Homeopathy somehow got linked with parents not immunizing their children. In addition, the homeopathic remedies do contain chemicals that one's primary care physician should be told about. There have been cases where people have been harmed taking medicines without proper supervision, as many of these medicines are available over the counter at health food stores. The American Medical Association considers homeopathy to be a sham and the remedies have been viewed as unethical.[11]

Homeopathy is based on two premises. The first is that "like cures like." The second is the "law of minimum dose."

"Like cures like" refers to using the same substance that causes a disease in well people to cure similar symptoms in people who are ill. The homeopath does an extensive intake interview where symptoms and issues are discussed. The homeopath will recommend certain homeopathic medicines, which are usually pellets placed under the tongue, which contain a dilute form of some compound. One example was shared with me by a woman who used homeopathy successfully for menopause symptoms that included migraine headaches. Lesser symptoms included hot flashes, night sweats, and leg cramps. The homeopath prescribed a tincture of snake venom (this is the controversial part). The homeopath recommended taking the pellets every four hours the first day and then decreasing to once or twice a day on day two. On day three only one dose was recommended. The woman reported her migraines stopped and she had fewer hot flashes and night sweats. The leg cramps eventually went away once she began taking magnesium and calcium. Where "like cures like" in this example is not clear. Homeopaths explain it is a complex decision-making process to choose the right "remedy" for the patient.

The "law of minimum dose" means that the lowest possible medication dose will be the most effective. This is why pellets may contain one drop of a medicine diluted many times before it is applied to the pellets. It is the "essence" provided by the medication that induces healing. Less is more from a homeopathic perspective. This philosophy is in contrast to conventional medicine where more equals better results or more profound influence.

Homeopathy has been around for some time. There is considerable information out there for those of you who would like to understand it in more depth than is allowed in this section.

ACUPUNCTURE

Acupuncture is a very old traditional form of Chinese medicine. It utilizes small needles that are inserted in the skin at precise points for the purposes of stimulating "flow" or "qi" in the body.

Acupuncture is used for depression, anxiety, smoking cessation, migraine headaches, pain, and nausea. There are many more uses, but these are the areas where there is the most literature and firsthand accounts by people who have used it.

Unlike homeopathy, acupuncture is endorsed by the U.S. National Institute of Health for use with certain conditions.

Traditional Chinese medicine is based on an understanding of disease as being a state of disharmony or being out of balance. By stimulating body energy of qi along what are called meridian lines, energy blocks are loosened and removed.

There are a number of acupuncture types, including: cosmetic acupuncture for mini facelifts, acupressure (a needleless approach), moxibustion (using a mugwort stick that is burned near the skin), scalp acupuncture, and electro acupuncture (for nerve stimulation).

Acupuncture is popular throughout the United States, with heavy usage on the West Coast and in the western states.

With issues of loss, grief, and trauma, acupuncture has been used to balance the body and lessen or remove anxiety that is often associated with these concerns.

HYPNOSIS

Hypnosis is also referred to as hypnotherapy or hypnotic suggestion. It is known for successful use in smoking cessation. It is also used for pain management, anxiety, and behavioral control.

Hypnosis is best when practiced by licensed professionals. The goal of hypnosis is to place the person in a trance-like state free from distraction. This results in a focused ability to concentrate. In this deep and relaxed, yet focused, state the hypnotherapist will make suggestions to you about how to change your behavior or how to better control anxiety. Suggestions may also be made about a special situation you are struggling with. If one is trying to stop smoking or trying to cope with chemotherapy, the hypnotherapy may help you reach a calmer state. With the hypnotherapy-induced tools, you will have more energy to expend in a positive fashion toward actualizing that goal.

Many medical facilities, hospitals, and cancer units use hypnotherapy. Be sure to use a licensed professional.

ANIMAL-ASSISTED THERAPIES

Humans are animals. We also bond with other creatures not of our own species. This can include dogs, cats, birds, dolphins, and horses, to name just a few. Let's look at some of the ways that animals are used to assist people with loss, grief, fear, anxiety, depression, learning disabilities, phobias, trauma, and more. In her riveting memoir, *A Stolen Life: A Memoir*, Jaycee Dugard writes of how animal-assisted therapy helped her. [12]

Animal-assisted therapy uses animals as a form of treatment. Animals are used in individual psychotherapy practices, in equine-assisted therapy centers, at eating disorder clinics and inpatient centers, at therapeutic adolescent boarding school facilities, in prisons, nursing homes, hospital and outpatient hospital settings, and in psychiatric institutions. There is a large range of issues for which animals are available to help humans step through to a better place of cognitive, emotional, and behavioral functioning. Some private practice mental health therapists have dogs present in the therapy room as a comfort for clients. Other clinicians may have birds or cats. It is thought that the animal's presence relaxes most people. Of course, this would not hold true for someone who had been bitten by a dog or other animal.

Many of my clients over the years have had special-assist animals that go where their human goes. These clients fly with their cockatoos and sleep with their golden labs. They go to the doctor with their Burmese cat and feel safer with their cockatiel.

Animals can be used to help the disabled. Animals are used to assist with grief. We use the services and compassion of animals to help us feel less lonely. Animals are also used to detect cancer and they can often tell when someone is dying. Animals help in the rehabilitation of war veterans. They are used to help convicts in prison learn to connect empathically and to care about others.

I went to a training session some years back at an equine therapy center. There were ten mental health therapists present. We were being taught how smart these animals are. In one exercise we were instructed to stand in the center of the corral. Two horses were let into the space. One was a respectful horse that meandered around checking us out. The other was a bit of a nosy body. The nosy body approached each therapist, and each of us handled the intrusion in our own way. I stepped back, I asked it to go away, and I finally created significant distance between the horse and me, after giving him a pet or two. The horse went around to each of us and settled on one therapist with golden red hair. She didn't shoo the horse away. The horse was pushing against her and nibbling at her neck and hair. She laughed nervously claiming, "The horse must really like me." This went on for some time and it actually felt as though the horse was molesting her.

Low and behold. The exercise, we were then told, was about the horse finding who in the group had a history of sexual abuse. Remember, we were all trained therapists and this was OK under the circumstances. It turned out that the golden-haired therapist had a history of sexual abuse as a child and the rest of us did not have that history. The equine therapist pointed out that horses show you what you are struggling with. The rest of us therapist really didn't care for a massive creature, unknown to us, pushing, licking, roughly nudging, and otherwise forcing a confrontation. It was different for the golden-haired therapist, who let the horse do whatever he wanted.

In equine therapy this is not the scenario that would take place. It is an example of the way an animal's wisdom can be used to help us and our human helpers understand what we need help with.

NOTES

1. Phelan, "Transcendental Meditation," 5–20.
2. Paturel, "Meditation as Medicine," 30–33.

 3. Gaynor, *Meditations and Music.*
 4. Yin Yang House, "What Styles of Healing."
 5. www.tomatis.com
 6. Gaynor, *The Healing Power of Sound.*
 7. Ortiz, *The Tao of Music.*
 8. *Women's Health,* "Types of Yoga."
 9. Stillpoint Center, "What Is Cranial Sacral."
10. National Institute of Health, "Homeopathy."
11. Shaw, "Homeopathy."
12. Dugard, *A Stolen Life.*

Chapter Eighteen

Unhealthy Coping and the Dangers of Self-Medicating

Problems are not the problem; coping is the problem. —Virginia Satir

We make up horrors to help us cope with the real ones. —Stephen King

Life is about adapting. We either adapt or we die. It is the same in mental health. We can adapt by way of healthy coping mechanisms or we can adapt with unhealthy coping strategies. Both help keep us alive. Some ways people cope create further tragedy and trauma. This chapter will look at the things we want to avoid. It is not a judgment against people who cope by way of maladaptive choices. Most of these folks are looking to find another way. They either don't believe they can or they haven't had the right combination of support to help them see that it is possible.

SELF-MEDICATING

We have all heard these words. Self-medicating refers to using street drugs, alcohol, or prescription drugs to "medicate" yourself; for some, they dull the pain, they help them forget, or they assist in the coping process. It can also mean using other things such as gambling, pornography, shopping, and over- or under-eating as a way to soothe oneself. Self-medicating is dangerous because the methods used can be dangerous and usually simply mask the underlying problems, which will eventually surface. When loss and grief are too much to bear, working with a professional, rather than self-medicating, is safer, more effective, and longer lasting.

Self-medicating is used for depression, anxiety, restlessness, and to fill a void within one's self. Any number of reasons can be given for self-medicating but the chief complaints are anxiety, depression, and an overall sense of unhappiness. We have therapy and psychiatric medications that can and do help with all of these problems. We also have a host of wonderful alternative therapies that have been used for a very long time to address such concerns. When we employ a knowledgeable professional we guarantee a measure of safety and it is one step in building a supportive, helping team around you.

Many people who are dealing with loss and grief choose, whether consciously or unconsciously, to self-medicate. Some feel so alone they don't know how to reach out. Others may feel that to ask for help is a sign of weakness. Still others fall into patterns and habits that seem to soothe their pain but end up putting it aside for another day. And others may not know how to reach out, or to whom to reach. We know everyone grieves in his or her own way and it is certainly more than acceptable to seek out support, but many feel it shows weakness. Just getting over it is not an option either. For most people grief involves some type of process. If grief becomes complicated or traumatic grief, all the more reason to seek assistance. The thing to keep in mind is that we don't "get over" things; we learn to cope or accept those things with increased mastery over time.

Self-medicating is an unhealthy coping strategy that almost always makes things worse rather than better. It is like putting a bandage on a broken leg. It will look like you are attending to the problem, but you aren't.

FORMS OF SELF-MEDICATING

Nicotine and alcohol are legal drugs widely used throughout the world. We have all heard that nicotine is one of the most addictive substances there is. It is. Physicians and researchers have determined that nicotine is pharmacologically and behaviorally just as addictive as the street drug heroin. Alcohol abuse and dependence is responsible for so many family, interpersonal, legal, traumatic, psychological, and financial problems. Even though alcohol is legal it creates more problems than illegal drug use as its use and abuse it much more widespread.

NICOTINE

Nicotine comes from the tobacco plant, which is in the nightshade family of plants. Other nightshade plants include tomatoes, eggplant, and potatoes. Apart from tobacco (*nicotiana tabacum*), other nightshade plants include belladonna (*atropa belladonna*) and the mandrake plant (*mandragora officinum*). The mandrake plant contains hallucinogenic tropane alkaloids, which makes it popular in rituals where hallucinating is the desired outcome. Belladonna is extremely toxic and can cause hallucinations and delirium.

Nicotine is both a depressant and a stimulant. It is often used as a form of self-medicating. People may begin smoking due to grief and loss, they increase smoking during times of grief, and it becomes a coping mechanism that is unhealthy and dangerous. Studies have shown that individuals with psychiatric disorders have greater sensitivity to nicotine dependence.[1] Complicated grief, traumatic grief, and bereavement are considered psychiatric diagnoses. The symptoms often involved in grief, such as depression, anxiety, and other psychiatric conditions, can predispose individuals to this form of self-medicating. Often, when involved in the initial assessment for psychotherapy I ask when someone first started to smoke cigarettes. Typically they were young, but not always. Some people begin smoking in their teen years and this is a great time of loss, change, transition, and uncertainty. Adolescent years are filled with self-doubt. Add to the normal scheme of how things can play out during adolescence life, events such as the death of a friend, an illness in the family, the death of a parent, or economic loss that places a hardship on the family. A young person, without knowing it, seeks out self-medicating. Some of the easiest drugs to find include cigarettes.

During times of grief the habit of smoking feels necessary and smoking typically increases. Someone who smoked a pack a day may suddenly find they are smoking two packs a day. I knew a man who was diagnosed with bladder cancer. Bladder cancer is one of the cancers directly associated with smoking (to clarify, you can get bladder cancer if you don't smoke, but most people with bladder cancer have a history of smoking). This gentleman was told by his urologist to stop smoking. The man, riddled with fear of having cancer, did not stop. After several invasive treatments to resect, cauterize, and remove the bladder tumors, he still did not stop smoking. His smoking level increased due to stress, issues related to loss of health and his former state of vigor, and grief over his life and what was ahead.

I do hear of people who never smoked until, as an adult, something traumatic took place. It might have been the death of a parent or a breakup of a romantic relationship that served as the trigger to begin smoking.

Smoking may begin in response to a loss such as weight gain or feeling a need to have help losing weight. Nicotine has long been known to be an appetite suppressant. In the 1940s and 1950s smoking was recommended for woman to lose weight.[2] Cigarette use "exploded" following World War I and marketing to women first began in the 1920s with Marlboro's "Mild as May" cigarette being recommended for women.[3]

Nicotine acts at the level of the central nervous system providing a stimulatory response.[4] It functions as an MAO (monoamine oxidase) inhibitor, which allows dopamine to increase. Dopamine helps us feel more relaxed and positive. It can also elevate your mood. Once dopamine is increased the nicotine enters the reward system of the brain, where it contributes to physiological reinforcement.

As most people know, cigarette use or the use of other tobacco products such as cigars can result in bronchitis, emphysema, ulcers, and high blood pressure. Tobacco use has a contributory connection to a vast number of cancers including lung cancer, bladder cancer, throat and mouth cancer, and colon cancer.

ALCOHOL

Alcohol is in the drug class known as a sedative hypnotic. Alcohol acts as a depressant on the central nervous system in the first few drinks. After a few drinks, alcohol can act as a stimulant.[5] This may account for why some heavy drinkers start out being cordial and become mean or dangerous after too many drinks. A certain level of alcohol creates an excitatory response in the body. When involved with losses and grief, individuals may feel uncomfortable with these feelings, which can range widely from sadness to rage and onward to serious depression and obsessive thoughts or compulsive behaviors. Alcohol, like other drugs, can change what a person feels. This is why it is widely used to "soothe" symptoms and to take a person away from "the now." I have known many people who began drinking at times of transition (loss) during adolescence. As adults they relate what it was that drew them into drinking to soothe feelings of despair. Often they relate that parents were fighting or parents were not listening to them. They may also relate that there was a breakup with a significant person in their life or that the family moved to a new town. One teen I worked with began drinking to "fit in," but later found it functioned to take him away from his feelings. So, even after he achieved "fitting in," he continued to drink and drank excessively any time something "went wrong." This could be receiving a C on an exam or a negative interaction with a peer. Remember, loss is anything that will require change. Even a C for someone who receives A's is a loss.

Sustained use or large amounts of alcohol increases the risk of liver disease, it impairs your digestive system, it can destroy brain cells, it causes damage to the central nervous system, creates malnutrition, and is a contributory agent to many diseases. Some of the diseases linked to alcohol use are pancreatitis, alcohol-induced dementia, cardiovascular disease, cancer, reproductive problems, stomach ulcers, obesity, and anorexia.

Alcoholism or alcohol dependence is a major health problem in the United States. "Alcohol is now the third leading cause of the global burden of disease and injury."[6] The World Health Organization (WHO) reports 2.5 million alcohol-related deaths annually worldwide.[7] Alcohol dependence leaves behind a legacy of destroyed individuals and families. It wreaks havoc with self-esteem, causes depression, and creates untenable anxiety states. It weakens your immune systems and takes away your health. Legal issues typically go hand in hand with excessive drinking. DUI (driving under the influence) and DWI (driving while intoxicated) statistics are staggering in all of the states in the United States. Other crimes are tied to alcohol use. People die from alcohol poisoning, they kill others while under the influence of alcohol, and alcohol dependence and abuse is tied to intimate partner abuse (domestic violence) and child abuse.

"The National Council on Alcoholism and Drug Dependence notes that individuals who were drinking at the time of an offense annually commit three million crimes. Two-thirds of those crimes were classified as simple assaults."[8]

Alcoholism may take the form of daily drinking, daily intoxication, binge drinking, or even social drinking. The key to understanding alcoholism is within the concepts of dependence and abuse. Social drinkers may feel they don't have an alcohol problem. They may rationalize that they have only a couple of drinks each day and perhaps more when company is over. Alcoholism is not determined by how many drinks a person has but by the problems it creates. If even one person in your family has trouble with your drinking, and it is a legitimate issue such as you being loud, inattentive, scary, or unable to help the family, then you have an alcohol problem. If consequences are created due to your drinking (any type of consequences) then there is a problem. "Alcoholism in the mental health profession is usually described as any drinking that interferes with one's social, familial, occupational, or obligatory functioning. This is a broad definition and it suggests that if drinking has created consequences in your life, you may have an alcohol problem."[9]

Frequently we see people increase alcohol consumption at times of despair or unhappiness. Many of my female clients report increases in alcohol use at times of marital distress. Most of my female clients increased drinking alcohol when their spouse was diagnosed with a serious illness such as cancer. Mothers I work with increased alcohol consumption following the death of their child. If someone already drinks alcohol and a life event presents that translates to loss and requires grief, there is a high likelihood that alcohol may be abused or dependence may be established due to the grief.

MARIJUANA

Marijuana, or *Cannabis sativa*, is known by street names such as pot, weed, Mary Jane, and many other terms. It is a widely used illegal drug. In recent years it has been approved for medical use and both Washington state (2012) and Colorado (2013) have legalized the use of cannabis. Cannabis use has a very long history dating back to the third millennium BC.[10] Marijuana is a psychoactive drug with stimulant, depressant, and hallucinogenic properties.

Marijuana is not ranked by the National Institute of Drug Abuse as a highly addictive substance. The most addictive of six substances ranked was nicotine, followed by heroin, alcohol, cocaine, caffeine, and ending with cannabis as the least addictive.[11] Still, due to its widespread use, particularly among developing adolescents, it is considered a concern. A 2012 cohort study in the Proceeding of the National Academy of Sciences states, "It was found that the persistent, dependent use of marijuana before age 18 was associated with lasting harm to a person's intelligence, attention and memory, and were suggestive of neurological harm from cannabis. Quitting cannabis did not appear to reverse the loss. However, individuals who started cannabis use after the age of 18 did not show similar declines."[12]

Marijuana is often used to dull pain. Every user has a different experience, with some reporting a reduction of anxiety and others reporting an increase in anxiety. Those who find it helps with anxiety often use it for trauma, issues related to loss and grief, and to numb feelings.

CAFFEINE

Caffeine is included here as a drug due to its inclusion as an addictive drug studied by the NIDA (National Institute for Drug Addiction). Caffeine is a psychoactive drug with stimulant properties. It is found in a variety of plants, most notably the tea plant and the coffee plant. The Food and Drug Administration consider ordinary consumption of caffeine safe. It is considered toxic in doses over 10 grams.

The DSM V, due out for publication in 2013, has included caffeine as an addictive substance and modified Caffeine Use Disorder criteria from the earlier DSM IV–TR. Hundreds of studies exist where caffeine use, dependence, and abuse are tied to mental health disorders, bereavement, and grief. It is a coping mechanism with certain risks attached to its use and overuse, as well as protective factors associated with its mild to moderate use.

Caffeine use has been studied where pregnancy and miscarriage are concerned. The March of Dimes recommends no more than one cup (12 ounces) of coffee per day when pregnant.[13] Pregnancy is a time of great anticipation, but also a time of stress. Many women combat stress by using the stimulant caffeine. There are conflicting studies as to whether caffeine use during pregnancy increases the risk of miscarriage.

What we do know is that caffeine is a stimulant and stimulants provide energy. When a person is recovering from alcohol dependence or abuse, caffeine is often substituted to offset the depression that follows cessation of alcohol. This is why it is usual to see coffee and cigarettes at AA or NA meetings. Even though recovery is a great thing it represents a change and change signals loss and loss involves stress, as well as a certain amount of grief.

Caffeine use has been studied with cancer, sleep, and inflammatory markers such as Il-6 (interleukin). Chronic inflammation, in particular among the elderly, is associated with morbidity. A recent study shows that certain health factors and choices such as the consumption of caffeine had an effect on increasing the Il-6 marker.[14] Caffeine is related to insomnia and poor sleep also increases the Il-6 marker.

People do use caffeine as part of the loss, grief, and bereavement process and it is considered unhealthy by most researchers unless the consumption is very mild (one cup or 12 ounces). Purdue University[15] as well as many health centers such as the Mayo Clinic[16] instruct people who are dealing with grief to limit the use of caffeine.

Caffeine has gone up and down over the years in terms of being seen as a health risk or health benefit. Moderate consumption is currently believed to have some health benefits with certain types of cancer and Parkinson's disease, and some people find caffeine use reduces anxiety. On the other hand, many people report insomnia and increases in anxiety with caffeine consumption.

COCAINE

Cocaine is derived from the coca plant. It is an illegal substance. It functions as a powerful nervous system stimulant with effects lasting from fifteen minutes to thirty minutes depending on the way it is ingested and the dose taken. It is taken to produce feelings of euphoria and to provide energy. Anxiety and restlessness, in addition to insomnia, are produced when "coming down" off cocaine. Individuals frequently use alcohol to "come down" as one substance offsets the other. This was vividly portrayed in the Denzel Washington film *Flight.*

Cocaine is often used to alter one's mood. In doing so the user is not thinking about problems as they are replaced with energy and an overall positive feeling. People who are grieving, dealing with singular or multiple losses, and those with trauma history use cocaine to step aside from the debilitating effects of emotional grief. As with all self-medicating, the results are short-term where relief is concerned. Additionally, new problems are generally created to add to the list of losses and issues in general.

Cocaine is considered the second most popular recreational drug in the United States, with marijuana being the most popular.

HEROIN

Other names for heroin include smack, horse, brown, black tar, and H. There are also localized names for it. Diamorphine is the name used for the medical use of this drug. It can be used to treat heart attacks and severe pain associated with traumatic injury such as a very serious automobile accident.

Heroin is illegal. The United Nations 2005 estimate was that there were more than 50 million regular users of heroin, cocaine, and synthetic drugs worldwide.[17] Heroin is used for euphoria and relaxation.

Often associated with inner-city poor people, heroin is widely used in small towns and suburbia. It is highly addictive and involves an unfriendly withdrawal period. Pax and Chris Prentice wrote a useful book, *The Addiction Cure*.[18] There is one chapter written by Pax Prentice about when he was a heroin user. It is worth the read and riveting with details about how strong a hold addiction can have on a person. The book is also valuable for reframing addictions outside of the more accepted twelve-step model.

PRESCRIPTION DRUGS

Prescription drugs are used off-label for many things. People have found that pain medications produce euphoria and that anxiety medications do reduce anxiety. There are three classes of prescription drugs most often abused by people in the United States. These include narcotic painkillers, sedatives and tranquilizers, and stimulants.

Narcotic painkillers include drugs such as oxycodone, hydrocodone, Oxycontin, Percodan, Percocet, hydromorphone, propoxyphene, and meperidine.

Sedatives and tranquilizers include benzodiazepines, sleep medications, and barbiturates. All cause sedation, reduced anxiety, lowered inhibitions, and often, impaired memory.

Simulants include amphetamines such as Adderall, Dexedrine, and biphetamine. Other stimulants include methylphenidates such as Concerta or Ritalin.

Prescription drug abuse has been on the increase. Children and adolescents can easily obtain such drugs from the home medicine cabinet. Recent restrictions are now limiting the prescribing of these drugs. When prescribed by a family physician, the patient will also be required to see a psychiatrist or specialist for the drug to be continued. The Mayo Clinic defines prescription drug abuse as "the use of a prescription medication in a way not intended by the prescribing doctor, such as for the feelings you get from the drug. Prescription drug abuse or problematic use includes everything from taking a friend's prescription painkiller for your backache to snorting or injecting ground up pills to get high. Drug abuse may become ongoing and compulsive, despite the negative consequences."[19]

Nearly five million teenagers admitted abusing or using nonprescribed prescription drugs in a survey conducted among U.S. teens in 2013.[20] This survey notes that this number includes 24 percent of high school students. This represents a 33 percent increase from 2008. This study further identifies problems with parental attitudes. Namely, some parents assume that abuse or use of prescription drugs is less dangerous than that of street drugs. Parents don't intervene and may condone the use of prescription drugs for the alleviation of any discomfort. The study also found that parents did not object to their children's use of certain drugs such as Ritalin and Adderall if the drugs improved their student's grades or performance at school. At times young people obtain prescription drugs from their parent's medicine cabinets, from their parents directly, or from friends who found them at home or bought them from street dealers. A health care professional I once knew would put Valium in her baby's bottle with formula in order to put the infant to sleep when he was cranky.

Health care professionals deal with loss and grief every day. They are the caregivers, and trauma is what they do. There is no special training that makes professionals immune to the suffering of others or to the suffering they will experience helping others. In a recent study, in 2013 health care professionals are reported to be abusing anesthesia drugs as a form of self-medicating.[21] Propofol (Diprivan) is an anesthesia drug used in surgery. It grabbed the headlines following the death of Michael Jackson, who was administered the drug, in combination with others, prior to his death. Propofol is a sedative that "puts people to sleep" for surgery or other types of medical interventions. Propofol is not a sleep medication, for insomnia, for stress, trauma, or loss and grief. Yet, it is used by professionals for sleep. This study showed that those identified as abusing this drug were typically women with a history of depression and a history of childhood sexual or physical abuse. If the grief associated with child abuse is not dealt with, it increases the likelihood of later problems with substance abuse and dependence.

The elderly are also at risk for self-medicating using prescription medications. Often an elderly person will visit a doctor due to a sprain, broken or fractured bone, or another painful condition. It is the duty of medical professionals to reduce suffering, and pain is a form of suffering. Let's assume that Bill broke his hip. He underwent hip replacement therapy at the age of sixty. All went well, but there was severe pain following this serious procedure. He was given Oxycontin and then hydrocodone. His pain didn't diminish and the doctor kept prescribing, as recovery can be lengthy after some surgeries. In the meantime his wife was diagnosed with cancer and died within two months of the diagnosis. Bill referred himself to counseling because he was unable to get off the pain medication. He also spoke of considerable grief that he was "stoned the entire time my wife was dying." He felt he had abandoned her and felt he had been "weak." He was also fearful of coming off the prescription drugs and felt if he was not on the drugs he would be punished for his use of them during her illness. He figured it was better to be "high" if he was due a payback than sober. In time Bill worked through these issues and was able to get off the prescription drugs. It did take, as is often the case, communication between therapist and doctor to arrive at a method of doing a step-down off the drugs.

Individuals over the age of sixty-five make up about 13 percent of the population in the United States; they use more than 33 percent of all prescriptions filled. Older adults are at risk for self-medicating due to depression, losses that accompany aging, illness, and very often a shrinking social network. In addition, as we age our liver functions less well when it comes to filtering out what we ingest. Many older Americans are on more than one medication. The same medications in a younger person, with a younger liver, might be fine. In an older person medications can take a long time to leave the body, therefore posing a risk for overmedication. With painkillers, even if taken as prescribed, the older person may find they are "high" due to the liver not functioning at an optimum level. In no time, they become unintentionally addicted.

Individuals who are dealing with trauma, loss, and grief are vulnerable to using prescription drugs to numb the painful feelings. Often this is not the answer and is, at best, only a short-term solution when monitored by a psychiatrist or specialist. Most health professionals monitor drugs that are given for conditions where the identifying problem is grief. Antidepressants are not addictive. Many anxiety prescriptions are not addictive either. The prescription drugs that are primarily abused are sedatives and tranquilizers, painkillers, and stimulants. If one is very upset due to a loss and the associated grief, there may be problems with anxiety where a sedative would help. There may be problems with lethargy, apathy, and depression, but typically we wouldn't use a stimulant to help a person with grief. There are classes of antidepressants that are stimulating rather than sedating and these might be a good choice. We would not use a painkiller for any reason with grief unless the grief was related to the person's own medical trauma. This is when physicians and patients dialogue about risks and benefits. Sometimes an addiction is acceptable. If the person is dying from cancer, of advanced age and infirm, as with other medical conditions this is a dialogue of importance between physician and patient.

INTRUSIVE THOUGHTS, AVOIDANCE, HYPERAROUSAL, AND NUMBING OF RESPONSES

All of these alarming terms refer to posttraumatic stress, posttraumatic stress disorder, trauma, and traumatic stress. When trauma or PTSD goes untreated the result is a composite of coping mechanisms that are less than desirable. Remember how earlier we spoke about life and mental health being about survival? We have many choices for how to survive, but surviving is the goal. Certain things such as traumatization and repeat traumatization leave a person with a set of coping strategies that do the job of surviving, but continue to place the person at risk for further harm by nature of the coping mechanisms themselves.

Intrusive thoughts are a form of reexperiencing the traumatic event. This may take the form of flashbacks (memories that come in flashes of images), recurring distressing or disturbing dreams, a subjective reexperiencing of the event (feeling it in your body or feeling like it is happening again), or any intense psychological or physiological response that reminds you of the traumatic event. This can include thoughts of a loved one and things related to his or her death, dying, illness, or other things.

Avoidance happens when you avoid a place, person, or thing associated with a traumatic event. It also applies to avoidance of thoughts or feelings related to the event and talking about the event. It can also apply to avoiding certain behaviors such as traveling, going to the grocery store, driving a car, and any number of behaviors that may become associated with the event and thereby produce unwanted memories, flashbacks, distress, and in essence intrusive thoughts.

Hyperarousal refers to being overly aroused or easily emotionally aroused. Sometimes the word hypervigilance is used for hyperarousal. They are not the same. Both involve a heightened state of sensory awareness and sensitivity, which is exaggerated in intensity. Hyperarousal may cause a person to lose contact with reality and reexperience the prior trauma as though it were taking place again in the here and now. In hypervigilance the person remains aware of his surroundings and of time, place, and person, but is busy scanning for threats that are reminders of the past trauma. It is hypervigilance that is most connected to PTSD and different types of anxiety disorders. When hypervigilance and hyperarousal overlap it results in a form of dissociation typically due to PTSD and referred to as *the thousand-yard stare*.

The danger of not seeking professional help for PTSD, complicated or traumatic grief, and trauma is that of a cascade of unwanted physiological and psychological responses that make life even more difficult and dangerous.

RELATIONSHIP DAMAGE CONTROL

Relationships take a hit every time we experience a major loss, trauma, or life event that challenges us. We live in relation to others. These people are our people and they may be parents, children, siblings, partners, spouses, cousins, aunts, uncles, and grandparents. When something happens to one it affects everyone. Some of you may be saying, "Right." I know there are families that are disconnected, separated by geography, and separated emotionally over time. This doesn't mean they don't care. Creating distance in families is not unlike creating distance in posttraumatic stress disorder and the concept of avoidance we just discussed. Some families avoid each other in order to avoid some old family pain. They think they are protected from those old traumas and painful events if they distance themselves from the people who were a part of the past. But it doesn't really work. Just because you don't see your sister or brother doesn't mean you aren't being affected by the old trauma woven into your family's tapestry of time.

We want to safeguard our relationships with others. As we discussed in this book, our social networks are a big part of what increases longevity, helps to ward off pain, assists us with trauma and illness, and contributes to an overall wellness.

One safeguard is to be aware that everything that hurts you will hurt your loved ones as well. Sometimes the loved ones will say things that are hurtful such as, "Don't you think you should be over that by now," I would hesitate to apply a literal interpretation to such comments. I think what loved ones mean is, "This is hurting me too. Can we not keep dealing with it?"

Another safeguard is to recognize that everyone handles stress differently. Some folks embrace it, some externalize it, and some internalize it. It feels unsafe and uncomfortable for all concerned. Your partner may go inward and become silent. Resist the urge to interpret this as uncaring. Ask instead. Ask your partner what she is feeling and then sit still and really listen.

We need our people and they need us. We don't want to let trauma, loss, and grief rob us of the very things that make life meaningful. Yet, there are many people in this country who don't have another. They live alone and often they will die alone. It is not anyone's fault, but sometimes people lose everyone before it is their turn to die. Sometimes people are estranged from family and they feel they cannot reach out for help. Other times people don't marry and then find themselves sick and alone at age sixty or seventy with no children, siblings, or partner.

I knew a man who never married. He was, in his youth, a playboy sort, by his own description. He never saw the point of marriage. When he turned seventy he became very ill. In counseling he spoke about "the foolishness of my youth and thinking I would always be able to call the shots by myself." He wished he had married.

A woman I worked with came to counseling because her husband was just diagnosed with an aggressive cancer. They had been married over thirty years and had chosen not to have children. The husband was given six months to live. The woman was in a panic and said, "If only we had had children I wouldn't have to do this all by myself."

There are many reasons people find themselves without anyone. In these situations it is important to make community and culture work for you. It is harder, but it can be done. Church, organizations, volunteer positions, Hospice Foundation, counselors, and adult community programs can help connect you to others. All it takes is one person and the network is on the way to being built around you. Most people believe there is always room to invite another into their life. I live in the southwestern United States. It is amazing how the communities around my town work to help anyone in need. Those who are alone need not be, as organizations exist that will send someone to your house every day to spend a little time with you.

NOTES

1. Dierker and Donny, "The Role of Psychiatric Disorders," 439–446.
2. University of Dayton, "The History of Tobacco."
3. Kluger, *Ashes to Ashes.*
4. Mongelluzzo, *The Everything Guide to Self-Esteem*, 124.
5. Ibid.
6. Nauert, "Study Examines Alcohol."
7. National Council on Alcoholism and Drug Dependence, "2.5 Million Alcohol-Related Deaths."
8. Mongelluzzo, *The Everything Guide to Self-Esteem*, 125.
9. Ibid.
10. Rudgley, *Lost Civilizations.*
11. Hilts, "Relative Addictiveness."
12. Journalist's Resource, "Persistent Cannabis Users."
13. March of Dimes, "Caffeine in Pregnancy."
14. Okun et al., "Sleep Variability," 142–150.
15. Purdue University, "Coping with Grief and Loss."
16. Mayo Clinic, "Fatigue."
17. British Broadcasting Corporation, "The Global Drugs Trade."
18. Prentiss and Prentiss, *The Alcoholism and Addiction Cure.*
19. Mayo Clinic, "Prescription Drug Abuse."
20. National Institute of Health, "Prescription Drug Abuse."
21. National Institute of Health, "More Healthcare Professionals,"

Bibliography

Abbas, Amineh, and Jenny Macfie. "Supportive and Insight-oriented Psychodynamic Psychotherapy for Posttraumatic Stress Disorder in an Adult Male Survivor of Sexual Assault." *Clinical Case Studies* 12 (2013). doi:10.1177/1534650112471154.

Altschuler, Jenny, and Barbara Dale. "On Being an Ill Parent." *Journal of Clinical Child Psychology and Psychiatry* 4 (1999): 23–37.

American Pregnancy Association. "Stillbirth: Surviving Emotionally." Accessed March 13, 2013, from www.americanpregnancy.org/pregnancyloss/survivingemotionally.html

American Psychological Association. "Psychodynamic Psychotherapy Brings Lasting Benefits through Self-Knowledge." Accessed April 13, 2013, from www.apa.org/news/press/releases/2010/01/psychodynamic-therapy.aspx

Archer, John. *The Nature of Grief: The Evolution and Psychology of Reactions to Loss.* London: Brunner-Routledge, 1999.

Armony, Jorge L. "Current Emotion Research in Behavioral Neuroscience: The Role(s) of the Amygdala." *Emotion Review* 5 (2013). Accessed March 24, 2013, from HighWire. doi:10.1177/1754073912457208.

Arrom, Silvia M. *Containing the Poor: The Mexico City Poor House, 1774 – 1871.* Durham, NC: Duke University Press, 2000.

Avila, Elena, and Joy Parker. *Woman Who Glows in the Dark.* New York: Tarcher Penguin, 1999.

Baer, Roberta D., Susan C. Weller, Javier Garcia De Alba Garcia, Mark Glazer, Robert Trotter, Lee Pachter, and Robert E. Klein. "A Cross-cultural Approach to the Study of the Folk Illness Nervios." *Culture, Medicine, and Psychiatry* 27 (2003): 315–337.

Baker, A. A. "Granny Battering." *Modern Geriatrics* 8 (1975): 20–24.

Baro, F., M. Keirse, and M. Wouters. "Spousal Bereavement in the Elderly," *Health Promotion International* 1 (1986).

Blasco, Maribel, and Ann Varley. "Intact or in Tatters? Family Care of Older Women and Men in Urban Mexico." *Journal of Gender and Development* 8, no. 2 (2000): 47–55. ProQuest.

Boker, Pamela. *Grief Taboo in American Literature: Loss and Prolonged Adolescence in Twain, Melville, and Hemingway.* New York: New York University Press, 1997.

Bowlby, J. "Process of Mourning." *International Journal of Psychoanalysis*, 42 (1961): 317–339.

Bowlby, John, in Archer, John. *The Nature of Grief: The Evolution and Psychology of Reactions of Loss.* London: Brunner-Routledge, 1999.

Bonanno, George A. *The Other Side of Sadness.* New York: Basic Books, 2009.

Brett, Elizabeth. "The Classification of PTSD." In *Traumatic Stress: The Effects of Overwhelming Experience on Mind, Body, and Society*, edited by Bessel A. van der Kolk, Alexander McFarlane, and Lars Weisaeth. New York: Guilford Press, 1996.

British Broadcasting Corporation. "The Global Drugs Trade." Accessed April 20, 2013, from www.news.bbc.co.uk/hi/english/static/in_depth/world/2000/drugs_trade/default

Burrows, Rachel D., Janine J. Slavec, Douglas W. Nangle, and April C. O'Grady. "ERP, Medication, and Brief Hospitalization in the Treatment of an Adolescent with Severe BDD." *Clinical Case Studies* 12 (2012). doi:10.1177/1534650112460911.

Burston, G. "Do Your Elderly Patients Live in Fear of Being Battered?" *Modern Geriatrics* 7 (1977): 54, 55.

Burton, Nanette [Mongelluzzo]. *Entering Adulthood: Understanding Depression and Suicide.* Santa Cruz, CA: ETR & Associates, 1990.

Burton, Robert. *The Anatomy of Melancholy.* New York: New York Review Books, 2001.

Burton, Robert, and Holbrook Jackson. *The Anatomy of Melancholy.* London. 2013.

Cavera, Robert S., Leah Jacobs, and Robert W. Motta. "Experimental Exposure Therapy for Posttraumatic Nightmares." *Clinical Case Studies* (2013). doi:10.117/1534650113475701.

Center for International Rehabilitation Research Information & Exchange (CIRRIE). "Mexican Culture and Illness." Buffalo: State University of New York, 2001. Accessed November 20, 2005, from www.cirrie.org/p15

China Ministry of Culture. "Hanging Coffins in Gongxian." Accessed January 19, 2013, from www.chinaculture.org/gb/en_curiosity/2004-10/26/content_62633.htm

Cohen, Judith A., and Anthony P. Mannarino. "Supporting Children with Traumatic Grief: What Educators Need to Know." *School Psychology International* 32 (2011): 117–131.

Crelinsten, Ronald D., and Alex P. Schmid, eds. *The Politics of Pain: Torturers and Their Masters.* Leiden, The Netherlands: Center for the Study of Social Conflicts, 1993, p. 122

Crelinsten, Ronald D., and Alex P. Schmid, eds. *The Politics of Pain: Torturers and Their Masters.* The Netherlands: Leiden University, Leiden Institute for Social Scientific Research, 1993, p. 20.

Davis, Dona L., and Setha Low, eds. *Gender, Health, and Illness: The Case of Nerves.* New York: Hemisphere, 1989.

Desmond, Adrian J., and James Moore. *Darwin.* New York: Warner Books, 1991.

DeVinne, P. B., ed. *American Heritage Dictionary.* Boston: Houghton Mifflin, 1982.

Dierker, L., and E. Donny. "The Role of Psychiatric Disorders in the Relationship between Cigarette Smoking and DSM IV Nicotine Dependence among Young Adults." *Oxford Journals: Nicotine and Tobacco Research* 10, no. 3 (2008): 439–446. doi:10.1080/14622200801901898.

Doumas, Diana, Gayla Margolis, and Richard John. "The Intergenerational Transmission of Aggression across Three Generations." *Journal of Family Violence* 9 (1994): 157–175.

Dugard, Jaycee L. *A Stolen Life: A Memoir.* New York: Simon & Schuster, 2011.

Duran, Beyhan. "Developing a Scale to Measure Parental Worry and Their Attitudes toward Childhood Cancer after Successful Completion of Treatment: A pilot Study." *Journal of Pediatric Oncology* 28 (2011): 154–168.

Edgerton, Robert B. *Sick Societies: Challenging the Myth of Primitive Harmony.* New York: Free Press, 1992.

Eisenberger, N. I., M. D. Lieberman, and K. D. Williams, "Does Rejection Hurt? An fMRI Study of Social Exclusion," *Science* 302, no. 5643 (October 10, 2003): 290–292.

EMDR Institute. "What Is EMDR?" Accessed April 10, 2013, from www.emdr.com/general-information/what-is-emdr/what-is-emdr.html

Fadiman, Anne. *The Spirit Catches You and You Fall Down: A Hmong Child, Her American Doctors, and the Collision of Two Cultures.* New York: Farrar, Straus & Giroux, 1998.

Fernandez, Shantel, Lisa Demarni Cromer, Cameo Borntrager, Rachael Swopes, Rochelle F., Hanso, and Joanne L. Davis. "A Case Series: Cognitive-Behavioral Treatment (Exposure, Relaxation, and Rescripting Therapy) of Trauma-related Nightmares Experienced by Children." *Clinical Case Studies* 12 (2013). doi:10.1177/1534650112462623.

Figley, Charles R., ed. *Treating Compassion Fatigue*. New York: Routledge, 2002.

Finkler, Kaja. "Gender, Domestic Violence, and Sickness in Mexico." *Journal of Social Science and Medicine* 45 (1997): 1147–1160.

Freud, Sigmund, and James Strachey. *Three Essays on the Theory of Sexuality*. New York: Basic Books, 1962.

Freud, Sigmund. *Totem and Taboo*. New York: Dover, 2011

Freud, Sigmund. *On Murder, Mourning and Melancholia*. UK: Penguin Limited, 2007.

Gaynor, Mitchell L. *The Healing Power of Sound: Recovery from Life-Threatening Illness Using Sound, Voice, and Music*. Boston: Shambhala Publications, 2002.

———. *Meditations and Music for Sound Healing: A Leading Oncologist Explores the Healing Power of Sound (Sound Medicine)*. Roslyn, NY: Relaxation Company, 2006.

Gilbert, Kathleen R. "We've Had the Same Loss, Why Don't We Have the Same Grief?" *Death Studies* 20 (1996): 269. Accessed March 1, 2013. doi:10.1080/07481189608252781.

Glover, Jonathan. *Humanity: A Moral History of the Twentieth Century*. New Haven, CT. Yale University Press, 1999.

Gonzalez-Crussi, F. *The Day of the Dead: And Other Mortal Reflections*. New York: Harcourt Brace, 1993.

Gore, Al. *An Inconvenient Truth*. DVD. Directed by Davis Guggenheim. Hollywood, CA: Paramount Classics, 2006.

Green, Lorraine, and Victoria Grant, "Gagged Grief and Beleaguered Bereavements? An Analysis of Multidisciplinary Theory and Research Relating to Same Sex Partnership Bereavement," *Sexualities* 11 (2008): 275–300.

Harlow, Harry F. "Love in Infant Monkeys." *Scientific American* 200 (1959): 68–74.

Hilts, Philip J. "Relative Addictiveness of Drugs." *New York Times*, August 2, 1994. Accessed April 20, 2013.

Home School Legal Defense Association. "Homeschooling Research." Accessed March 12, 2013, from www. hslda.org/research/faq.asp#1

Horowitz, Mardi J. *Stress Response Syndromes: PTSD, Grief, and Adjustment Disorders*. 4th ed. Northvale, NJ: Jason Aronson, 1997.

Hospice Foundation. "Shattering Eight Myths about Grief." Accessed April 1, 2013, from www. hospicefoundation.org/8griefmyths

———. "Eight Myths about Children and Loss." Accessed April 1, 2013, from www. hospicefoundation.org/pages/page.asp?page_id=171403

Hugo. DVD. Directed by Martin Scorsese. Hollywood, CA: Paramount Pictures, 2011.

Humane Society. "Coping with the Death of Your Pet." October 3, 2012. Accessed March 1, 2013, from www.humanesociety.org/animal/resources/tips/coping_with_pet_death.html

Institoris, Heinrich, and Jakob Sprenger. *The Malleus Maleficarum of Hei nrick Kramer and James Sprenger.* Translated by M. Summers. New York: Dover, 1971.

Joanna Briggs Institute. www4.rgu.ac.uk/files/BereavementFinal

Journalist's Resource. "Persistent Cannabis Users Show Neuropsychological Decline from Childhood to Midlife." Accessed April 20, 2013, from http://journalistresource.org/studies/society/heal

Kazak, Anne E., and Lamia P. Barakat. "Brief Report: Parenting Stress and Quality of Life during Treatment for Childhood Leukemia Predicts Child and Parent Adjustment after Treatment Ends." *Journal of Pediatric Psychology* 22 (1997): 749–758.

Khamsi, Stephen. "Healing of Pre and Perinatal Trauma." Accessed December 5, 2005, from www.birthpsychology.com/healing/review2

Kissane, David P., Sidney Block, David Dow, Ray Snyder, Patrick Onghena, Dean McKenzie, and Christopher Wallace. "The Melbourne Family Grief Study, I: Perceptions of Family Function in Bereavement." *American Journal of Psychiatry* 153 (1996): 650.

Kleinman, Arthur. *The Illness Narratives.* New York: Basic Books, 1988.

Kluger, Richard. *Ashes to Ashes: America's Hundred-Year Cigarette War, the Public Health, and the Unabashed Triumph of Philip Morris.* New York: Alfred A. Knopf, 1996.

Konigsberg, Ruth D. *The Truth about Grief.* New York: Simon & Schuster, 2011.

Kramer, Heinrick, and James Sprenger, *Malleus Maleficarum of Heinrick Kramer and James Sprenger.* Translated by M. Summers. New York: Dover, 1948.

Kroesen, Kendall W. "Es otra cosa: Emotions and Worldview in a Mexican Town." PhD diss., University of San Diego, 1997. *Dissertation Abstracts International*-A, 58 (03): 957. ProQuest document no. 739785431.

Kross, Ethan, M. G. Berman, W. Mischel, E. E. Smith, and T. D. Wager. "Social Rejection Shares Somatosensory Representations with Physical Pain." *Proceedings of the National Academy of Sciences, U.S.* 108, no. 15 (2011): 6270–6275.

Kubler-Ross, E. *On Death and Dying.* New York: Scribner, 1997.

Kulkarni, Madhur R., Sandra Graham-Bermann, Sheila A. M. Rauch, and Julia Seng. "Violence in Childhood as Correlate of Adulthood PTSD." *Journal of Interpersonal Violence* 26 (2010): 1264. Accessed March 30, 2013, from HighWire. doi:10.1177/0886260510368159.

Lewis, C. S. *A Grief Observed.* San Francisco: Harper & Row, 1989.

Lindemann, Erich. "Symptomatology and Management of Acute Grief." *American Journal of Psychiatry* 104 (1944): 141–148.

Lucas, Richard E. "Time Does Not Heal All Wounds: A Longitudinal Study of Reaction and Adaptation to Divorce." *Psychological Science* 16 (2005). doi:10.1111/j.1467-9280.2005.01642.x.

——. "Adaptation and the Set-Point Model of Subjective Well-Being: Does Happiness Change after Major Life Events?" *Current Directions in Psychological Science* 16 (2007): 75–79.

MacGregor, Peggy. "Grief: The Unrecognized Parental Response to Mental Illness in a Child," *Journal of Social Work* 39 (1993): 160. Accessed March 1, 2013. doi: 10.1093/sw/39.2.160.

Mahler, Margaret S., Fred Pine, and Anni Bergman. *The Psychological Birth of the Human Infant Symbiosis*. New York: Basic Books, 1995.

March of Dimes. "Caffeine in Pregnancy." Accessed from www.marchofdimes.com/pregnancy/nutrition_caffeine.html

Mayo Clinic. "Fatigue." Accessed from www.mayoclinic.com/health/fatigue/MY00120/DSECTION=causes

——. "Prescription Drug Abuse." Accessed from www.mayoclinic.com/print/prescription-drug-abuse/DS01079/METHOD=print&DSECTION=all

McNicol, Kirsten, Peter Salmon, Bridget Yound, and Peter Fisher. "Alleviating Emotional Distress in a Young Adult Survivor of Adolescent Cancer: A Case Study Illustrating a New Application of Metacognitive Therapy." *Clinical Case Studies* 12 (2012). doi:10.1177/1534650112461298.

Mettler, Fred. "Chernobyl's Living Legacy." International Atomic Energy Agency. Accessed March 12, 2013, from www.iaea.org/Publications/Magazines/Bulletin/Bull4

Mongelluzzo, Nanette Burton. "Street Stories of Mexico: A Comparative Case Study of Elderly Beggars." PhD diss., Saybrook University, 2006. Ann Arbor, MI: ProQuest, 2006.

——. "Abigail Goodspeed and Oliver Twist: A Tale of Changing the Course of Events." First published at Psych Central, 2012. http://blogs.psychcentral.com/angst-anxiety/2012/01/abigail-goodspeed-and-oliver-twist-a-tale-of-changing-the-course-of-events/

——. The Everything Guide to Self-Esteem. Avon, MA: Adams Media, 2013.

Morris, William, ed. *The American Heritage Dictionary*. Boston: Houghton Mifflin, 1982.

Nagy, Maria. "The Child's View of Death." In *The Meaning of Death*, edited by Herman Feifel. New York: McGraw Hill, 1969.

National Cancer Institute. "Grief, Bereavement, and Coping with Loss (PDQ)." Accessed February 23, 2013, from www.cancer.gov/cancertopics/pdq/supportivecare/bereavement/Patient/page1/AllPages#4

National Center for Education Statistics. "Fast Facts Homeschooling." Accessed April 1, 2013, from, http://nces.ed.gov/fastfacts/display.asp?id=91

National Council on Alcoholism and Drug Dependence. "2.5 Million Alcohol-Related Deaths Worldwide Annually." *Global Status of Alcohol and Health 2011*, World Health Organization. Accessed April 20, 2013, from http://www.ncadd.org/index.php/in-the-news/155-25-million-alcohol-related-deaths-worldwide-annually

National Funeral Directors Association. "Ten Common Myths-Realities about Grief." Accessed April 3, 2013, from http://nfda.org/grief-resources/understanding-death-a-grief/43.html

National Institute of Health. "Homeopathy: An Introduction." Accessed April 22, 2013, from http://nccam.nih.gov/health/homeopathy

———. "More Healthcare Professionals Abusing Anesthesia Drug: Study." Accessed from www.nlm.nih.gov/medlineplus/news/fullstory_135293.html

———. "Prescription Drug Abuse Up among U.S. Teens: Survey." Accessed from www.nlm.nih.gov/medlineplus/news/fullstory_136171.html

Nauert, Rick. "Study Examines Alcohol Use Patterns Worldwide." Psych Central, March 5, 2013. Accessed April 20, 2013, from www.psychcentral.com/news

Ness, Patrick. *A Monster Calls: Inspired by an Idea from Sibhan Dowd.* New York: Candlewick Press, 2013.

Nuland, Sherwin B. *How We Die: Reflections on Life's Final Chapter.* New York: Vintage, 1995.

Nunn, K. P. "Neurofuturity: A Theory of Change." *Clinical Child Psychology and Psychiatry* 11, no. 2 (April 2006): 183–190.

O'Brien, Tim. *The Things They Carried.* New York: Penguin, 1990, p. 86.

Okun, M., et.al. "Sleep Variability, Health-related Practices, and Inflammatory Markers in a Community Dwelling of Older Adults." *Psychosomatic Medicine: A Journal of Biobehavioral Medicine* 73, no. 2 (2011): 142–150.

Ortiz, John M. *The Tao of Music: Sound Psychology: Using Music to Change Your Life.* York Beach, ME: Samuel Weiser, 1997.

Ott, Carol H., Sara Sanders, and Sheryl T. Kelber. "Grief and Personal Growth Experience of Spouses and Adult-Child Caregivers of Individuals with Alzheimer's Disease and Related Dementias." *The Gerontologist* 47 (2007): 798–809.

Pan American Health Organization (PAHO), World Health Organization (WHO), and American Association of Retired Persons (AARP). "Midlife and Older Women in Latin America and the Caribbean." Washington, DC: Author, 1989.

Parkes, C. M., and R. J. Brown. "Health after Bereavement: A Controlled Study of Young Boston Widows and Widowers." *Journal of Psychosomatic Medicine*, 34, No. 5 (1972): 449–461.

Paturel, Amy. "Meditation as Medicine." *Neurology Now* 8 (2012): 30–33.

Paz, Octavio. *The Labyrinth of Solitude*. New York: Grove Press, 1985.

Phelan, Michael. "Transcendental Meditation: A Revitalization of an American Civil Religion." *Archives de Sciences Sociales des Religions* 24 (1979): 5–20.

Pilisuk, Marc, and Jennifer Rountree. *Who Benefits from Global Violence and War: Uncovering a Destructive System*. Westport, CT: Praeger, 2008.

Poe, Edgar Allan. Letter to Sarah Whitman, 1848.

Prentiss, Chris, and Pax Prentiss. *The Alcoholism and Addiction Cure: A Holistic Approach to Total Recovery*. Malibu, CA: Power Press, 2007.

Pressman, David L., and George A. Bonanno. "With Whom Do We Grieve? Social and Cultural Determinants of Grief Processing in the United States and China." *Journal of Social and Personal Relationships* 24 (2007): 729–746.

Preston, Richard. *Panic in Level 4*. New York: Random House, 2008.

Purdue University. "Coping with Grief and Loss." Accessed from www.purdue.edu/odos/aboutodos/Grief.pdf

Radford, Scott K. "Grief, Commiseration, and Consumption Following the Death of a Celebrity." *Journal of Consumer Culture* 12 (2012): 137–155.

Rauch, S. L., L. M. Shin, and E. A. Phelps. "Neurocircuitry Models of Posttraumatic Stress Disorder and Extinction: Human Neuroimaging Research—Past, Present, and Future." *Biological Psychiatry* 60, no. 4 (2006): 376–382.

Robertson, J. R. *Edgar A. Poe: A Study*. UK: Haskell House Pub Ltd, 1970.

Rosenbaum, Brenda. "With Our Heads Bowed: Women, Society and Culture in Chamula, Chiapas, Mexico." PhD diss., 1987. *Dissertation Abstracts International*-A, 48 (04), 971. Accessed September 24, 2004, from ProQuest Digital Dissertations database.

Rubel, Arthur J., Carl O'Nell, and Rolo Collado-Ardón. *Susto: A Folk Illness*. Berkeley: University of California Press, 1991.

Rudgley, Richard. *Lost Civilizations of the Stone Age*. New York: Free Press, 1998.

Sadock, Benjamin J., Virginia Sadock, and Harold Kaplan. *Synopsis of Psychiatry*. New York: Lippincott Williams & Wilkins, 2003.

Salgado de Snyder, Victoria N., Maria Jesus Diaz-Perez, and Victoria D. Ojeda. "The Prevalence of Nervios and Associated Symptomatology among Inhabitants of Mexican Rural Communities." *Culture, Medicine, and Psychiatry* 24 (2000): 453–470.

Sanders, C. M. *The Mourning After: Dealing with Adult Bereavement*. New York: Wiley and Sons, 1989.

Sanders, Catherine M., in Archer, John. *The Nature of Grief: The Evolution and Psychology of Reactions of Loss.* London: Brunner-Routledge, 1999.

Santora, Neil. "Relative Addictiveness of Drugs." *New York Times*, August 2, 1994. www.Tfy.drugsense.org

Sarton, May. *As We Are Now: A Novel.* New York: W. W. Norton, 1973.

Scarry, Elaine. *The Body in Pain.* New York: Oxford University Press, 1985.

Scharff, Kate. *Therapy Demystified: An Insider's Guide to Getting the Right Help (Without Going Broke).* New York: Marlowe, 2004.

Schoenberg, Bernard, Arthur Carr, David Peretz, and Austin Kutscher, eds. *Loss and Grief: Psychological Management in Medical Practice.* New York: Columbia University Press, 1970.

Schumer, Fran. "After a Death, the Pain That Doesn't Go Away." New York Times, September 28, 2009. Accessed March 30, 2013, from www.nytimes.com/2009/09/29/health/29gireif.html

Servan-Schreiber, David. *Anticancer: A New Way of Life.* New York: Viking, 2009.

Shaw, D. M. "Homeopathy Is Where the Harm Is: Five Unethical Effects of Funding Unscientific Remedies." *Journal of Medical Ethics* 36 (2010): 130, 131. doi:10.1136/jme.2009.034959.

Shay, Jonathan. *Achilles in Vietnam: Combat Trauma and the Undoing of Character.* New York: Simon & Schuster, 1994, p. 67.

Shedler, Jonathan. "The Efficacy of Psychodynamic Psychotherapy." American Psychological Association, Vol. 65, No. 2, 2010.

Shemesh, Eyal, Jeffrey Newcorn, Lori Rockmore, Benjamin Shneider, Sukru Emre, Bruce Gelb, Robert Rapaport, Sally Noone, Rachel Annunziato, James Schmeidler, and Rachel Yehuda. "Comparison of Parent and Child Reports of Emotional Trauma Symptoms in Pediatric Outpatient Settings." *Pediatrics* 115 (2005): e582–e589. doi:10.1542/peds.2004-2201.

Shepherd, Dean A. "Learning from Business Failure: Propositions of Grief Recovery for the Self-Employed." *Academy of Management Review* 28 (2003): 318–328.

Smith, Sophia K., Sheryl Zimmerman, Christianna Williams, Habtamu Benecha, Amy Abernethy, Deborak Mayer, Lloyd Edwards, and Patricia Ganz. "Post-Traumatic Stress Symptoms in Long-Term Non-Hodgkin's Lymphoma Survivors: Does Time Heal?" *Journal of Clinical Oncology* 29 (2011). doi:10.1200/JCO.2011.37.2631.

Soika, Karin U. *Sati: A Project on the Indian Ritual of Widow Burning.* Accessed March 8, 2005, from www.soika.com/links/projekte/esati.htm

Sontag, Susan. *Regarding the Pain of Others.* New York: Picador, 2003.

Staub, Ervin. *The Roots of Evil: The Origins of Genocide and Other Group Violence.* Cambridge: Cambridge University Press, 1989.

Stillpoint Center. "What Is Cranial Sacral (Craniosacral) Therapy (CST)?" Accessed April 22, 2013, from www. stillpointbalance.com

Stirling, John Jr. et al., "Understanding the Behavioral and Emotional Consequences of Child Abuse." *Pediatrics* 122 (2008): 667.

Stone, Alan A., and Sue Stone. *The Abnormal Personality through Literature*. Englewood Cliffs, NJ: Prentice Hall, 1966.

Suris, Alina, Lisa Lind, Michael Kashner, Patricia Borman, and Frederick Petty. "Sexual Assault in Women Veterans: An Examination of PTSD Risk, Health Care Utilization, and Cost of Care." *Psychosomatic Medicine: Journal of Biobehavioral Medicine* 66 (2004): 749–756.

Tapp, Nicholas. "Hmong Religion." *Asian Folklore Studies* 48 (1989): 59–94.

Thannhauser, Jennifer E. "Grief-Peer Dynamics: Understanding Experiences with Pediatric Multiple Sclerosis." *Journal of Qualitative Health Research* 19 (2009): 766–777. Accessed March 10, 2013. doi:10.1177/1049732309334859.

Tolle, Eckhart. *Practicing the Power of Now.* Novato, CA: New World Library, 1999, p. 91.

Tout, Ken. *Ageing in Developing Countries*. New York: Oxford University Press, 1989.

United Nations Division for the Advancement of Women (UNDAW). Convention on the Elimination of All Forms of Discrimination against Women, United Nations, New York, January 27, 2005.

University of Dayton. "The History of Tobacco." Accessed from http://academic.udayton.edu/health/syllabi/tobacco/history.htm#combo

van der Kolk, Bessel A., Alexander McFarlane, and Lars Weisaeth, eds. *Traumatic Stress: The Effects of Overwhelming Experience on Mind, Body, and Society.* New York: Guilford Press, 1996.

Wald, Jaye. "Implementation and Outcome of Combining Interoceptive Exposure with Trauma-related Exposure Therapy in a Patient with Combat-related Posttraumatic Stress Disorder." *Clinical Case Studies* 9 (2010). Accessed April 1, 2013, from HighWire. doi:10.1177/1534650110137387.

Walker, Barbara. *The Crone: Woman of Age, Wisdom, and Power.* San Francisco: Harper & Row, 1985.

Walter, Tony. *On Bereavement: The Culture of Grief.* Buckingham, UK: Open University Press, 1999.

Weil, Andrew. "What Is Integrative Medicine?" Accessed from drweil.com/drw/u/ART02054/Andrew-Weil-Integrative-Medicine.html

Wikipedia. "Hmong Funeral." Accessed March 28, 2013, from http://en.wikipedia.org/wiki/Hmong_funeral

———. "Hurricane Katrina." Accessed from http://en.wikipedia.org/wiki/Hurricane_Katrina

———. "List of School Shootings in the United States." Accessed March 18, 2013, from www.wikipedia.org/wiki/List_of_school_shootings_in

———. Rome Statute of the International Criminal Court, in "Crimes against Humanity." Accessed March 22, 2013, from http://en.wikipedia.org/wiki/Crimes_against_humanity

Women's Health. "Types of Yoga." Accessed April 20, 2013, from www.womenshealthmag.com/yoga/types-of-yoga

Women's United Nations Report Network (WUNRN). "The Status of Widows in South Asia." Accessed August 14, 2005, from www.wunrn.com/news/general/stories/032905

World Bank. "How Poor are the Old? A Survey of Evidence from 44 Countries." Vol. 1. Washington, DC: World Bank, 2000. Accessed March 5, 2005, from www.worldbank.org

World Health Organization (WHO). Global Status of Alc. "2.5 Million Alcohol-related Deaths Worldwide Annually." Accessed April 20, 2013, from www.ncadd.org/index.php/in-the-news/155-25-

———. "Suicide Prevention (SUPRE)." Accessed January 5, 2012, from www.who.int/mental_health/prevention/suicideprevent/en/

World Health Organization (WHO) / International Network for the Prevention of Elder Abuse (INPEA). "Missing Voices: Views of Older Persons on Elder Abuse." Accessed January 7, 2005, from www.inpea.net/links.html

World Nuclear Association. "Fukushima Accident 2011 (updated March 2013)." Accessed March 15, 2013, from www.world-nuclear.org/info/Safety-and-Security/Safety-of-Plans/Fukushima-Accident-2011/#.UUvTXxk1Y8Y

Yin Yang House. "What Styles of Healing and Energy Work Are Practiced?" Accessed April 21, 2013, from www.yinyanghouse.com

Index

About the Author

Nanette Burton Mongelluzzo has been active in the mental health community for over thirty years. She is a practicing psychotherapist working with children, teens, adults, couples, and families. Nanette works with anxiety, depression, loss and grief, bereavement, cancer, posttraumatic stress disorder, eating disorders, self-mutilation, suicide-risk, and adjustment-related mental health issues. She is active in her community and offers community-based workshops on all things mental health. Her life work orients around understanding, developing, and fostering good mental health in children, teens, and adults. She is featured as a radio and television guest on local broadcasting outlets. She teaches graduate level courses in professional counseling and blogs for *Psych Central*. Dr. Burton-Mongelluzzo is the author of *Entering Adulthood: Understanding Depression and Suicide*, 1990; *Street Stories of Mexico: A Comparative Case Study of Elderly Beggars*, 2006; and *The Everything Guide to Self-Esteem*, 2012.